New Technologies for Education

New Technologies for Education

A Beginner's Guide

Third Edition

Ann E. Barron
University of South Florida

Gary W. Orwig
University of Central Florida

1997
LIBRARIES UNLIMITED, INC.
Englewood, Colorado

To our families:
David, Brenda, Julie, and Paula Barron;
Joyce Orwig and Jennifer and Steven Waid;
and to our "sisters" and "brothers" in education.

Libraries Unlimited, Inc.
P.O. Box 6633
Englewood, CO 80155-6633
1-800-237-6124

Interior Illustrations: Janice Holt and Roy Winkelman
Production Editor: Kay Mariea
Copy Editor: Thea de Hart
Proofreader: Ann Marie Damian
Indexer: Christine Smith
Typesetter: Kay Minnis

Library of Congress Cataloging-in-Publication Data

Barron, Ann E.
    New technologies for education : a beginner's guide / Ann E. Barron, Gary W. Orwig. -- 3rd ed.
    xv, 295 p. 22x28 cm.
    Includes bibliographical references and indexes.
    ISBN 1-56308-477-5
    1. Educational technology--United States. 2. Teaching--Aids and devices. I. Orwig, Gary W., 1945-   . II. Title.
LB1028.3.B37   1997
371.3'078--dc20   96-39108
                                                     CIP

Contents

2
Compact Disc–Read Only Memory (CD-ROM)
(continued)

3
Interactive Videodisc

4

Digital Audio

4

Digital Audio

(continued)

5

Digital Images and Video

6

Presentation and Hypermedia Programs

7
Local Area Networks

8

Telecommunications

9
Teleconferencing and Distance Learning

10
The Computer as an Assistive Technology

Preface

The third edition of *New Technologies for Education: A Beginner's Guide* offers an updated look at the technologies that are affecting education, including the World Wide Web, wireless LANs, multimedia, and videoconferencing. Designed for all educators who are interested in the instructional applications of technology, this book provides an overview of compact disc technologies, videodiscs, digital audio, digitized video, hypermedia, local area networks, telecommunications, teleconferencing, and assistive technologies. The advantages, disadvantages, and educational applications of each technology are presented, along with detailed graphics and generous glossaries. Each chapter also provides a scenario to illustrate implementation techniques, a copy-ready brochure for in-service training workshops, and abundant resource information.

New Technologies for Education is written for all educators who are interested in bridging the technology gap. By educators we mean teachers, trainers, school library media specialists, and educational administrators. The book is intended as an introduction to new technologies for those currently employed in the teaching profession as well as for those who are planning a career in education or training.

ORGANIZATION AND USE

New Technologies for Education can be used as a resource book, as a guide for in-service education, or as a textbook. As a resource, this book contains a wealth of information. Each chapter begins with a "real-life" scenario that shows the implementation of technology in an educational setting. A list of topics provides an outline of the chapter's contents. Detailed graphics throughout the book provide configurations and illustrations of hardware, software, and the like. In addition, each chapter contains generous appendixes with contact information for software and hardware vendors, up-to-date reference materials, and easy-to-understand glossaries. A detailed index for the entire book provides easy access to specific topics and information.

The book is also designed for use in conjunction with in-service training for a wide variety of technologies. To facilitate in-service workshops, each chapter was written to be independent of the others, although relevant topics are cross-referenced. In addition, most chapters include a copy-ready brochure that summarizes the topic. These brochures may be copied and distributed for educational purposes, such as in-service training. Terminology specific to each technology is also provided at the end of the chapters and can be incorporated into teacher workshops.

As a textbook, *New Technologies for Education* is appropriate for multimedia and technology courses at the undergraduate and graduate levels. Throughout the book, emphasis is placed on the educational applications of technology. In addition, the advantages and disadvantages of each technology are discussed to provide relevant examples for teacher training.

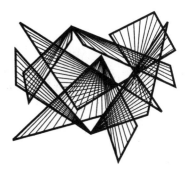

1

Teaching with New Technology

A Scenario

The students in Mr. Gurrell's seventh-grade class were engaged in reviewing their electronic portfolios. The process began last September when he announced the following guidelines:

- All students would be expected to assemble an electronic portfolio of their work by May 10.

- Students would be responsible for deciding what material would be added to their electronic record and justifying each element.

- The projects should document achievements in communication skills, logic, aesthetics, research, personal interests, and community involvement.

- HyperStudio would be used to organize and structure the portfolios.

- At the end of the year, each portfolio would be stored on a recordable CD-ROM; the next year the student would add his or her eighth-grade portfolio to the CD-ROM.

This was the first year that his class had assembled this type of assessment record, and Mr. Gurrell was impressed with the degree of involvement and enthusiasm displayed by the students. Instead of passively dreading report-card day, the students were active participants in the construction of a record of their accomplishments through telecommunications, video, sound, and other media.

John linked his HyperStudio portfolio to the World Wide Web page he had created. His Web page linked to all the sites on the Internet that contained information about AIDS. Through his Web page, students throughout the world could read about the latest AIDS research, view the statistics, and receive prompt, candid answers from experts by sending E-mail messages.

In her portfolio, Melissa included some of the papers she had written for English class and a digital recording of the song she had played in the music contest. She knew her parents would be thrilled to have a recording of the event even though she had only received a third-place ribbon.

1

Ravi, Nora, Mike, and Lenor scanned in photos from the Math/Science Fair. Their project had focused on optical illusions, and it had been easy for them to incorporate some of the graphics and charts into their HyperStudio stacks. They also included some buttons with questions that would provide feedback to users about their interpretations of the illusions.

The basketball and volleyball teams were also documented in several portfolios. Dennis, the self-appointed class cameraman, had videotaped parts of the city tournament, and several members of the teams incorporated short digital movies of their contributions.

Yes, portfolio assessments are very different from the normal A, B, C, D, F evaluations. Rather than trying to fit students neatly into a bell curve, the portfolios encouraged the students to be creative, selective, and responsible for their own knowledge and performances. The focus was to visually document the students' progress for parents and to produce a record for future reference. Technology was merely the tool that made it possible.

From automatic-teller machines and voice mail to cars that "talk" to us, our social and professional lives are inundated with technology. In this chapter, we examine the trends of using technology in schools and outline the benefits that technology can offer education. Topics of the chapter include

- Trends in technology
- Benefits of technology in education
- Suggestions for implementing technology in schools
- Resources for further information

TRENDS IN TECHNOLOGY

New Technologies for Education: A Beginner's Guide investigates the advantages, disadvantages, and educational applications of several different technologies that fall within the domains of multimedia instruction and networks. *Multimedia instruction* can be loosely defined as educational programs integrating some, but not necessarily all, the following media in an interactive environment controlled by a computer: text, graphics, animation, sound, and video. Multimedia programs contain "links and tools that let the user navigate, interact, create, and communicate" (Hofstetter 1994, 6). *Networks* consist of computers and other devices that are connected by cables, telephone systems, satellites, or other means to provide enhanced communication and research capabilities.

Technology in all areas is evolving at a rapid pace, fueled by faster, smaller, more powerful, and less expensive components that are easier to use. Laptop computers with built-in CD-ROM drives, modems, and fax units are more powerful and less expensive than the mainframe computers of just a few years ago. The integration of television, telephone, and computer technologies is also changing the way we live. Telephone "operators" are often voice-recognition systems; you can see and hear someone in another country via the Internet; and in some places it is possible to touch the television screen to order a movie or interact with a computer program that is transmitted to your house via cable television.

Information is becoming more accessible and transmittable, and some are referring to the present as the Communication Age (Betts 1994). Important skills for students include the ability to utilize technology to access, analyze, filter, and organize multidimensional information sources.

It has been difficult for our educational system to keep pace with the rapid advances in multimedia technology and information access. Many of our schools have changed little, and many teachers continue to emphasize the same instructional strategy, lectures, and the same technique, using a chalkboard, as educators in the 1920s. Fortunately, there are some bright spots on the horizon. Recent reports indicate that access to computers and other technologies is improving for schools, and there is increased access to computers, CD-ROMs, and international networks. More than half of the school districts responding to a survey from Quality Education Data, Inc., indicated that they were using educational multimedia for instruction (Looking ahead: A report on the latest survey results 1995). In addition, the ratio of students to computers has dropped to almost 10:1, down substantially from a few years ago (Hayes and Bybee 1995; Quality Education Data 1995), and half of the nation's public schools have at least one computer connected to the Internet (Milone 1996).

The government has also shown increased interest and commitment to national education standards, technology, and access for schools to the National Information Infrastructure (NII). The Goals 2000: Educate America Act, passed by the U. S. Senate and signed by President Clinton, is a major initiative to integrate technology into the content standards and plans of our nation's schools (MacDonald 1994). Another proposal, President Clinton's new school construction initiative, will help connect all classrooms to the information superhighway (Updates on legislation, budget, and activities 1996).

BENEFITS OF TECHNOLOGY IN EDUCATION

Integrating technology into education can be challenging, frustrating, time-consuming, and expensive. A common question often surfaces: Is it worth it? Indeed, Brunner and McMillan (1994) stated that "if we had a nickel for every reporter who called us at the Center for Children and Technology to ask us if our research proves that technology raises test scores, we wouldn't have to apply for any more government grants" (22).

Reporters, parents, and teachers may be disappointed when they discover that measuring the effectiveness of the new, diverse technologies in education is often more complicated than administering standardized tests. Many of the educational multimedia programs are designed in an open-ended, exploration format, and assessment of these programs through multiple-choice tests does not provide adequate answers about their effectiveness. Also, many of the new networking technologies have not been fully analyzed. The number of variables present with the integration of multimedia and educational networks complicates the research process; however, the following benefits can be presented based on the attributes of the technologies, teachers' perceptions, and published research.

Instructional effectiveness. One benefit of multimedia instruction is an increase in student achievement. The *Report on the Effectiveness of Technology in Schools: 1990-1994* detailed the results of several empirical research studies that found significant positive effects on student achievement (Sivin-Kachala and Bialo 1994). The research included findings in the areas of reading, writing, mathematics, science, and programming languages (Kulik and Kulik 1991; Bangert-Drowns 1993; McNeil and Nelson 1991; Ryan 1991).

Active learning. Interactive technologies provide stimulating environments that encourage student involvement in the learning process. For example, instead of reading about Martin Luther King Jr. in a book, students can hear his speeches, witness his marches, and analyze documents related to civil rights through multimedia. History can become more meaningful and more relevant.

Apple Classrooms of Tomorrow (ACOT) is a long-term research project sponsored by Apple Computer, the National Science Foundation, and the National Alliance for Restructuring Education. This study revealed that students actively involved with technology benefited in many ways. For example, the students had a "higher degree of social awareness and self-confidence; they [were] more independent and [had] more positive attitudes about learning and themselves; they [were] able to experiment and problem solve with greater ease; they [saw] themselves as collaborators and experts; and they [had] a positive orientation about the future" (Apple Computer 1991, 3).

Critical thinking. The structure and the use of technology can promote higher-level thinking skills (Vockell and Van Deusen 1989). Some programs, such as the Jasper Woodbury series, are designed specifically to encourage problem-solving skills (Cognition and Technology Group 1993). The use of technology such as hypermedia and telecommunications also affects thinking skills. For example, one of the most highly rated incentives for using telecommunications with students includes increasing students' inquiry and analytical skills (Honey and Henriquez 1993).

Individualization. Students are different, and they learn and develop in different ways at varying rates. We educators deceive ourselves if we think that 30-plus students will learn the same material in the same amount of time. Technology offers students diversity and self-paced learning, allowing them to progress at an appropriate rate in a nonthreatening environment (Peck and Dorricott 1994).

A dramatic shift from whole-class instruction to small-group and individual instruction has been documented with the integration of technology. When computers have been introduced into the curriculum, teacher-led (lecture) activities have decreased from 70 percent to less than 10 percent (Wilson et al. 1994).

Motivation. Motivating students is a constant challenge in education. Technology can inspire students (and teachers) by making learning exciting and relevant. Researchers often find that with technology students are more successful, more motivated to learn, and they have increased self-confidence and self-esteem (Sivin-Kachala and Bialo 1994; O'Connor and Brie 1994). In the Apple Classrooms of Tomorrow study in Columbus, Ohio, the average rate of student absenteeism was cut almost in half among the 216 students who took part in a technology-enriched environment (Dwyer 1994).

Flexibility for students with special needs. Technology offers many advantages for students with special needs. Modified presentation strategies have been effective with learning-disabled and low-achieving students, and adaptive devices are available to provide alternate inputs and outputs for assistive needs (Woodward and Gersten 1992; Skinner 1990). Studies have found that students with special needs also perceive computer-based instruction as less threatening (Swan et al. 1990).

Technology enables students with disabilities to communicate with others and to express themselves in writing. Technologies such as voice recognition, text-to-speech synthesis, and adaptive hardware and software are providing means for all students to reach their potential. "More and more success stories are pouring in about how technology, combined with effective practice, can help students with disabilities overcome barriers to their success" (Zorfass, Corley, and Remz 1994, 62).

Cooperative learning. Well-structured cooperative-learning activities can foster "the development of leadership abilities, a sense of teamwork, and improved self-esteem" (Strommen 1995, 27). By introducing technology into the educational environment, teachers can increase teacher-student interactions and promote learning that is more student centered and cooperative (Interactive Educational Systems Design 1994). Technology can be used to enhance and encourage cooperative learning in our schools through small groups using a single computer, network-based instructional programs (such as *Wagon Train 1848* by MECC), or collaborative projects on the Internet.

Experts caution, however, that just because students are sharing a computer does not mean that cooperative learning is taking place. David Dockterman of Tom Snyder Productions offers the following guidelines for implementing cooperative-learning activities:

- Students are cooperating, not just taking turns.

- The content of the collaboration is about the content you want to teach.

- The software is structured to promote interaction (Dockterman 1995, 33).

Communication skills. Communication skills can be enhanced by using technology in small groups and by integrating telecommunications into the curriculum. Research reviews indicate that networks can affect learning indirectly by providing unique opportunities for students to practice, demonstrate, and critique communication skills (Cohen and Riel 1989; Wright 1991).

Multisensory delivery. One benefit of multimedia instruction is that it provides information through multiple sensory channels, allowing students with various learning styles to assimilate and apply the knowledge (Holzberg 1994). Research in learning styles indicates that some students learn better through specific modalities such as audio, visual, or kinesthetic (Barbe and Swassing 1979; Dunn and Dunn 1978). In other words, one student may be an audio learner and benefit most when instruction is delivered through sound and narration. Another student may be a visual learner and benefit most when information is conveyed through pictures and text.

Multicultural education. Telecommunications make it possible to expand classroom "walls" and to link students and teachers in national and international exchanges. These interactions enable students from vastly different backgrounds to build cultural bridges by investigating common problems from different perspectives. Students in distant countries such as Russia, Iceland, China, and the United States can communicate daily about life-styles, politics, science, and global issues (Barron and Ivers 1996).

Although it is certainly possible for these students to exchange letters via regular mail service, feedback through computer networks is generally more meaningful because it is fast and the students can remain focused on the ideas, projects, and interchanges. In addition, the cost of communicating is minimal in comparison to international postal rates or telephone charges. "Indeed, never before could teams of students, thousands of miles apart, engage in a dialogue through which they jointly construct a model of their respective economics, cultural surroundings, or ecologies, and then collaboratively test its implications" (Salomon 1991, 43).

Technology alone is not the determining factor in effective education. The important issue is what is done with the technology: The instructional methods must be based on sound learning principles (Clark 1989). There is also evidence that the teacher is a critical variable in the effectiveness of computers (Collis 1989). As technology continues to advance, we must learn to use it wisely to motivate, instruct, and challenge students. Unfortunately, "the computer can be misused as easily as it can be powerfully applied" (Rockman 1992, 15).

IMPLEMENTATION

Integrating technology into education is not an easy task. Although the price of software and hardware is decreasing, it is still difficult for schools to afford resources sufficient to meet the demands. In addition, educators must make a constant effort to keep abreast of the latest developments. This section provides some suggestions for implementing technology:

Determine your instructional goals and objectives, then locate the technology to support them. In other words, select the technology to fit your curriculum, not vice versa. Many times we become entranced with a new program or piece of hardware only to find that it does not come close to addressing the objectives. Technology, like other teaching tools, must be implemented only where appropriate.

Seek support from administrators. Talk to your administrators and keep them informed about your instructional goals and technology needs. "Even in difficult budget times, you can be confident that if you can directly link your requests for technology to the attainment of specific and highly valued student goals, you will get support from both administrators and community members" (Dyrli and Kinnaman 1994a, 18).

Form partnerships with local businesses, universities, and students' parents. Partnerships can provide donations of equipment, expertise, and time—all of which can be valuable additions to your quest to integrate technology in the classroom (Wiburg 1994).

Acquire technology in increments. Hardware and software are changing so rapidly that they may be obsolete or "second generation" by the time you and the teachers in your school learn to use them (Dyrli and Kinnaman 1994b). Purchase technology in increments, learn to use it, integrate it into the curriculum, and then investigate additional resources.

Visit other schools and ask other educators for advice. One of the best ways to acquire ideas on the integration of technology into a classroom is to visit other schools. Most teachers are more than willing to share their successes and lessons learned in the classroom. In addition, some states and districts have established model technology schools to test implementation techniques. Do not be afraid to ask questions of fellow teachers, other professionals, and students. Advances in technology are constant and overwhelming, and no one has all the answers.

Provide in-service training sessions. To meet the training demand for emerging technologies, most districts, regions, and states have instituted in-service workshops and seminars for teachers. These activities are usually excellent avenues for learning about new developments. If possible, plan workshops that emphasize hands-on training, provide well-planned materials for future reference, include lesson-integration strategies, and promote interchanges with other teachers (Harris 1995).

Provide training for teachers on the software and hardware that is available at their schools. One mistake that school districts may make is to bring in outside experts, who arrive with their own hardware and software. Although it is beneficial to see what others are doing, the training sessions should focus on the technology that the teachers will have available even after the expert leaves (Siegel 1995).

Provide follow-up support and coaching. Support for teachers after in-service training is essential (Office of Technology Assessment 1995). The support should consist of technical troubleshooting expertise as well as pedagogical ideas for integrating technology into the curriculum (Tally 1995).

Involve the students, and capitalize on their expertise. It is not uncommon for some students in a class to be more comfortable with new technologies than the teacher. This situation can be a real plus because the students' expertise can be tapped to train other students. Student involvement provides valuable assistance for the teacher and helps to build students' self-esteem.

Investigate public-domain and shareware sources. Education money is tight, and most schools cannot afford all the software they need. Public-domain software is available at no cost and may be freely copied. Shareware, however, is almost always copyrighted and should not be considered free. If you try a shareware program and intend to use it, send the registration fee to the author of the program. This payment constitutes the license to continue using the program, and you will receive information about updates.

Investigate technical support and documentation. Access to quality documentation and technical support is invaluable for any buyer of hardware or software. Be sure the vendors are reputable and have a history of reliable service. A toll-free number is especially important for the integration of technologies purchased from a distant source.

Subscribe to magazines and journals. There is a wealth of periodicals focusing on technology in education. These publications are a great means for keeping up with the latest developments and releases. In addition, research, integration ideas, and product reviews are provided. A list of periodicals is included in the list of resources at the end of this chapter, along with contact information. Many of the publications are available at little or no cost to qualified professionals.

Balance "high tech" with "high touch." The integration of technologies will not replace classroom teachers because technology cannot provide a teacher's compassion or ability to analyze an individual student's learning needs. Instead, teachers can use technology as another tool for presenting and providing access to knowledge. Human beings—teachers—remain the essential factor for providing high touch in an increasingly high-tech world (Kinnaman 1994; Cornell and Bollet 1989).

Be flexible and ready for change. We must accept that we cannot force technology to fit neatly into our traditional paradigms. For technology to foster collaboration, cross-discipline explorations, and complex problem solving, we may have to adjust our school schedules to accommodate it. Likewise, the evaluation of technology-based projects requires a new look at the assessment of student and teacher performance (Means and Olson 1994).

CONCLUSION

In the fast-approaching twenty-first century, the adult lives of our children and our students will be drastically different from the lives of their parents and teachers. The integration of technology into school curricula is no longer a luxury; it is a prerequisite to survival in a future that will be driven and supported by technology (Mageau and Chion-Kenney 1994).

Integrating new technologies is not a cure-all for education, but indicators attest that new technologies can help in restructuring our classrooms with activities that promote collaboration and can provide effective tools for interpretive skills, information management, and open inquiry. Technology can also provide an excellent avenue for student motivation, exploration, and instruction in a multisensory, diverse world. Technology, however, is only a tool. The challenge rests with educators to effectively integrate it in appropriate places throughout the curriculum.

EDUCATIONAL TECHNOLOGY RESOURCES

Beyond Computing
590 Madison Avenue
New York, NY 10022
847-564-1385

Boot
Imagine Publications
1350 Old Bayshore
Brisbane, CA 94005
415-468-4869

CD-ROM Professional
Online, Inc.
462 Danbury Road
Wilton, CT 06897-2126
800-248-8466

Classroom Connect
Wentworth Worldwide Media
P.O. Box 10488
Lancaster, PA 17605
800-638-1639

Collegiate Microcomputer
Rose Hulman Institute of Technology
5500 Wabash Avenue
Terre Haute, IN 47803
812-877-1511

Computers in the Schools
Haworth Press
10 Alice Street
Binghamton, NY 13904-1580
607-722-5857

ED-TECH Review
P.O. Box 2966
Charlottesville, VA 22902
804-973-3987

Educational Technology
Educational Technology Publications
720 Palisade Avenue
Englewood Cliffs, NJ 07632
201-871-4007

Educational Technology Research and Development (ETR&D)
Association for Educational Communications and Technology
1025 Vermont Avenue NW, Suite 820
Washington, DC 20005
202-347-7834

Electronic Learning
Scholastic, Inc.
555 Broadway
New York, NY 10012
212-505-4900

Hypernexus: Journal of Hypermedia and Multimedia Studies
International Society for Technology in Education
1787 Agate Street
Eugene, OR 97403-1923
800-336-5191

Information Technology and Libraries

American Library Association
50 E. Huron Street
Chicago, IL 60611-2795
312-944-6780

Instruction Delivery Systems

Communicative Technology
    Corporation
50 Culpeper Street
Warrenton, VA 22186
800-457-6812

Interactive Teacher

Millennium Publishing
118 N. Monroe Street, Suite 300
Tallahassee, FL 32301
904-425-1351

Internet World

Mecklermedia Corporation
20 Ketchum Street
Westport, CT 06880-5808
203-226-6967

Journal of Computers in Math and Science Teaching

Association for the Advancement of
    Computing in Education
P.O. Box 2966
Charlottesville, VA 22902
804-973-3987

Journal of Computing in Childhood Education

Association for the Advancement of
    Computing in Education
P.O. Box 2966
Charlottesville, VA 22902
804-973-3987

Journal of Computing in Higher Education

Lederle Graduate Research Center
P.O. Box 2593
Amherst, MA 01004-2593
413-545-4232

Journal of Computing in Teacher Education

International Society for Technology in
    Education
1787 Agate Street
Eugene, OR 97403-1923
800-336-5191

Journal of Educational Computing Research

Baywood Publishing
26 Austin Avenue, Box 337
Amityville, NY 11701
800-638-7819

Journal of Educational Multimedia and Hypermedia

Association for the Advancement of
    Computing in Education
P.O. Box 2966
Charlottesville, VA 22902
804-973-3987

Journal of Educational Technology Systems

Baywood Publishing
26 Austin Avenue, Box 337
Amityville, NY 11701
800-638-7819

Journal of Interactive Instruction Development

Communicative Technology Corporation
50 Culpeper Street
Warrenton, VA 22186
800-457-6812

Journal of Research on Computing in Education

International Society for Technology in
    Education
1787 Agate Street
Eugene, OR 97403-1923
800-336-5191

Journal of Technology and Teacher Education

Association for the Advancement of
    Computing in Education
P.O. Box 2966
Charlottesville, VA 22902
804-973-3987

Learning and Leading with Technology

International Society for Technology in
    Education
1787 Agate Street
Eugene, OR 97403-1923
800-336-5191

Library Hi Tech Journal
Pierian Press
P.O. Box 1808
Ann Arbor, MI 48106
313-434-5530

Mac Addict
Imagine Publications
1350 Old Bayshore Highway
Brisbane, CA 94005
415-468-4869

Mathematics and Computer Education
MATYC Journal
P.O. Box 158
Old Bethpage, NY 11804
516-822-5475

Media & Methods
1429 Walnut Street
Philadelphia, PA 10102
800-555-5657

Multimedia and Videodisc Compendium
2819 Hamline Avenue North
St. Paul, MN 55113
612-639-3973

Multimedia Monitor
P.O. Box 26
Falls Church, VA 22040-0026
703-241-1799

Multimedia Producer
Knowledge Industry Publications, Inc.
701 Westchester Avenue
White Plains, NY 10604
914-328-9157

MultiMedia Schools
462 Danbury Road
Wilton, CT 06897
202-244-6710

Multimedia World
501 Second Street
San Francisco, CA 94107
415-281-8650

NewMedia
HyperMedia Communications
901 Mariner's Island Boulevard,
    Suite 365
San Mateo, CA 94404
415-573-5170

Online
Online, Inc.
462 Danbury Road
Wilton, CT 06897-2126
800-248-8466

Optical Information Systems Magazine
Mecklermedia Corporation
11 Ferry Lane West
Westport, CT 06880-5808
203-226-6967

PC Graphics & Video
201 E. Sandpointe Avenue
Santa Ana, CA 92707
714-513-8400

PC Novice
120 W. Harvest Drive
Lincoln, NE 68521
800-424-7900

Presentations Magazine
50 S. Ninth Street
Minneapolis, MN 55402
800-328-4329

Satellite Scholar
P.O. Box 3508
Missoula, MT 59806
406-549-4860

Syllabus
Syllabus Press
1307 S. Mary Avenue
Sunnyvale, CA 94087
800-773-0670

Technology and Learning
Peter Li, Inc.
330 Progress Road
Dayton, OH 45449
800-543-4383

TechTrends
Association for Educational
    Communications and Technology
1025 Vermont Avenue NW, Suite 820
Washington, DC 20005
202-347-7834

Telecommunications
685 Canton Street
Norwood, MA 02062
617-356-4595

Telecommunications in Education
International Society for Technology in
　Education
1787 Agate Street
Eugene, OR 97403-1923
800-336-5191

T.H.E. Journal
Technological Horizons in Education
150 El Camino Real, Suite 112
Tustin, CA 92680-3670
714-730-4011

Wired
544 Second Street
San Francisco, CA 94107
415-276-5000

REFERENCE LIST

Apple Computer. (1991). *Apple classrooms of tomorrow: Philosophy and structure and what's happening where.* ERIC Document Reproduction Service No. ED340349.

Bangert-Drowns, R. L. (1993). The word processor as an instructional tool: A meta-analysis of word processing in writing instruction. *Review of Educational Research* 63(1): 69–93.

Barbe, W. B., and R. H. Swassing. (1979). *Teaching through modality strengths: Concepts and practices.* Columbus, OH: Zaner-Bloser.

Barron, A. E., and K. S. Ivers. (1996). *The Internet and instruction: Ideas and activities.* Englewood, CO: Libraries Unlimited.

Betts, F. (1994). On the birth of the communication age: A conversation with David Thornburg. *Educational Leadership* 51(7): 20–23.

Brunner, C., and K. McMillan. (1994). Beyond test scores. *Electronic Learning* 14(1): 22–23.

Clark, R. E. (1989). Current progress and future directions for research in instructional technology. *Educational Technology Research and Development* 37(1): 57–66.

Cognition and Technology Group at Vanderbilt University. (1993). The Jasper experiment: Using video to furnish real-world problem-solving contexts. *Arithmetic Teacher* 40(30): 474–78.

Cohen, M., and M. Riel. (1989). The effect of distant audiences on students' writing. *American Educational Research Journal* 26(2): 143–59.

Collis, B. (1989). *Using information technology to create new educational situations.* ERIC Document Reproduction Service No. ED310793.

Cornell, R. A., and R. M. Bollet. (1989). High touch in the high tech world of education: Impact '89. *Educational Media International* 26(2): 67–72.

Dockterman, D. (1995). Yes, but is it cooperative? *Electronic Learning* 14(4): 33.

Dunn, R., and K. Dunn. (1978). *Teaching students through their individual learning styles: A practical approach.* Reston, VA: Reston.

Dwyer, D. (1994). Apple classrooms of tomorrow: What we've learned. *Educational Leadership* 51(7): 4–10.

Dyrli, O. E., and D. E. Kinnaman. (1994a). Gaining access to technology: First step in making a difference for your students. *Technology and Learning* 14(4): 16–20.

———. (1994b). Moving from successful classrooms to successful schools. *Technology and Learning* 14(6): 46–54.

Harris, J. (1995). Teaching teachers to use telecomputing tools. *ERIC Review* 4(1): 2–4.

Hayes, J., and D. L. Bybee. (1995). Defining the greatest need for educational technology. *Learning and Leading with Technology* 23(2): 48–50.

Hofstetter, F. T. (1994). Is multimedia the next literacy? *Educator's Tech Exchange* Winter 6–13.

Holzberg, C. S. (1994). The new multimedia: What researchers say about multimedia. *Electronic Learning* 13(8): 55–62.

Honey, M., and A. Henriquez. (1993). *Telecommunications and K-12 educators: Findings from a national survey.* New York: Center for Technology in Education, Bank Street College of Education.

Interactive Educational Systems Design. (1994). *Report on the effectiveness of technology in schools.* Washington, DC: Software Publishers Association.

Kinnaman, D. E. (1994). Remember the human element in your technology planning. *Technology and Learning* 14(5): 62.

Kulik, C. C., and J. A. Kulik. (1991). Effectiveness of computer-based instruction: An updated analysis. *Computers in Human Behavior* 7(1–2): 75–94.

Looking ahead: A report on the latest survey results. (1995). *Technology and Learning* 15(4): 20–25.

MacDonald, J. T. (1994). Goals 2000: Educate America act. *T.H.E. Journal* 21(10): 10.

Mageau, T., and L. Chion-Kenney. (1994). Facing the future. *Electronic Learning* 14(2): 37–40.

McNeil, B. J., and K. R. Nelson. (1991). Meta-analysis of interactive video instruction: A 10-year review of achievement effects. *Journal of Computer-Based Instruction* 18(1): 1–6.

Means, M., and K. Olson. (1994). The link between technology and authentic learning. *Educational Leadership* 51(7): 15–18.

Milone, M. N. (1996). More schools on the information superhighway. *Technology and Learning* 16(8): 27.

O'Connor, J., and R. Brie. (1994). Mathematics and science partnerships: Products, people, performance and multimedia. *Computing Teacher* 22(1): 27–30.

Office of Technology Assessment. (1995). *Teachers and technology: Making the connection.* Washington, DC: U.S. Congress.

Peck, K. L., and D. Dorricott. (1994). Why use technology? *Educational Leadership* 51(7): 11–14.

Quality Education Data. (1995). *Technology in public schools*. Denver, CO: Peterson's Guides.

Rockman, S. (1992). *Learning from technologies: A perspective on the research literature*. U.S. Office of Technology Assessment, ERIC Document Reproduction Service No. ED361499.

Ryan, A. W. (1991). Meta-analysis of achievement effects of microcomputer applications in elementary schools. *Educational Administration Quarterly* 27(2): 161–84.

Salomon, G. (1991). Learning: New conceptions, new opportunities. *Educational Technology* 31(6): 41–44.

Siegel, J. (1995). The state of teacher training. *Electronic Learning* 14(8): 43–53.

Sivin-Kachala, J., and E. R. Bialo. (1994). *Report on the effectiveness of technology in schools: 1990-1994*. Washington, DC: Software Publishers Association.

Skinner, M. E. (1990). The effects of computer-based instruction on the achievement of college students as a function of achievement status and mode of presentation. *Computers in Human Behavior* 6: 3512–360.

Strommen, E. (1995). Cooperative learning: Technology may be the Trojan horse that brings collaboration into the classroom. *Electronic Learning* 14(4): 24–35.

Swan, K., F. Guerrero, M. Mitrani, and J. Schoener. (1990). Honing in on the target: Who among the educationally disadvantaged benefits most from what CBI? *Journal of Research on Computing in Education* Summer: 381–403.

Tally, B. (1995). Developmental training: understanding the ways teachers learn. *Electronic Learning* 14(8): 14–15.

Updates on legislation, budget, and activities: Summary of President Clinton's school construction initiative. Available late summer 1996 at: gopher://gopher.ed.gov:70/11/update/pres.

Vockell, E., and R. M. Van Deusen. (1989). *The computer and higher-order thinking skills*. Watsonville, CA: Mitchell.

Wiburg, K. (1994). Integrating technologies into schools: Why has it been so slow? *Computing Teacher* 21(5): 6–8.

Wilson, B. G., R. Hamilton, J. L. Teslow, and T. A. Cyr. (1994). *Technology making a difference: The Peakview Elementary School study*. Syracuse, NY: ERIC Clearinghouse on Information and Technology.

Woodward, J., and R. Gersten. (1992). Innovative technology for secondary students with learning disabilities. *Exceptional Children* 58(5): 407–21.

Wright, W. (1991). International group work: Using a computer conference to invigorate the writing of your students. In *The English classroom in the computer age*, ed. W. Wresch, 100–103. Urbana, IL: National Council of Teachers of English.

Zorfass, J., P. Corley, and A. Remz. (1994). Helping students with disabilities become writers. *Educational Leadership* 51(7): 62–66.

RECOMMENDED READING

Ambrose, D. W. (1991). The effects of hypermedia on learning: A literature review. *Educational Technology* 31(12): 51–54.

Barksdale, J. M. (1996). New teachers: Why schools of education are still sending you staff you'll have to train in technology. *Electronic Learning* 15(5): 38–45.

Baule, S. (1995). Providing for technological support: Help! *Technology Connection* 2(2): 12.

Bell, S. M. (1995). Rules to train by. *Electronic Learning* 15(1): 1.

Burks, J. (1994). Classroom education + interactive multimedia = formula for revolution. *Multimedia World* 1(5): 52–69.

Cummings, L. E. (1995). Educational technology—A faculty resistance view. *Educational Technology Review* 4(Autumn): 13–18.

Dalton, D. (1990). The effects of cooperative learning strategies on achievement and attitudes during interactive video. *Journal of Computer-Based Instruction* 17(1): 8–16.

Davies, K. J. (1995). From dreams to reality—Implementing a computer plan. *Learning and Leading with Technology* 23(2): 54–55.

Dickinson, D. (1994). Multiple technologies for multiple intelligences. In *Multimedia and learning: A school leader's guide,* ed. A. Ward, 42–48. Alexandria, VA: National School Boards Association.

Dyrli, O. E., and D. E. Kinnaman. (1994). Preparing for the integration of emerging technologies. *Technology and Learning* 14(8): 92–100.

Eichleay, K., and C. Kilroy. (1994). Hot tips for inclusion with technology. *Computing Teacher* 21(4): 38–40.

Fletcher, J. D. (1990). *The effectiveness of interactive videodisc instruction in defense training and education.* Arlington, VA: Institute for Defense Analyses, Science and Technology Division (IDA paper P-2372).

Kanning, R. G. (1994). What multimedia can do in our classrooms. *Educational Leadership* 51(7): 40–44.

Kearsley, G. (1993). Educational technology: Does it work? *Ed-Tech Review* (Spring-Summer): 34–36.

Kinnaman, D.E. (1995). Schools need good teachers and good technology. *Technology and Learning* 15(8): 98.

Kozma, R. B. (1991). Learning with media. *Review of Educational Research* 61(2): 179–211.

Moore, D. M., R. J. Myers, and J. K. Burton. (1994). What multimedia might do . . . and what we know about what it does. In *Multimedia and learning: A school leader's guide*, ed. A. Ward, 29–41. Alexandria, VA: National School Boards Association.

O'Neil, J. (1995). Technology and schools: A conversation with Chris Dede. *Educational Leadership* 53(2): 6–11.

Orwig, A. H. (1994). Begin with teachers and watch students benefit. *Technology and Learning* 15(1): 74–76.

Paul, D. (1994). An integration/inservice model that works. *T.H.E. Journal* 21(9): 60–62.

Riel, M., and L. Harasim. (1994). Research perspectives on network learning. *Machine Mediated Learning* 4.

Rock, H. M., and A. Cummings. (1994). Can videodiscs improve student outcomes? *Educational Leadership* 51(7): 46–50.

Rutherford, L. H., and S. J. Grana. (1995). Retrofitting academe: Adapting faculty attitudes and practices to technology. *T.H.E. Journal* 23(2): 82–86.

Schlechter, T. (1990). The relative instructional efficiency of small group computer-based training. *Journal of Educational Computing Research* 6(3): 329–41.

Technology planning process: Tips for making it work. (1995). *Technology and Learning* 15(8): IBM3–IBM5.

Tolman, M. H., and R. A. Allred. (1991). *The computer and education: What research says to the teacher.* ERIC Document Reproduction Service No. ED335344.

Tuttle, H. G. (1995). From productivity to collaboration. *MultiMedia Schools* 2(3): 38–42.

Verity, J. W. (1994). The information revolution: How digital technology is changing the way we work and live. *Business Week* (May 18): 10–18.

Weiss, J. (1994). Keeping up with the research. *Technology and Learning* 14(5): 30–36.

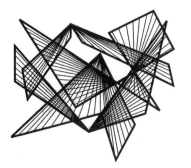

2

Compact Disc–Read Only Memory (CD-ROM)

A Scenario

Ms. Magill was proud of the effort the students in her class had put into their reports for Social Studies. Using PowerPoint, they had each created a multimedia presentation that contained a mixture of text, graphics, audio, and video clips about a country. The only problem was that most of the files for the project were quite large, and with 42 students in the class, the storage area on the computer drives was now full. To make room on the drives for the other classes, the files from Ms. Magill's class would have to be deleted. However, before deleting the files, Ms. Magill decided she would record a CD-ROM to archive the files for future reference.

She began the process by using the computer network to move all the files to one computer. The computer she selected for recording the CD-ROM was fast, with a large hard drive. She knew that speed was important when recording a CD-ROM. (In a previous attempt, she had tried to use a slower computer and had ruined several blank compact discs in the process.) This time, she selected the fast computer, and after all the files were assembled on the same hard drive, she connected the CD-recordable drive.

The next step was to make sure that the files were arranged exactly the way she wanted them to appear on the finished CD-ROM. In other words, she had to carefully examine the file structure and the way the windows appeared. She knew that once the CD-ROM was recorded, this view would remain the same because CD-ROM discs cannot be changed.

After Ms. Magill investigated the possible formats for the CD-ROM, she decided to create the disc in ISO 9660. She had learned that the ISO 9660 format could be read by either an MS-DOS or a Macintosh computer. (Because the presentations had been created with Power-Point, she would add the PowerPoint viewer for Macintosh and Windows to the CD-ROM.) After all the files were arranged on the hard disk in the structure she wanted, Ms. Magill opened the software-recording program on the computer to run a test session. This session did not actually record on the blank disk, but it informed her of a few errors in the file names and structures.

After correcting the errors, she was ready for the "real thing." Ms. Magill placed the blank compact disc in the recorder, crossed her fingers, clicked the Record button, and waited as the files were copied from the hard drive to the compact disc.

When the files were finished recording, Ms. Magill tested the new disc in a CD-ROM drive and could hardly believe that it actually worked. As a techno novice, she had not even used a CD-ROM program until two years ago. Now she had successfully recorded a compact disc to store her students' files!

Compact Disc–Read Only Memory (CD-ROM) technology was first produced in 1986—more than 10 years ago. It has been so successful that most computers are now purchased with built-in CD-ROM players, and there are thousands of inexpensive, commercial titles on the market. This technology, more than any other, has changed the way we store and retrieve information in education and information services. This chapter includes

- An overview of CD-ROM technology
- Educational applications for CD-ROM
- Search and retrieval strategies for CD-ROM
- Configurations for CD-ROM hardware
- Advantages and disadvantages of CD-ROM
- Recording a compact disc
- Related compact disc technologies
- Evaluation and implementation techniques
- Resources for further information

INTRODUCTION

The information explosion and the development of multimedia technologies have created a need to store large amounts of text, audio, video, and graphics files in a small amount of space. Another challenge lies in being able to find and retrieve the desired information quickly and accurately. CD-ROM technology has met these challenges by providing a small, inexpensive disc that can store more than 650 megabytes of data—equivalent to several hundred diskettes or the entire text of a 20-volume encyclopedia. (See fig. 2.1.)

CD-ROM is a close cousin to the compact discs with audio (CD-Audio) that were developed by Philips and Sony in 1982. Both technologies store information on small plastic discs that are 4.72 inches in diameter. The primary difference between CD-Audio and CD-ROM is that CD-Audio is designed to store only music and audio recordings; CD-ROM discs can store a variety of digital media, such as text, graphics, video, or audio. Both technologies encode the digital information on the disc with a laser beam, and a laser beam is used to read the discs. CD-ROM discs are durable because there is no contact or wear on the disc when it is played. The information on the discs is permanent and cannot be modified or erased.

Storage Device	Capacity	Equivalent
Floppy Disks	1.4 MB	720 pages of text
Hard Disk Drive	200 MB	100,000 pages of text
CD-ROM	650+ MB	325,000 pages of text

Figure 2.1. Capacities of Various Storage Devices.

EDUCATIONAL APPLICATIONS

A CD-ROM disc can store information in a variety of formats for a variety of applications. Most CD-ROM applications for education fall within one of the following categories: encyclopedias, reference sources, periodical databases, multimedia instruction, interactive books, games, music, computer software, and clip media.

Encyclopedias

One of the most useful and exciting applications of CD-ROM technology is the ability to store an encyclopedia on a single disc—yes, every word—along with a rich array of charts, graphics, pictures, video, and sound. The information in the encyclopedia can be retrieved quickly by multiple, interlinked access routes, such as time lines, picture catalogs, sound files, or textual searches. In addition, students can make notes as they study the information, save text to diskettes, print the files, or set electronic bookmarks to record their paths.

Examples:

Several encyclopedias are available for schools; all provide a fast, efficient, inexpensive alternative to manually searching a text-based encyclopedia. The *New Grolier Multimedia Encyclopedia* is available for Macintosh and MS-DOS computers and includes text, sound, pictures, video clips, multimedia essays, and powerful search techniques. The 1996 version also includes a link to CompuServe for students who want to conduct online research.

Another popular encyclopedia is *Compton's Interactive Encyclopedia* by Soft-Key International. *Compton's,* like most of the other encyclopedias, offers several alternative access routes to information, such as keyword searches, media catalogs, an atlas, and a time line. Whichever route is taken, links are available to obtain the full text of each article. The encyclopedia can also link to America Online for Internet-related research.

Information Finder, an electronic version of the *World Book Encyclopedia,* provides text and graphics. It also offers competitive pricing, powerful search techniques, and a fast and efficient interface. The *World Book Dictionary,* with more than 140,000 definitions, is available from within the encyclopedia.

Encarta Encyclopedia by Microsoft is noted for its wealth of sounds and images. It also contains powerful search tools and an interactive game that encourages users to search the encyclopedia for answers to questions in a variety of content areas.

There are also several simplified encyclopedias for younger students. For example, *Explorapedia* by Microsoft offers titles such as *The World of Nature* and *The World of People.* Both titles allow students to conduct research or engage in a variety of games and activities related to the topics.

Other Reference Sources

Some CD-ROM discs are dedicated to general-reference sources such as dictionaries, atlases, and telephone directories. Other CD-ROMs focus on content-specific reference sources and offer extensive information about a particular topic.

Examples:

Have you ever wished for a dictionary that could pronounce words that were unfamiliar to you? The *Macmillan Dictionary for Children* by Simon and Schuster Interactive and *My First Incredible Amazing Dictionary* by Dorling Kindersley Multimedia pronounce words, provide definitions, and include illustrations. The *Macmillan Dictionary* includes 12,000 words, 1,000 illustrations, and 400 sound effects.

Street Atlas USA by DeLorme provides detailed street maps for all 50 states. Searches can be conducted by street names, phone exchanges, or zip code. You can zoom in on a street or E-mail the map to other *Street Atlas* owners.

Picture Atlas of the World CD-ROM by National Geographic Society provides physical and cultural atlases of countries throughout the world. One of the features of the program enables students to assemble the media elements to create a report or presentation.

JFK Assassination: A Visual Investigation and *Vietnam: A Visual Investigation* by Medio Multimedia are two examples of content-specific titles. Both of these programs provide an abundance of information for students in the form of news footage, photographs, official documents, and interviews with prominent people. Through the information in these programs, students can examine the issues and draw their own conclusions on the events that shaped history.

Periodical Databases

One of the first, and still one of the most important, applications for CD-ROM is the storage of large periodical databases. Prior to CD-ROM, these databases were usually stored in huge indexes in libraries or on mainframe computers. Computers and modems could be used to access the mainframe computers, but the expense was high, and many schools did not have the necessary hardware or telephone lines. (See chapter 8 for more information on telecommunications and modems.)

Some of the indexes now available on CD-ROM contain the full text of the articles; others provide only the bibliographic information and abstracts. CD-ROM databases are invaluable because of the time they save in searching for relevant information.

Examples:

The Education Resources Information Center (ERIC) is a national bibliographic database for educational literature. ERIC references more than 775 professional journals and 300,000 documents from other sources, such as conference papers and research studies. The information in ERIC is acquired from a nationwide network of 16 clearinghouses. Several different companies are currently supplying the search software for ERIC and distributing the database on CD-ROM. These companies include SilverPlatter and Knight-Ridder Information Services, Inc. (See this chapter's resource list for contact points and suppliers for CD-ROMs.)

There are numerous other education databases on CD-ROM. For example, SIRS (Social Issues Resources Series) is a service that provides timely information about a variety of issues. The SIRS CD-ROM contains a selection of articles from newspapers, magazines, government publications, and journals, and SIRS *Discoverer* offers full-text articles and graphics selected from more than 300 magazines and newspapers.

Other popular reference applications include *Text on Microfiche (TOM)* and *InfoTrac* by Information Access Company, which offer access to magazine articles; *NewsBank* by NewsBank, a popular newspaper index with full-text articles and microfiche; and *First Search* by Online Computer Library Catalog (OCLC).

Multimedia Instruction

In the past, the majority of educational software programs were distributed on floppy diskette. Now, CD-ROMs are being used to deliver most of the instructional programs. With CD-ROM, the instruction can include more graphics, sounds, video, and interactivity. In addition, many of the programs on CD-ROM can be used on either Macintosh or Windows computers. Multimedia instruction on a CD-ROM can range from a mathematics lesson with sound and pictures to an interactive textbook for language arts or science. The diversity and quantity of multimedia instructional programs is enormous and increasing daily.

Examples:

Reader Rabbit's Interactive Reading Journey (Learning Company) is a primer designed for grades K-2 that helps children learn to read. It contains 40 online stories with instruction and activities to reinforce reading comprehension and phonics.

Math Workshop (Broderbund Software) engages students in the world of mathematics through intriguing problems and motivational activities. The program is designed for grades 1-4 and includes several adjustable levels of difficulty.

A.D.A.M. (Animated Dissection of Anatomy for Medicine) (A.D.A.M. Software) allows students to examine the human anatomy. The program offers features that can zoom, rotate, and dissect the human body layer by layer. Detailed illustrations and interactive animations make this an intriguing program for students.

The *Rosetta Stone Language Library* by Fairfield Language Technologies provides interactive instruction in Spanish, French, German, Russian, or English. In each version, the student may select Run (sequential lessons), Tutorial (quizzes), Diction (practice with written and spoken language skills), or Browse (pictures, text, and voice).

Interactive Books

Storybooks can come alive on CD-ROM. With the increased storage space, it is possible to include graphics, sounds, and animation along with the text of a book. In addition, the books can be interactive, allowing students to click on words for definitions, pronunciations, animation, or links to another section of the book.

Examples:

George Shrinks is an example of a illustrated, animated title from the HarperCollins Interactive Storybook series. Throughout the story, students can select one of the following options: Read and Play, Look and Listen, Pick-a-Screen, or Sing Along.

Broderbund Software also produces electronic books, including *Just Grandma and Me, Just Me and My Dad,* and *Arthur's Teacher Trouble.* These books contain lively animation, talking characters, music, and sound effects. Children can click to explore the text and pictures and can hear translations in English, Spanish, or Japanese.

Discis Books by Discis Knowledge Research offer a series of tales for children by popular authors such as Beatrix Potter. These books appear on screen with the original text and illustrations and are enhanced with narration that is synchronized with highlighted words. Options are provided to translate individual words or phrases into several foreign languages and to provide pronunciations or definitions.

Nonfiction interactive books are also available. The series Wonders of Learning CD-ROM Library by the National Geographic Society includes five titles: *Animals and How They Grow, The Human Body, Our Earth, A World of Animals,* and *A World of Plants.* This series is designed for elementary students and provides audio in English and Spanish.

Other examples of interactive books include *Wiggleworks* from Scholastic, Inc., *Bravo Books* from Computer Curriculum Corporation, *Alistair and the Alien Invasion* by Simon and Schuster Interactive, and *How the Leopard Got His Spots* by Microsoft.

Games and Activities

In addition to the popular consumer games such as *Myst* by Broderbund Software and *The Seventh Guest* by Virgin Interactive, there are several educational games on the market. Many of the educational games on CD-ROM are expanded versions of existing floppy disk-based titles. The enhancements involve adding music or digitized speech and improving the quality and quantity of on-screen graphics, animation, and video.

Examples:

The Oregon Trail II by MECC is available on CD-ROM for Macintosh and MS-DOS computers. In this familiar game, players learn about geography, history, and science as they cross the country. The CD-ROM versions offer increased interactivity, graphics, and sounds over the previous software versions. Similar programs for the Yukon Trail and the Amazon Trail are also available from MECC.

Thinkin' Things Collection by Edmark Corporation includes five learning activities: Frippletration, Toony's Tunes, Snake Blox, 2-3D Blox, and Oranga Banga's Band. These interactive activities help to develop thinking, reasoning, and musical skills for young students.

The Carmen SanDiego series by Broderbund Software has been expanded to include *Carmen SanDiego Junior Detective*. Similar to the programs designed for older students, the Junior edition teaches geography skills through a captivating mystery game. The main difference between the Junior edition and the previous editions is the emphasis on audio and graphics for nonreaders.

The popular videodisc program *Science Sleuths* is now available on CD-ROM from Videodiscovery. The CD-ROM version includes an online notebook and six levels of difficulty with a different solution for each level. To solve the mystery, students must use logic and mathematical skills, along with a scientific approach to research the problem with the online tools, charts, and information.

Other applications such as *Encarta* by Microsoft and *Exotic Japan* by Voyager include a game as one of their components. In these and similar games, the students can click on a button, leave the game, and branch to the information on the CD-ROM to find the answer. The student can then return directly to the point of departure in the game.

Music

Some of the popular CD-ROM applications are actually audio CDs with software programs that can access and play specific sections. This combination of software and audio provides wonderful possibilities for interactive music.

Examples:

CD Companion: Beethoven's Ninth Symphony by Voyager and Microsoft consists of Macintosh or Windows software and an audio recording of the Ninth Symphony. The set offers a blend of musical education and entertainment about the life and works of Ludwig van Beethoven. The menu on the software offers access to five parts:

1. "A Pocket Guide" provides an overview of the symphony and enables users to hear any of the major sections.

2. "Beethoven's World" covers the social, political, and historical environment in which the symphony was created.

3. "The Art of Listening" selects portions of the symphony for general study.

4. "A Close Reading" provides a detailed examination of the work. Users can analyze each bar of music and hear examples from the compact disc.

5. "The Ninth Game" is a question-and-answer game for one to four players.

The Beethoven program is part of the Multimedia Composer series, which also includes several similar musical applications: *Stravinsky: The Rite of Spring*; *Schubert: The Trout Quintet*; *Richard Strauss: Three Tone Poems*; and *Mozart: The Dissonant Quartet*. All the programs contain the same components as the Beethoven application as well as unique features.

Microsoft also offers a program called *Musical Instruments* that allows students to "play" more than 200 musical instruments and listen to 1,500 sound samples. The program includes information about the origin and culture of each instrument.

Computer Software
and Application Programs

CD-ROM is an ideal medium for distributing computer programs. One CD-ROM disc can replace numerous computer diskettes at a fraction of the cost. Distribution through CD-ROM is advantageous because installing a large program (such as *Microsoft Office*) from a CD-ROM is much faster than installing from numerous diskettes. In addition, CD-ROM is read only; therefore the master discs will never be erased by mistake.

Examples:

The *PD-ROM (Public Domain ROM)* is published twice a year by the Berkeley Macintosh Users Group. This CD-ROM contains more than 600 megabytes of public-domain software that can be copied and used without charge.

Other popular shareware discs are *Info-Mac* by Pacific HighTech and *Shareware Breakthrough* by MEI/Micro Center.

Clip Art and Clip Media

Computer graphics and sounds usually produce large files and can be difficult to distribute on floppy diskettes. CD-ROM is an excellent medium for storage and distribution of these files. QuickTime and Video for Windows movies (small movies that play on a computer screen) are also being distributed on CD-ROM because of the enormous file sizes required (see chapter 5 for more information about QuickTime, Video for Windows, and digital video). Most of the art, movies, sounds, and fonts sold commercially as clip media are royalty free and allow unlimited use as long as the contents are not resold.

Examples:

Clip art can be purchased for any computer platform in black and white or in full color. These images provide an inexpensive, easy means of enhancing newsletters, hypermedia programs, or posters. *Corel Gallery* by Corel Corporation provides 15,000 clip-art images, 500 fonts, 500 photographs, 75 sound clips, and 10 video clips that can be used on such things as brochures, multimedia presentations, instructional materials, and greeting cards.

Innovative Media's *Sonic Waves 3000* is a CD-ROM set that contains thousands of sound effects, music clips, and speeches. The audio clips are stored in digital audio format, and a digital audio editor is included to allow the user to modify the sound clips.

Another example of audio collections on CD-ROM is the *Janus Professional Sound Library* by Janus Interactive. This 10-disc set provides 10,000 royalty-free sounds related to animals, households, industry, nature, offices, recreation, social gatherings, and transportation.

SEARCH AND RETRIEVAL
OF INFORMATION

The power of electronic reference discs such as encyclopedias and databases lies not only in the rapid access to a particular subject, such as Florida, but in the ability to use *Florida* as a keyword and find every occurrence of the word in the source. Because CD-ROMs contain such a large amount of data, sophisticated techniques are used to create indexes that enable users to find the desired information efficiently. Most CD-ROM reference sources, such as encyclopedias, allow the user to search for information in at least two ways: the browse search and the keyword search.

Browse Search

A *browse search* is similar to looking through an alphabetical index. All the titles or words are listed in order, and after you locate a title of interest, you can go directly to the article. The advantages of using a browse-search technique are that it is easy and it makes materials accessible to novice users. It also provides a quick overview of the topics available for review.

A disadvantage of browse searching is that in many cases you can search only for titles. If the word that interests you is not in a title, no references will be found. Another limitation is that you cannot search for combinations of words or phrases. Therefore, the topics located may be broad in scope.

Keyword Search

A *keyword search* is more powerful than a browse search because it allows you to search the contents of all the articles or records for a specific keyword or phrase. Keyword searches usually provide a list of all the articles that contain the keyword and the number of hits (occurrences) of the keyword in each article. Figure 2.2 contains the results of a keyword search for the words *CD-ROM* and *network* in an electronic encyclopedia. Note that there are 12 occurrences of the word *CD-ROM* in 7 different articles and 39 occurrences of the word *network* in 16 different articles. When these search terms are combined, there are only three articles that include both of the words.

Logical Connectors

An advantage of keyword searching is that logical connectors can be used to narrow or broaden the search. In these searches, sometimes referred to as *analytic* or *Boolean*, three familiar words—and, or, not—are used to specify the relationships of the keywords.

The *and* connector is used to narrow a search and include all essential keywords. In other words, to retrieve information on education in Washington, you would want only the articles that include *education* and *Washington*. In this case, the *and* connector—*education and Washington*—serves to narrow the search to the articles or references that contain both keywords. Note in the diagram in figure 2.3 that the *and* connector retrieves only the articles common to both words.

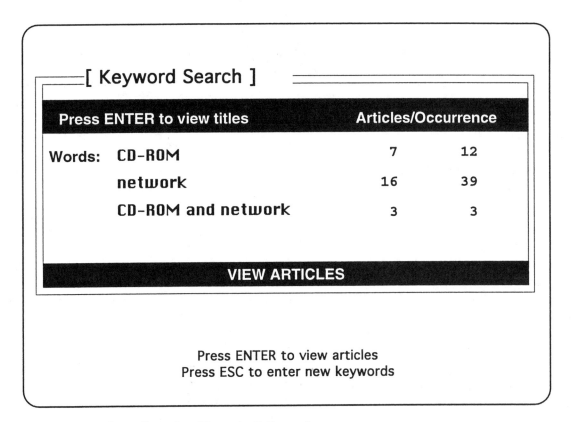

[Keyword Search]

Press ENTER to view titles	Articles/Occurrence	
Words: **CD-ROM**	7	12
network	16	39
CD-ROM and network	3	3
VIEW ARTICLES		

Press ENTER to view articles
Press ESC to enter new keywords

Figure 2.2. Results of a Keyword Search.

The *or* connector is used to broaden a search. The *or* connector is usually employed to provide access to articles that contain synonyms, either of which would be of interest. In the previous example, articles on *instruction* as well as *education* might be pertinent. Therefore, the search could be broadened to include *education or instruction*. Other examples of appropriate uses of the *or* connector might be

car or automobile

graphic or illustration

doctor or physician

identical or monozygotic

Figure 2.4 on page 28 contains a diagram illustrating the *or* connector. Note that the hits will include all the articles that contain either or both of the keywords.

The *not* connector is used to narrow a search by excluding similar uses of the same word. For example, in the case of searching for information on education in the state of Washington, the search

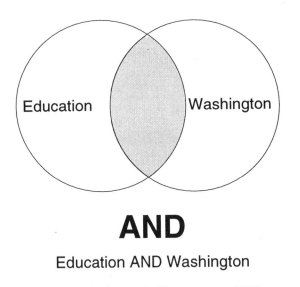

AND

Education AND Washington

Figure 2.3. Search Strategy—AND Connector.

would find occurrences of articles and information on educational practices in Washington, D.C., as well as Washington State. To eliminate Washington, D.C., you can narrow the search with the *not* command and exclude all references to D.C., as in *Washington not D.C.* The *not* connector is illustrated in figure 2.5. Note that any article containing information about Washington, D.C., will be eliminated.

Other examples of appropriate uses of the *not* connector include

pitcher not baseball

China not country

tennis not table

Martin and Luther not King

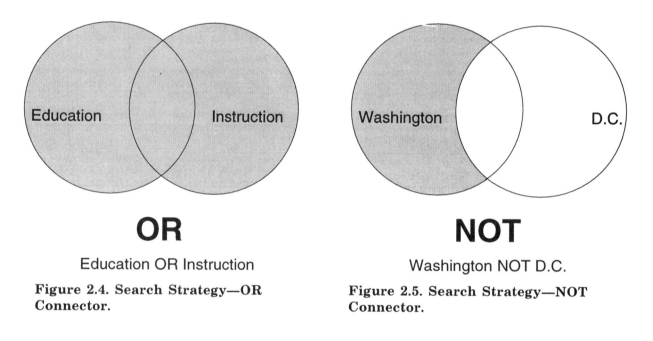

Figure 2.4. Search Strategy—OR Connector.

Figure 2.5. Search Strategy—NOT Connector.

Additional Search Techniques

A variety of other techniques are commonly used to search for text on a CD-ROM reference source. The basic structure and use of these techniques are similar in most applications. However, the exact computer commands may vary.

Truncation

If you are seeking data about professions in Mexico, you would probably want to include *employment* as a keyword. Additional keywords could be *employ, employee, employer, employed, employs, employers,* and so on. Instead of entering all these related words, you can use *truncation.* When a word is truncated—cut off at the root of the essential part—the search accepts alternate endings. In this example, if the keyword was *employ,* the references to all words that begin with *employ* would be retrieved. If you wanted to be a little more specific, then *employer* could be used, resulting in retrieval of references to only *employer* and *employers*.

Wild Cards

The use of wild cards is similar to truncation. The difference is that wild cards provide alternate spellings *within* a word or phrase rather than at the end. As an example, suppose you were looking for references to women in the Olympics. One of your keywords would be *women,* but you would also want to include references to *woman.* Instead of using *women* and *woman* as keywords, you can use a wild card—usually a \$, *, ?, or similar character, such as *wom\$n*—for the fourth character. The search will now yield *woman* and *women.*

Proximity Searches

The *proximity* of two words can be an important consideration when designing a search strategy. For example, if you want information about compact disc technology, you would enter the two keywords: *compact* and *disc.* Unfortunately, you may also retrieve articles about *disc* brakes in *compact* cars. To minimize the possibility of unwanted articles, specify the proximity of the words. For example, you could specify that the words appear in the same sentence.

HARDWARE CONFIGURATION

To display the information on a CD-ROM disc, a CD-ROM player must be connected to a computer and monitor. Most players are designed to be connected to either a Macintosh or an MS-DOS computer. With the proper access software, the computer can read the data on the CD-ROM disc as if it were a hard drive. In other words, you can do a directory listing or even copy files from the CD-ROM disc to a diskette or hard drive. To provide efficient access to the information on the disc, most CD-ROM reference applications provide software programs to search or index the information on the disc. This software is usually located on the CD-ROM disc; in some cases, some of the files may have to be installed onto your hard drive. Headphones or speakers are also needed to hear the audio on the discs.

A CD-ROM system requires

- A computer and monitor
- CD-ROM drive
- CD-ROM disc
- Speakers or headphones (for audio)

CD-ROM drives can be internal or external. (See fig. 2.6 on page 30.) The internal drives may be built into the computer when it is purchased, or they may be installed in place of a floppy-disk drive. Internal drives are compact and do not require any desk space; however, they limit the portability of the player. External drives have their own housing and are easier to move from one computer to another.

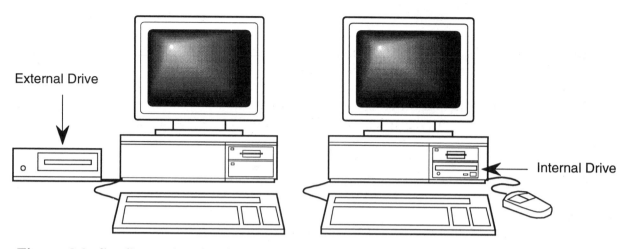

Figure 2.6. Configuration for CD-ROM.

CD-ROM drives are available with a variety of speeds. The oldest, slowest drives are called *single* speed. In this case, speed refers to the *data-transfer rate* of the drive. A single-speed drive can transfer information at 150 kilobytes per second (K/sec); a double speed, at 300K/sec; a quad speed, at 600K/sec; six speed (6X) at 900K/sec; and an eight speed (8X) at 1200K/sec. Single-speed drives are now obsolete. It is best to purchase the fastest drive you can afford, especially if the program contains large files such as video.

Another function of the speed of a CD-ROM drive is the *access time*. The access time is expressed in the number of milliseconds (ms) it takes the laser beam to move into position and locate the desired information on the disc. A standard access time a few years ago was 700ms; rates of less than 150ms are common now. The access time is especially important for applications that require numerous searches, such as database programs.

Macintosh

A CD-ROM player can be connected to any Macintosh computer through the SCSI (Small Computer Systems Interface, pronounced "skuzzy") port on the back of the computer. The required interface cable is generally included with the purchase of the CD-ROM player. For the computer to recognize and interact with the player, CD-ROM access files must be loaded into the systems folder of the Macintosh. The access files alert the computer to the presence of the CD-ROM and provide the software protocols necessary to read the data on the CD-ROM. In most cases, the required CD-ROM software is provided with the CD-ROM drive. An "install" program helps to ensure that the files are located in the correct folders.

When purchasing a CD-ROM application for a Macintosh computer, note the display requirements. Some of the CD-ROM programs specify 256 colors or a 14-inch monitor. Make sure your system can meet the requirements before purchasing the program. Also, many of the newer programs require at least a double-speed or quad-speed player.

MS-DOS

To connect a CD-ROM player to an MS-DOS computer, an additional card (board) may have to be installed in the computer. After the card has been installed, an interface cable connects the CD-ROM player to the card.

Some of the digital audio cards, such as Sound Blaster, provide a connection port for CD-ROM drives. In this case, the CD-ROM cable is connected to the digital audio card and you do not need to install an additional computer board. (See chapter 4 for more information on digital audio cards.)

Another possibility is that the computer may contain a SCSI port. In this case, the CD-ROM drive can connect to the SCSI port, and installing an additional board in the computer will not be necessary.

A software program with CD-ROM extensions must be added on the start-up drive of the computer. These extensions allow the computer to communicate with the CD-ROM player as if it were an additional hard drive (an "install" program is usually supplied with the player).

When purchasing a CD-ROM application for an MS-DOS computer, be sure that the program is compatible with your computer monitor. If the CD-ROM program offers color graphics and photographs, check to make sure that your monitor can display the required number of colors and has the necessary resolution.

Another consideration is whether the program requires Microsoft Windows, a graphic interface to MS-DOS computers that works well on fast computers—those that are at least a 486 processor. Almost all the CD-ROM programs on the market require Windows, so you may have to purchase a new computer or upgrade your computer to be able to run the applications.

Audio Output from CD-ROM

Most CD-ROM players have the ability to play CD-quality audio, and many of the applications incorporate audio into the programs. Two different formats—CD-Audio and digitized audio—can be used to store sound, voice, and music on a CD-ROM. The hardware required depends on the format incorporated.

CD-Audio

Compact disc-audio (CD-Audio) is the format used to record popular, high-quality music discs. This format can be placed on a CD-ROM and played through a CD-ROM player without any additional hardware. The audio on the CD-ROM is amplified through the player and output to either headphones or speakers attached to the CD-ROM player. (See fig. 2.7 on page 32.)

If CD-Audio and text or graphics are stored on the same compact disc, they are placed in different locations. This results in a slight search-time lag between displaying text or graphics and playing the audio. For example, a picture of Beethoven may be displayed and then the laser beam will move to another part of the disc to play the music.

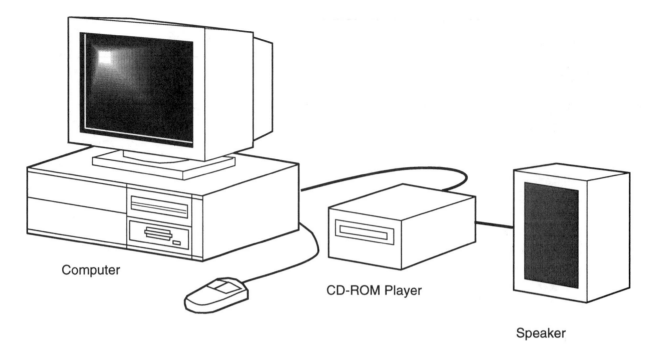

Computer

CD-ROM Player

Speaker

Figure 2.7. CD-Audio Output from CD-ROM Player.

Digitized Audio

An alternative format for storing audio on a CD-ROM is digitized audio. This format can be stored at various quality levels to conserve space. If the audio requirements are primarily for narration, digitized audio is often implemented because it requires less storage space than high-quality CD-Audio (see chapter 4 for more details on digital audio).

To play digitized audio from a CD-ROM, the sound must be routed through an audio card or component in a computer. If a Macintosh computer is used, the sound comes through the computer's built-in speakers. If an MS-DOS computer is used, the audio must be sent to a digital audio board in the computer, which will then output the audio to an external speaker or headphones. (See fig. 2.8.)

Jukeboxes and CD-ROM Towers

Many libraries and media centers install minichangers, jukeboxes, or tower players on a computer network to deliver applications that require more than one disc or to provide access to several different CD-ROMs. A *minichanger* generally refers to a CD-ROM desktop drive with one drive mechanism and the ability to swap between 4 and 18 discs. A *jukebox* is a CD-ROM system that can hold up to 500 CD-ROM discs. Between one and four minichanger mechanisms are used to access and play the desired discs in the jukebox. With a minichanger or a jukebox, only very few discs can be accessed at a given time. Also, there will be a delay between applications because the drive mechanisms must physically switch one disc out and switch another one in.

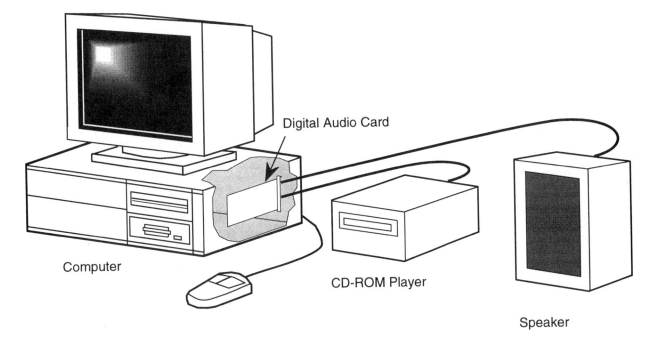

Figure 2.8. Digitized Audio Output from CD-ROM Player.

If your school needs fast, simultaneous access to more than one disc, a CD-ROM *tower* may be a better choice. A tower houses several CD-ROM players—usually between 2 and 40—in a single case, and all players may be accessed at the same time. (See fig. 2.9.)

Daisychaining CD-ROM Drives

Several individual CD-ROM drives can be connected to one computer by *daisychaining* the drives with connecting cables. In this configuration, the drives

Figure 2.9. CD-ROM Tower.

are each assigned a different number, and the computer can recognize up to six different drives (or other devices). Daisychaining CD-ROM drives is most common with Macintosh computers and MS-DOS computers that have a SCSI port. (See fig. 2.10 on page 34.)

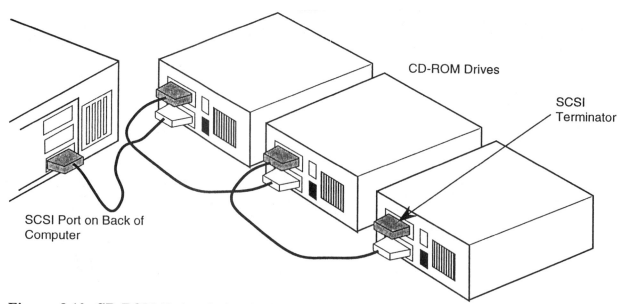

Figure 2.10. CD-ROM Daisychained Through a SCSI Port.

Networks

It is possible for several computers to share a CD-ROM if the appropriate hardware and software are connected to a network. There are several advantages to networking CD-ROM drives, including:

- Access. An entire school can access the CD-ROM titles located in the media center or another central location;

- Cost. It is usually less expensive to obtain a network license for titles than to purchase separate copies for each computer;

- Security. It may be difficult to keep track of CD-ROM discs that are used on separate computers. With a CD-ROM network, the drives are generally located in a secure area near the file server.

There are, however, some constraints to consider before you decide to network your collection of CD-ROMs, including:

- Speed. CD-ROMs on a network can be quite slow if the demand is high. Only about six to eight users can access one disc at the same time while still maintaining an acceptable access rate.

- Complexity. To operate a CD-ROM network, one must have a good understanding of computer networks and CD-ROM systems.

- Multimedia. Running multimedia files over a network can be a problem. If sound files are played, every workstation will have to have an audio card for MS-DOS computers. Also, video files do not transfer well—primarily because it is difficult to sustain the transfer rates of the large files on a network that must meet demands from simultaneous users.

Some general-purpose network operating system software, such as Novell NetWare, have built-in support for networking CD-ROMs. There are also network software systems that are specifically designed for accessing CD-ROM on a network (see chapter 7 for more information about networks).

ADVANTAGES AND DISADVANTAGES OF CD-ROM

Although CD-ROM technology offers many benefits to schools and libraries, it is not appropriate for every situation. The following are some of the features and limitations of CD-ROM technology for education.

Advantages of CD-ROM

Storage capacity. Each CD-ROM disc can hold approximately 650 megabytes of data, graphics, or sound. That capacity is equivalent to hundreds of floppy disks and more than an entire printed encyclopedia.

Portability. CD-ROM discs are small and lightweight, making them an ideal medium for transporting data.

Durability. CD-ROM discs are durable and encoded in plastic. Although they should be handled with care, fingerprints and slight scratches will not usually impair their performance. In addition, the discs are read with a laser beam, so there is no direct contact or wear on the disc as it is played.

Low cost of replication. CD-ROMs cost less than a dollar to reproduce after the master is created. CD-ROM technology has the potential to save money and trees!

Inexpensive hardware. The cost of CD-ROM drives has decreased dramatically in the past few years.

Availability of titles. The number of CD-ROM titles has increased recently. The several thousand commercial titles now available include a wide range of reference materials and multimedia applications.

Cross-platform titles. Although many of the CD-ROM applications operate on only a Macintosh or only an MS-DOS computer, there is a trend toward creating cross-platform titles. These programs are called hybrid, and they will work on both platforms.

Speed. Although the access time of CD-ROM drives may be slightly slower than that of hard drives, the speed of the search time compared to manual methods is impressive.

Disadvantages of CD-ROM

Cost of subscriptions. Some CD-ROM reference applications require a subscription fee for updates. These fees are often as high or higher than the original purchase price. Many schools have purchased a CD-ROM application only to find that they cannot afford the subscriptions.

Lack of standards for retrieval software. There is little consistency among CD-ROM applications. For example, in one application, *Help* may be accessed with the F1 key, but in another application, *Help* is Control H. Techniques for using wild cards, truncation, and logical connectors also vary widely from application to application.

Installation. Installation of the hardware is generally straightforward; however, installing the software can be frustrating. In the MS-DOS environment, two files must be changed to allow the computer to access the CD-ROM (autoexec.bat and config.sys). Although most install programs modify these two files automatically, there may be conflicts with other applications. In the Macintosh environment, the proper files must be placed in the system folder, and the correct versions of the system finder are required.

COMPACT DISC RECORDERS

Although CD-ROM discs are read only, you can now purchase a CD-R (Compact Disc-Recordable) drive at a reasonable price and record your own discs. CD-R discs are compatible with CD-ROM and can be played on regular CD-ROM players. With CD-R, you can record data on a blank disc and add additional data at a later date, but you cannot erase the disc or any information on it. The following steps provide some guidance for getting started in this area.

Step 1. Obtain the Hardware

To create a CD-ROM, you must have a computer with the storage capacity to hold the volume of data you plan to record (up to 650 megabytes). The processing speed of the computer and a number of other factors are also important if you plan to record a CD-R because the information must be sent to the recorder in a steady stream. If the data stream is interrupted, the CD-ROM disc will be useless.

Step 2. Gather the Information

A major step in creating a CD-ROM is determining what information you are going to put on the disc. Basically, anything that can be stored in digital form can be included in a CD-ROM application; most of the school projects center around large collections of text or multimedia. Although 600-plus megabytes may seem like a lot of information, when you begin to add video and sound, the limit can be quickly exceeded. If the information is not in digital form, you will need to convert it. In other words, you may need to scan the photographs and digitize the video and audio.

Step 3. Format the Data

Before the information is placed on the CD-ROM disc, it must be formatted to one of the CD-ROM standards—usually either ISO 9660 (International Standards Organization) or Apple HFS (Hierarchical File System). ISO 9660 is an international standard that can be read on MS-DOS, UNIX, and Macintosh computers. To achieve the cross-platform flexibility, the ISO 9660 requires strict adherence to file-naming and directory conventions, such as no more than eight characters in a file name.

The Apple HFS standard can be used to create Macintosh-only CD-ROM discs. This standard is the same file format used on all Macintosh floppy disks and hard disks. To produce a CD-ROM in HFS format, a hard drive is prepared with the files, icons, and windows adjusted to appear exactly the way you want the users to see the CD-ROM. (It is best to format or defragment the drive first.) Whatever views (name, icon, date, and so on) you select are the ones every user will see. Therefore, you should choose the views carefully and check the positions and sizes of each window.

Step 4. Run a Test

Before the final disc is produced, it is wise to run a test. Some of the CD-R software will allow you to test the "write" without actually recording on the disc. This test run can help to uncover errors in data transfer and file structure.

Step 5. Record the CD-ROM

There are two main choices for recording a custom CD-ROM: You can use a CD-Recordable (CD-R) drive, or you can send your files to a professional replicator. If you need more than 30 copies of the discs, a professional replication service may be a wise choice because they can record a master disc and quickly and inexpensively make the copies. On the other hand, if you are making only a handful of CDs, it is more cost efficient to record them yourself with a CD-R drive and a blank disc (blank CD-R discs are available at computer stores for about $10). After the software is formatted and the hardware is configured, the procedure is as easy as clicking *Record*.

OTHER COMPACT DISC TECHNOLOGIES

The first CD-ROM applications were released in 1985, and the success of CD-ROM has fostered the creation of many other technologies that incorporate compact discs. Although most of the technologies use the same-sized disc, in many cases they are incompatible—each application requires its own specific player and disc format.

CD-A (Compact Disc-Audio). CD-Audio was released in 1982, and it was the first standard for storing digital information on compact discs. CD-Audio discs store a maximum of 74 minutes of high-quality audio (usually music) on a compact disc. Almost all the players designed for other formats (CD-ROM, CD-i, and so on) can play CD-Audio discs. (See chapter 4 for more information on CD-Audio.) Audio stored in this format is often referred to as red-book audio and is of high quality.

Photo CD (Photographic Compact Disc). The Eastman Kodak Company created a standard for producing writable compact discs for storing photographic images. You can take regular 35mm slides or film negatives and have the pictures recorded onto a Photo-CD disc instead of developing them into slides or prints. The price for this development and storage is approximately $1.50 per image—a relatively inexpensive way to place photos on a compact disc. The Photo CDs are multisession, meaning you can add images later. For example, you may have 24 photos placed on a Photo CD on one date and then add another 24 at a later date.

Most Photo CDs hold a maximum of 100 pictures, each at five different resolutions. (See fig. 2.11.) In most cases, you will use the snapshot or standard size for display on a computer screen. It is also possible to request a Photo CD with more images—up to 800—all recorded at low resolution.

SIZE	RESOLUTION
Wallet	192 x 128
Snapshot	384 x 256
Standard	768 x 512
Large	1536 x 1024
Poster	3072 x 2048

Figure 2.11. Images on a Photo CD.

Almost all CD-ROM players are Photo CD–compatible. To display the images through a CD-ROM player, they must be imported into graphics programs such as Photoshop. Once they are opened on your computer, they can be altered and stored on the computer drive. Photo CDs are versatile because they are cross-platform, meaning you can read the disc from either a Macintosh or MS-DOS computer. Companies such as Corel market stock photography on Photo CDs at attractive prices.

CD-i (Compact Disc–Interactive). CD-i was developed by Philips in 1991 as an interactive audio, video, and computer system stored on a compact disc. The CD-i discs are the same size as CD-ROM and CD-A discs, but they are formatted in a different manner and are incompatible with CD-ROM players. CD-i players that are sold by Philips and other companies contain a built-in computer processor, and the output of a CD-i disc displays on a standard television set. Although there are not as many CD-i titles as there are CD-ROM titles, CD-i players are popular in some schools because the discs are self-booting and do not require any software installation. Students interact with the CD-i programs through a mouse or remote-control unit.

DVD (Digital Versatile Disc). Ten years ago, when CD-ROM was first introduced, 650-plus megabytes seemed like an enormous amount of storage space. However, as we add more digital audio and digital video to our multimedia products, a CD-ROM does not offer sufficient space. A new standard, Digital Versatile Disc, is now being developed that can store more than 4.7 gigabytes of information—about seven times as much as a CD-ROM. DVD can also store an entire two-hour movie on a single side of the disc.

The DVD players should be released in late 1996 or early 1997 by Toshiba, Sony, and Philips. Predictions are that the initial price of the players will be much higher than that of CD-ROM players. Eventually, though, the prices will drop, and the format is likely to be adopted by educational titles as well as distributors of movies (see chapter 5 for more information on DVD).

EVALUATION AND IMPLEMENTATION

The successful implementation of a new technology requires planning and research. The following suggestions are offered to assist schools in acquiring applications and workstations for CD-ROM.

1. Carefully analyze the content of the CD-ROM to ensure that it provides the scope, currency, and accuracy that are appropriate for the curriculum area, student needs, and grade level. If you are buying CD-ROM applications for elementary students or students with low reading levels, be sure to check the reading requirements of the text. In some cases the interface may appear user friendly, and there may be bells and whistles in the multimedia, but the text may be well beyond the scope of your readers.

2. Locate reviews of CD-ROM applications. Many of the periodicals listed in chapter 1, such as *CD-ROM Professional,* and *MultiMedia Schools,* provide in-depth reviews of current CD-ROM titles. Technology conferences and Internet news groups are also excellent places to find information on new applications.

3. Test the interface for ease of use. CD-ROM applications should allow the students to operate them without frustration. In general, look for uncluttered screens with sufficient prompts to assist in moving through the program and accessing the content.

4. Look for bundled packages of applications. Some of the best buys for CD-ROM applications are available in bundled packages. By analyzing the market, you can often get 6 or 10 applications for the same price as the one you are searching for. You must be careful, however, that the applications are indeed the full program rather than scaled-down models.

5. Check renewal fees. Many schools have purchased a CD-ROM application, such as a database, only to discover they cannot afford the subscription fees. Because information changes continuously, the updates may be more expensive than the original application.

6. Purchase a high-resolution color computer monitor. If you want to be able to take advantage of the multimedia programs, you will need a color monitor for a Macintosh and at least a VGA (video graphics array) monitor for an MS-DOS computer.

7. Attach headphones to the CD-ROM players. More applications are providing audio output for music or narration. Almost all CD-ROM players have outputs for headphones—a must if the application is to be used in a library or media center. Speakers will be required if a large group will be listening to the application.

8. Dedicate a machine for CD-ROM applications. Unless the use of CD-ROM is sporadic, it is usually best to dedicate a machine as a CD-ROM workstation. Limiting the use of the machine to CD-ROM applications will help eliminate the controversy caused by students seeking to pursue a variety of applications.

9. Set a time limit for students to use the CD-ROM workstation. Many libraries are finding time restraints necessary. Depending on the demand for the application, the limit may be anywhere from 15 minutes to 1 hour.

10. Set a limit on the number of printouts each student can make at one time. This gives more students an opportunity to use the CD-ROM. Limiting the number of printouts per student can also help to conserve paper.

11. Guard the discs. CD-ROM discs will not play in CD-Audio players. Unfortunately, however, students do not always realize the incompatibility. To avoid loss of or damage to CD-ROM discs, some schools have implemented procedures to help to protect the discs. For example, if only one application is being run on a computer, the CD-ROM player may be placed in a concealed area. If the discs must be changed, a checkout system may be required to keep track of the applications.

12. Provide job aids at the computer workstation. Because there are no standards for searching different CD-ROMs, students will need job aids, including command summaries, beside the workstation. Many of the applications supply a laminated set of commands for the user's reference.

13. Train a core of students. This is one of the most successful techniques for providing training on CD-ROM. Trained students can then help others use the technology.

CONCLUSION

CD-ROM technology has a strong base in the educational system because of its large storage capacity and low cost. CD-ROMs provide almost instant access to approximately 650 megabytes of text, graphics, video, and sound. The educational applications for CD-ROM cover a wide range of programs, including electronic encyclopedias, multimedia databases, games, clip media, and electronic storybooks.

With an installed base of more than 100 million CD-ROM players, it would appear that the CD-ROM industry is quite stable (Dyrli and Kinnaman 1995). However, new competition is looming on the horizon as DVD technology promises several times more storage space and the storage of two-hour movies with full-screen, full-motion delivery. Only time will tell if we are on the threshold of an enhanced CD or a new technology entirely.

CD-ROM GLOSSARY

access time. The time required to find and display information. Most CD-ROM drives have access times between 100 and 300 milliseconds.

autoexec.bat. The file in MS-DOS computers containing commands that are executed whenever the computer starts up.

Boolean search. The use of logical connectors—*and, or, not*—to search for a combination of words or phrases.

browse search. A search similar to looking through an alphabetical index. All the articles or words are listed in order.

caddy. A small plastic and metal case that is required by some CD-ROM drives to hold the compact disc when it is inserted into the drive.

CD-Audio (Compact Disc–Audio). A popular format for high-fidelity digital music. Each disc offers 74 minutes of programmable sound with no degradation of quality during playback.

CD-i (Compact Disc–Interactive). A system specification for an interactive audio, video, and computer system based on a compact disc as the storage medium. CD-i has a range of capabilities and is focused at the consumer market.

CD-R (Compact Disc–Recordable). A CD-ROM drive capable of recording compact discs in a format that is compatible with CD-ROM standards.

CD-ROM (Compact Disc–Read Only Memory). A prerecorded, nonerasable disc that stores approximately 650 megabytes of digital data.

compact disc. A 4.72-inch-wide plastic platter that stores digital data or music that is encoded and read by a laser or a light beam. Sometimes called *optical* discs.

compression. Technique used to store video images, sound, and so on, using fewer bits and therefore less disk storage space.

config.sys. The file in MS-DOS computers that contains information about the hardware configuration.

cross-platform. A software program that can run in the Macintosh and MS-DOS environments.

daisychain. Connecting more than one device, such as a CD-ROM, to the same computer port.

data-transfer rate. The number of kilobytes of information that can be transferred each second from the CD-ROM disc or other peripheral to the host computer. A single-speed CD-ROM drive has a data-transfer rate of 150K/sec; a quad-speed drive has 600K/sec.

disc. Usually refers to a videodisc or compact disc. Computer diskettes are generally referred to as *disks* (with a *k*), and videodiscs and other optical storage media are referred to as *discs* (with a *c*).

double-speed drive. A CD-ROM drive that transfers data at 300K/sec—twice as fast as the original CD-Audio discs.

download. The process of copying a file from a storage medium, such as a CD-ROM, to a computer diskette or hard drive.

DVD (Digital Versatile Disc). A second generation of the original CD-ROM format that will provide up to two layers of digital information on a single-sided compact disc. Storage will be up to 4.7 gigabytes for one layer and 8.5 gigabytes for two layers.

HFS (Hierarchical File System). The Apple HFS standard is used to create Macintosh-only CD-ROM discs; this standard is the same file format used on all Macintosh floppy disks and hard disks.

interface. A link between two components, such as a CD-ROM player and a computer.

ISO 9660. A format for CD-ROM data that was established by the International Standards Organization. This format, also known as High Sierra, approximates the MS-DOS style of naming files, and it can be used for Macintosh or MS-DOS discs.

jukebox. CD-ROM drives that can hold several discs and switch between them to play the one that is requested by the computer.

keyword search. A search that allows the user to search the contents of all the articles for a specific keyword or phrase. It usually provides a listing of the articles that contain the keyword and the number of hits, or occurrences, of the keyword in each article.

minichanger. A CD-ROM player that has one drive mechanism and several discs. The discs are switched in and out of the mechanism by demand from the computer.

mixed-mode CD-ROM. Compact discs that contain computer data and CD-Audio tracks. The computer data is generally recorded on the inner tracks of the disc, and the audio is recorded on the outer tracks.

MPC (multimedia personal computer). A hardware configuration standard for MS-DOS computers. To be termed an MPC workstation, the following components are required: 2MB of RAM, a hard drive, Microsoft Windows, a VGA monitor, a CD-ROM drive, and a digital audio board. (See chapter 4.)

MSCDEX (Microsoft Extensions). A software program by Microsoft Corporation that allows MS-DOS computers to communicate with a CD-ROM drive just like any other computer drive.

multisession player. A CD-ROM player that can read discs that were recorded at several different times. For example, Photo-CD discs are often recorded in several sessions.

optical disc. A disc that is encoded and read with a beam of light. Usually refers to a compact disc or videodisc. (*See also* compact disc.)

peripheral. Hardware that is controlled by a computer.

Photo CD (Photographic Compact Disc). Used by the Kodak Company to store photographic images on a compact disc.

proprietary controller interface. A computer interface that is designed to operate with a specific peripheral, such as a specific CD-ROM player.

proximity search. A search that specifies the closeness of the keywords within the article. For example, the user can specify that the keywords must be in the same paragraph or be less than five words apart.

quad-speed CD-ROM drive. A CD-ROM drive that has a data-transfer rate four times faster (600K/sec) than the original compact discs (150K/sec).

QuickTime. A file format that allows Macintosh computers to compress and play digitized video movies.

rewritable compact discs. Computer drives that allow you to write, erase, and rewrite on a compact disc.

SCSI (Small Computer Systems Interface). A standard for connecting external devices (such as CD-ROM drives) to a computer. SCSI interfaces allow more than one drive to be added (daisychained).

SCSI-2. An improved, updated form of SCSI.

single-session player. A CD-ROM player that can only read discs that were recorded in one session. If a multisession disc is played in this player, it will read only the part of the disc that was recorded first.

triple-speed CD-ROM drive. A drive that transfers data at 450K/sec—three times as fast as the original CD-Audio discs.

truncation. A search technique that allows for alternate endings.

VGA (video graphics array). A graphics-display adapter for MS-DOS computers that can display up to 256 colors simultaneously.

Video CD. Compact discs that are designed to deliver full-motion video. These discs can store up to 74 minutes of video; however, they require special video decoder hardware and sometimes software.

Video for Windows. A file format that allows MS-DOS computers with Microsoft Windows to compress or play digitized video movies.

wild cards. Search techniques that allow alternate spellings within words. For example, a wild card, such as the symbol *$*, can be used to search for *wom$n,* yielding either *woman* or *women.*

workstation. A unit that consists of a computer and peripherals that is used to deliver lessons or provide a work area.

WORM (Write Once–Read Many). Refers to a special technology that can record but not erase a compact disc.

CD-ROM RESOURCES

A.D.A.M. Software
1600 Riveredge Parkway
Atlanta, GA 30328
800-755-2326

Berkeley Macintosh Users Group
1442A Walnut Street, Suite 62
Berkeley, CA 94709-1496
510-549-2684

Bowker Electronic Publishing
245 W. 17th Street
New York, NY 10011
800-323-3288

Brodart Automation
500 Arch Street
Williamsport, PA 17705
800-233-8467

Broderbund Software, Inc.
500 Redwood Boulevard
Novato, CA 94948
800-521-6263

CD-ROM Directory
Online, Inc.
462 Danbury Road
Wilton, CT 06897-2126
800-248-8466

Claris Corporation
5201 Patrick Henry Drive
Santa Clara, CA 95052-8168
800-3CLARIS

Computer Curriculum Corp.
1287 Lawrence Station Road
Sunnyvale, CA 94041
800-227-8329

Corel Corporation
1600 Carling Avenue
Ottawa, Ontario K1Z 8R7
Canada
800-772-6735

D. C. Heath and Company
2700 N. Richardt Avenue
Indianapolis, IN 46219
800-334-3284

Davidson and Associates
19840 Pioneer Avenue
Torrance, CA 90503
800-545-7677

DeLorme Mapping
P.O. Box 298
Freeport, ME 04032
800-452-5931

Discis Knowledge Research
P.O. Box 66
Buffalo, NY 14223
800-567-4321

Disclosure, Inc.
5161 River Road
Bethesda, MD 20816
800-843-7747

Dorling Kindersley Multimedia
95 Madison Avenue
New York, NY 10016
800-356-6575

Eastman Kodak Company
343 State Street
Rochester, NY 14650
800-242-2424, ext. 53

EBSCO Electronic Information
P.O. Box 2250
83 Pine Street
Peabody, MA 01960-7250
800-653-2726

Edmark Corporation
P.O. Box 97021
Redmond, WA 98073
800-362-2890

EDUCORP Computer Services
7434 Trade Street
San Diego, CA 92121
800-843-9497

Encyclopaedia Britannica
310 S. Michigan Avenue
Chicago, IL 60604
800-554-9862

Fairfield Language Technologies
122 S. Main Street
Harrisburg, VA 22801
800-788-0822

Follett Software Company
809 N. Front Street
McHenry, IL 60050
800-323-3397

Grolier Interactive
Sherman Turnpike
Danbury, CT 06816
800-285-4534

HarperCollins Interactive
1000 Keystone Industrial Park
Scranton, PA 18512
800-424-6234

IBM Corporation
4111 Northside Parkway
Atlanta, GA 30327
800-IBM-4EDU

Information Access Company
362 Lakeside Drive
Foster City, CA 94404
800-227-8431

Innovative Media Corporation
631 E. Allen Street
Springfield, IL 62703
217-544-4614

Intellimation
P.O. Box 1911
Santa Barbara, CA 93116
800-368-6868

IntelliTools
55 Leveroni Court, Suite 9
Novato, CA 94949
800-899-6687

Janus Interactive
1600 N.W. 167 Place
Beaverton, OR 97006
800-766-0835

Jostens Learning Corporation
9920 Pacific Heights Boulevard
San Diego, CA 92121
800-521-8538

Knight-Ridder Information Services, Inc.
2440 El Camino Real
Mountain View, CA 94040
800-334-2564

Knowledge Adventure
45402 Dyer Street
La Crescenta, CA 91214
800-542-4240

LCSI
P.O. Box 162
Highgate Springs, VT 05404
800-321-5646

The Learning Company
One Athenaeum Street
Cambridge, MA 02142
800-227-5609

LOGAL Software, Inc.
125 Cambridge Park Drive
Cambridge, MA 02140
800-564-2587

Macmillan/McGraw-Hill
220 E. Danieldale Road
De Soto, TX 75115
800-442-9685

Macromedia
600 Townsend Street
San Francisco, CA 94103
800-945-4051

MAXIS
2 Theatre Square, Suite 230
Orinda, CA 94567
800-99-MAXIS

Medio Multimedia
2611 151st Place NE
Redmond, WA 98052
800-788-3866

MEI/Micro Center
1100 Steelwood Road
Columbus, OH 43212
800-634-3478

Microsoft Corporation
One Microsoft Way
Redmond, WA 98052
800-426-9400

Mindscape
88 Rowland Way
Novato, CA 94945
800-234-3088

Minnesota Educational Computing Corporation (MECC)
6160 Summit Drive North
Minneapolis, MN 55430
800-685-6322

National Geographic Society
Educational Services
P.O. Box 98019
Washington, DC 20090
800-368-2728

NautilusCD
7001 Metatec Boulevard
Dublin, OH 43017
800-637-3472

New Media Schoolhouse
Box 390 Westchester Avenue
Pound Ridge, NY 10576
800-672-6002

NewsBank
58 Pine Street
New Canaan, CT 06840
800-762-8182

OCLC (Online Computer Library Catalog)
6565 Fratz Road
Dublin, OH 43017-0702
800-848-5878, ext. 6251

Optical Information Systems
Mecklermedia Corporation
11 Ferry Lane West
Westport, CT 06880-5808
203-226-6967

Optical Publishing Association
P.O. Box 21268
Columbus, OH 43221
614-442-8805

Pacific HighTech
4530 Fortuna Way
Salt Lake City, UT 84124
801-261-1024

Philips Professional Products
1 Philips Drive
Knoxville, TN 37914
800-223-4432

PhotoDisc, Inc.
2013 Fourth Avenue
Seattle, WA 98121
800-528-3472

Sanctuary Woods
1825 S. Grant Street
San Mateo, CA 94402
800-943-3664

Scholastic, Inc.
730 Broadway
New York, NY 10003
800-325-6149

SilverPlatter Information, Inc.
100 River Ridge Drive
Norwood, MA 02062
800-343-0064

Simon and Schuster Interactive
1230 Avenue of the Americas
New York, NY 10020
800-223-2336

SmartStuff Software
P.O. Box 82284
Portland, OR 97282
800-671-3999

Social Issues Resources Series, Inc.
P.O. Box 2348
Boca Raton, FL 33427-2348
800-232-7477

SoftKey International
One Athenaeum Street
Cambridge, MA 02142
800-227-5609

Software Toolworks
60 Leveroni Court
Novato, CA 94949
800-234-3088

Sony Electronics
1 Sony Drive
Park Ridge, NJ 07656-8003
800-686-SONY

Sunburst Software
101 Castleton Street
Pleasantville, NY 10570
800-321-7511

Syracuse Language Systems, Inc.
719 E. Genesee Street
Syracuse, NY 13210
800-688-1937

3M Optical Recording Department
Building 223-5S-01
3M Center
Saint Paul, MN 55144-1000
800-336-3636

Thynx
141 New Road
Parsippany, NJ 07054
800-828-4766

Time Warner Electronic Publishing
409 Sherman Avenue
Palo Alto, CA 94306
212-522-4643

Todd Enterprises
31 Water Mill Lane
Great Neck, NJ 11021
800-832-2722

Tom Snyder Productions
80 Coolidge Hill Road
Watertown, MA 02172
800-342-0236

UMI (University Microfilms International)
300 N. Zeeb Road
Ann Arbor, MI 48106
800-521-0600

Videodiscovery, Inc.
1700 Westlake Avenue North, Suite 600
Seattle, WA 98109
800-548-3472

Virgin Interactive
18061 Fitch Avenue
Irvine, CA 92714
800-874-4607

Voyager Company
578 Broadway, Suite 406
New York, NY 10012
800-446-2001

World Book Publishing
101 N.W. Point Boulevard
Elk Grove Village, IL 60007
800-621-8202

CD-i Resources

AIMS Multimedia
9710 DeSoto Avenue
Chatsworth, CA 91311
800-367-2467

AMPED, Ltd.
220 Clipper Bay Drive
Alpharetta, CA 30202
770-475-3387

CD-i Professional
P.O. Box 158
Camden, ME 04915
207-338-1122

Edutech
P.O. Box 51760
Pacific Grove, CA 93950
800-451-4440

Optimum Resources
P.O. Box 23317
Hilton Head, SC 29925
800-327-1473

Philips Professional Products
10960 Wilshire Boulevard
Los Angeles, CA 90024
800-340-7888

Skillmaster TransforMedia
P.O. Box 596
Lake Zurich, IL 60047
800-451-1843

Sony Electronics, Inc.
3 Paragon Drive
Montvale, NJ 07645
800-686-SONY

REFERENCE LIST

Dyrli, E., and D. E. Kinnaman. (1995). Moving ahead educationally with multimedia. *Technology and Learning* 15(7): 46–51.

RECOMMENDED READING

Bunzel, T. (1996). The dawning of DVD. *Multimedia Producer* 2(4): 31–34.

Carter, B. J. (1995). CD-ROM mastering: What are your publishing options? *T.H.E. Journal* 22(7): 80–87.

Cazet, D. (1996). Early reading, electronic-style. *Technology and Learning* 16(5): 14–16.

Congress, M. (1996). CD-ROM in school libraries: Who uses what and why? *MultiMedia Schools* 3(3): 50–52.

Cury, J. O. (1996). Jukebox heroes. *Multimedia World* 3(6): 35.

Desmond, M. (1996). Why your next CD-ROM drive may be a recordable. *Multimedia World* 3(4): 16–17.

Doering, D. (1996). Choosing a CD-ROM network solution. *CD-ROM Professional* 9(3): 74–91.

Gisceglie, M. (1995). CD-i in the classroom. *Media & Methods* 32(2): S-6.

Graf, N. (1995). How to network CD-ROMs. *Media & Methods* 32(1): LS-16–LS-18.

Gray, J. (1995). Philips's compact disc-interactive gains in U. S. business, all European markets. *Multimedia Producer* 1(2): 57–58.

Holzberg, C. S. (1995). K-6 reference: New tools rule! *Electronic Learning* 15(1): 42–45.

Hurtig, B. (1996). Fast new CD-ROM drives. *NewMedia* 6(3): 40–56.

Ling, P. (1996). CD-ROM and multiplatform performance: The hybrid road. *CD-ROM Professional* 9(5): 38–48.

Lynch, P. J. (1995). PhotoCD: Digital photography anyone can use. *Syllabus* 8(8): 20–26.

Macciocca, J. M. (1996). The active life and energies of school libraries. *Media & Methods* 32(4): 26–30.

McBroom, G. (1995). Interactive CD yearbook and multimedia journalism. *Media & Methods* 32(1): 18–20.

McClanahan, G. (1995). Networking CD-ROMs: Some software considerations. *Multi-Media Schools* 2(32): 68–70.

Merrill, P. (1995). A survival guide for CD-ROM do-it-yourselfers. *Multimedia Producer* 1(6): 27–32.

Parham, C. (1995). CD-ROM storybooks revisited. *Technology and Learning* 15(6): 14–18.

Parker, D. J. (1996). DVD is just around the corner (but it is a very long block). *CD-ROM Professional* 9(5): 97–100.

Singer, L. A. (1995). CD-ROM storybooks: Variations on a theme. *MultiMedia Schools* 2(5): 48–50.

———. (1995). Choosing multimedia CD-ROM encyclopedias. *MultiMedia Schools* 2(4): 17–26.

Starrett, R. A. (1996). CD-recordable software and hybrid CDs. *CD-ROM Professional* 9(5): 50–55.

Wasson, G. (1996). Feel the burn. *MacUser* 12(1): 86–94.

COMPACT DISC READ ONLY MEMORY

An Overview Of

This brochure is an excerpt from:

New Technologies for Education

A Beginner's Guide

Third Edition

Dr. Ann E. Barron
University of South Florida

Dr. Gary W. Orwig
University of Central Florida

To obtain the complete book, contact:

Libraries Unlimited
P.O. Box 6633
Englewood, CO 80155-6633
800-237-6124

Educational Applications

Encyclopedias

An entire encyclopedia can be stored on a single CD-ROM disc (yes, every word). These applications can be searched for any word or combination of words. In addition, many electronic encyclopedias contain pictures, video, and sound.

Reference Databases

Library research is easier and faster with one of the many CD-ROM reference applications. Students and teachers can quickly retrieve titles and abstracts from databases such as *ERIC* on CD-ROM.

Multimedia Programs

Because CD-ROMs can store digital information in the form of text, graphics, sound, music, and video, they make an excellent medium for multimedia products. Multimedia on a CD-ROM can range from a storybook with sound and pictures to an interactive program for teaching science.

Computer Programs

CD-ROM discs are often used to store and deliver computer software. Several discs are available that provide public domain software. Students and teachers can preview the programs and then copy the selected software to a floppy diskette. Clip art and sound files are also distributed on CD-ROM discs.

- *Storage Capacity.* Each CD-ROM disc can hold more than 650 megabytes of text, graphics, sound, or digital video.

- *Portability.* CD-ROM discs are small and lightweight, making them an ideal medium for transporting data.

- *Durability.* CD-ROM discs are encoded in plastic and are very durable. Although they should be handled with care, fingerprints and slight scratches will not usually impair their performance.

- *Inexpensive Hardware.* The cost of CD-ROM drives has decreased dramatically in the past few years.

- *Availability of Titles.* Several thousand commercial titles are now available on CD-ROM discs.

- *Slow Data Access.* When compared to hard drives, CD-ROM drives are relatively slow in retrieving data.

- *Read Only.* CD-ROMs are read only, and they cannot be updated or changed in any way.

- *Lack of Interface Standards.* There is very little consistency among CD-ROM applications.

Configuration

CD-ROM discs require their own special player and cannot be played on an audio CD player; however, CD-ROM players can also play audio compact discs.

The CD-ROM player must be connected to a computer—either Macintosh, MS-DOS, or Apple II—with an interface cable. A computer monitor is used to display the data when it is retrieved from the CD-ROM. A keyboard, mouse, or other input device is required to interact with the CD-ROM.

CD-ROM Drive

When a CD-ROM player is connected to an MS-DOS computer, an additional card may have to be installed in the computer. CD-ROM players come in many shapes and sizes. Some players are external, and others may be built into the computer as an internal drive.

Storage Capacity

CD-ROM stands for Compact Disc-Read Only Memory. It is an information storage technology that uses a compact disc 4.72 inches in diameter. The discs are rugged and lightweight.

The storage capacity of a single CD-ROM disc is over 650 megabytes. That is equivalent to several hundred floppy diskettes or the entire text of a 20-volume encyclopedia.

STORAGE DEVICE	CAPACITY	EQUIVALENT
Floppy Disks	1.4 MB	720 pages of text
Hard Disk Drive	200 MB	100,000 pages of text
CD-ROM	650+ MB	325,000 pages of text

CD-ROM discs can store many types of digital information, including photographs, text, graphics, video, animations, and audio. Anything that can be stored on a computer diskette can also be stored on a CD-ROM.

CD-ROM is an optical storage medium that uses a tiny laser beam to store and retrieve the information on the disc. It is important to note that CD-ROM discs are read only. The information on the disc cannot be modified or erased.

3

Interactive Videodisc

A Scenario

The students in Ms. Brown's fifth-grade class were busy creating multimedia reports. The assignment was to present information to the class about the animals, insects, or fish they had studied. They could use videodisc images that were accessed with either barcodes or a computer program such as HyperCard or HyperStudio. The resources in the room included several inexpensive videodiscs, two videodisc players, and two computers with printers for making barcodes.

Sam's group was viewing a videodisc about mammals from the *Encyclopedia of Animals Series*. They used the *display* option on the remote-control unit so that they could write down the frame number of each picture they wanted to use in their report. After they decided exactly which images to include, they typed the frame numbers into the HyperCard template that Ms. Brown had created for the class. Each page of the HyperCard template had a video button where they could enter the beginning and ending frame numbers for each sequence and a text box where they could type in the descriptions or other information related to the image. The discussions were lively as the group debated about which of the animal pictures were best for their presentation.

Jill's and Jacob's groups had decided to use barcodes to access their images. First, they used the documentation that was supplied with the *Bio Sci* videodisc to select the images. The *Bio Sci* index listed all the frame numbers for the images, along with their common name and scientific name. Later, when the videodisc player was free, they would test out the numbers to make sure the images were appropriate. After they had the frame numbers listed, they used the *Bar'n'Coder* program on the computers to create the barcodes. It amazed them how easy it was to type in a frame number, print out a barcode, and, with a swipe of the barcode reader, display the corresponding image.

Jamal's group was using the *Insects* videodisc and HyperStudio for their project. Because HyperStudio includes video-control features, all they had to do was click on *begin* when they were on a frame where they wanted the video segment to start and click on *end* to record the frame number for the end of the video. They had a great time selecting the segments of the insects and watching them crawl all over the screen. When they had finished selecting a video clip, they clicked *try it* to ensure that they had selected the correct frames, and then *keep* to embed the commands into their presentation.

Anita had convinced her group to use the *Great Ocean Rescue* for their presentation. They spent some time going through the Teacher's Guide and were planning to have the class complete the Grief on the Reef mission. In addition to the structured materials, they planned to use the other side of the disc to add information about life on the reef.

When it was time for the presentations, Ms. Brown connected two television monitors to the videodisc player so that all the students would have a good view of the images. She was impressed by the amount of work the students had put into their projects and the amount of information they had acquired in the process. Even the typically unmotivated students could not help but become interested in the "giant" insects and the other high-quality images on the screen.

Videodisc technology currently offers the best quality for random-access, full-motion, full-screen video sequences. Videodisc players are affordable for schools, and they connect easily to regular television monitors. A variety of commercial videodisc programs are available for education, and many provide extensive support materials for teachers. This chapter provides

- An overview of videodisc formats and terminology
- Advantages and disadvantages of videodiscs
- Descriptions of the levels of interactivity
- Educational applications of videodiscs
- Repurposing videodiscs
- Creating a videodisc
- Selection and evaluation techniques
- Resources for further information

INTRODUCTION

Videodisc technology is an extension of videotape technology. The main difference is that the video information is stored on a hard, plastic disc instead of a tape. Also, videodiscs are read by a laser beam; this makes it possible to randomly search any segment and play it at slow or fast speeds. Videodiscs provide almost instantaneous access to full-motion video and quality sound.

Videodisc technology is not new. For more than 20 years it was successfully used in business and industrial training—though it has now almost disappeared in those environments. So why is it included in this book on new technologies for education? The main reason is that it did not become popular in schools until the 1990s. Now, even with the growth in the number of CD-ROM titles, videodiscs still have a vital role to play in education. Although they may be replaced by emerging digital video technologies (see chapter 5) in the near future, they currently offer the best option for full-screen, full-motion, high-quality video.

One reason for the sustained popularity of videodiscs in instructional settings is the multitude of available, reasonably priced educational discs. Teachers have discovered that videodiscs are an ideal medium for displaying high-quality images. Whether conducting a complex chemistry experiment or analyzing the formation of a tornado, with videodiscs teachers can completely control the sequence, rate, and duration of the presentation.

ADVANTAGES AND DISADVANTAGES OF VIDEODISCS

Videodiscs offer many advantages for schools over their videotape, film, and CD-ROM counterparts. However, videodiscs may not be the best medium for every situation. This section reviews the features and limitations of videodisc technology.

Advantages of Videodiscs

Access. Frames and segments on a videodisc can be accessed by using a remote-control unit, barcode reader, or computer. There is no need to fast-forward or rewind. The access is fast and precise. Unlike videotape, there is no need to remember to reset the counter to zero; the frame numbers on a videodisc are permanently encoded and do not change.

Cost. Although cost varies, many videodiscs are less expensive than the same programs on tape or film.

Durability. Because videodiscs are read with a laser beam and there is no direct contact, the images on the disc do not degenerate with use as they do with videotape. Even after many years of use, the video will look clean and sharp. Discs are made of rugged plastic—even fingerprints and small scratches do not affect them.

Quality. Videodiscs are generally recorded with 350 lines of resolution. VHS videotapes are recorded with only 200 to 250 lines of resolution. Therefore, videodiscs have a sharper appearance and better-quality picture. When you compare videodisc to CD-ROM, the videodisc quality is also higher in most cases because the images on a CD-ROM are often recorded at a low quality to save storage space.

Interactivity. Unlike videotape or film, a videodisc is relatively easy to control. Level III videodisc programs provide the interactivity and instant feedback of computer-assisted instruction with the visual and audio realism of a videodisc. Barcodes can also be used for interactive lessons.

Still frame. It is difficult to "pause" a videotape, and the tape may be damaged by doing so. Videodiscs can be halted on a still frame for hours with no damage. This provides individual access to every frame on the disc.

Dual audio tracks. Two audio tracks are available on all videodiscs. This means that you can have stereo sound or two separate tracks. In many of the programs, one track is recorded in English and the other in Spanish or another language.

Format standards. Although there are two different video formats—CLV and CAV—all videodisc players can play all laser standard videodiscs. The VHS versus BETA versus Umatic videotape format inconsistencies do not affect videodiscs.

Full-motion video. Although many CD-ROM titles are being produced that offer inexpensive access to a tremendous amount of information, the video on a CD-ROM is generally produced at less than full motion. Videodiscs play video at 30 frames per second with a realistic illusion of motion. On CD-ROM, the video is often recorded at only 15 frames per second or less, and the video appears jerky.

Full-screen video. Videotape and videodisc both display video on the entire screen, making it easier to project for a class. On a CD-ROM, most of the video is designed to display in $\frac{1}{4}$ or $\frac{1}{2}$ of the screen (see chapter 5 for more information about digital video).

Teacher support materials. It is not uncommon for a videodisc program to include a teacher's guide, barcode activities, lesson plans, and student work sheets.

Disadvantages of Videodiscs

Cost of interactive software. Some videodiscs—especially Level III programs—can be expensive because of the high production costs incurred for design and development of quality programs. Interactive CD-ROMs are generally less expensive.

Cost of hardware. Although the cost of videodisc players is declining, prices continue to limit the number of units within reach of schools. Players that connect to computers and provide remote-control units currently cost about $700. CD-ROM players are much less expensive.

Maintenance costs. It is not unusual to spend several hundred dollars to repair a videodisc player, and it can be difficult to find a repair shop locally. Players should be treated gently to minimize damage.

Lack of interface standards. Connecting a computer to a videodisc player for a Level III program can be frustrating. Different players require different interface cables and require different software drivers. Also, baud rates have to be set correctly.

Read only. Videodiscs are read only, which means that you cannot record on the disc. Videotape is much more flexible for recording and editing.

Limited motion sequences. Up to 54,000 still frames is a tremendous capacity for videodisc, but when this is translated into motion sequences, the limit is 30 minutes—much less than a videotape's capacity.

Computer storage requirements. If a Level III videodisc program is used, computer software is needed to run the program. In some cases, the amount of storage space required on a hard drive is enormous. Some programs require that up to 12 diskettes be loaded onto your hard drive. This quickly fills most drives available in schools. To solve this storage problem, a few of the videodisc programs have companion CD-ROMs that provide the interactive software portion of the program.

Video Frames

The video material on a videodisc is produced with a video camera and editing equipment just as it is for a videotape. After the master videotape is edited to a length of 30 or 60 minutes, it is recorded onto a hard, plastic videodisc. Once the videodisc is recorded, it cannot be changed in any way.

Both videotapes and videodiscs consist of a series of frames or pictures. When the tape or disc is in the play mode, it moves at a standard rate of 30 frames per second to create the illusion of motion. The difference between the storage of video frames on a videotape and a videodisc is illustrated in figure 3.1. On a videotape, video frames are stored in a linear pattern. You must fast forward or rewind to locate the section you want. On a videodisc, frames are stored in concentric circles and are read with a laser beam that can easily jump from one frame to another to provide almost instant access.

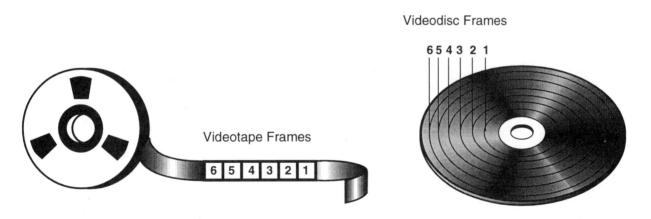

Figure 3.1. Videotape and Videodisc Frames.

The sound, or audio, on a videodisc is stored in two separate audio tracks that can be played separately or together for stereo. This feature provides the potential for having two different languages for the same video content or for having music on one track and narration on the other. The audio will play only if the videodisc is moving forward at the standard rate of 30 frames per second. If you play the disc faster, slower, or in reverse, there is no sound.

Videodisc Formats

There are two different videodisc formats. The most common format used in education is called CAV, for "constant angular velocity." On a CAV disc, each circle is an individual frame. Videodiscs that are recorded in this format have a capacity of 30 minutes of motion video on each side. An advantage of CAV discs is that a still frame (single picture) can be displayed. That means you can stop the videodisc on any single frame and display it for as long as you want without causing any damage to the videodisc. There are 30 minutes of motion on each side of the disc and 30 frames per second; therefore, you can access up to 54,000 individual frames if the disc is full (30 frames per second x 60 seconds per minute x 30 minutes per side = 54,000 frames per disc side).

Each frame on a 12-inch videodisc has a unique number in the range from 1 to 54,000. These numbers are automatically placed on the disc when it is recorded. If you know the number of a desired frame, you can use the remote-control unit to access it. Many of the educational videodiscs provide a list of frame numbers correlated with content so that the teacher can quickly access appropriate still images.

Another feature of a CAV videodisc is that you can "step"—move forward or back just one frame—by using the remote-control unit, barcode reader, or the videodisc player panel. This technique is useful if you want to analyze an event, such as the formation of a tornado. You can also "scan"—fast forward through the disc—and "play" at various speeds, forward or reverse.

The other format used for videodiscs is CLV, which stands for "constant linear velocity." A CLV disc is the same size as a CAV disc, but the video frames are stored in a different configuration; instead of one frame on each concentric circle, the frames are stored in a spiral pattern, and several frames or parts of frames may be on the same circle. This is good because more video can fit on a CLV disc—twice as much, or 60 minutes on each side—but it is also bad because many of the best features of videodiscs, such as the ability to still-frame and step-frame, are lost. Therefore, most CLV discs are used for movies and other applications that are designed to be played in a linear manner from beginning to end.

Instead of frame numbers, most CLV discs have embedded time codes. For example, you might search to 0:08.12, which would be 8 minutes and 12 seconds from the beginning of the disc. Because CLV discs cannot display still frames, when you search for a particular time code, the video starts playing from that point. Figure 3.2 summarizes some features of CAV and CLV videodiscs.

CAV and CLV videodiscs can have embedded chapter stops and picture stops. Chapter stops are much like chapters in a

Feature	CAV	CLV
Minutes per Side	30	60
Normal Play	Yes	Yes
Still-Frame	Yes	No
Step-Frame	Yes	No
Multispeed	Yes	No
Scan	Yes	Yes
Frame Search	Yes	No
Time Search	No	Yes
Chapter Search	Yes	Yes

Figure 3.2. Features of CAV and CLV Formats.

book: They divide the videodisc into linear segments. If a disc has chapter stops, a remote-control unit can be used to jump to the chapter you want. Picture stops are locations on the disc where the disc stops and displays a still frame. Many discs have picture stops at the beginning of the disc: A title screen appears and then the disc stops until the user presses *play* or issues another command.

LEVELS OF INTERACTIVITY

Three *levels of interactivity* are commonly used to refer to the delivery of videodisc programs. These levels—I, II, and III—provide varying amounts of control for the user and require different hardware configurations.

Level I

Level I interactivity refers to using the videodisc player without a computer. The disc access is controlled through either the control panel on the player, a remote-control unit, or a barcode reader. (See fig. 3.3.)

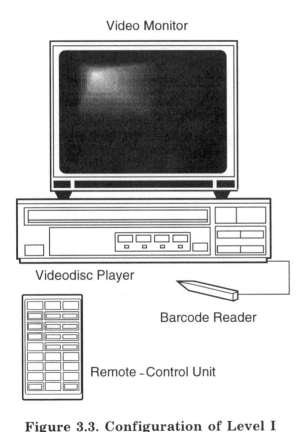

Figure 3.3. Configuration of Level I Interactivity.

Videodisc Player Control Panel

One way to control a Level I disc is through the control panel on the front of the disc player. Although the control panels for various models of players have different features, most panels provide at least some of the features shown in figure 3.4.

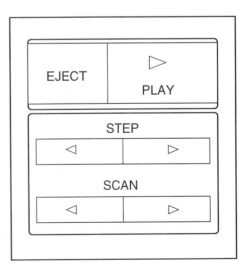

Figure 3.4. Control Panel on Videodisc Player.

Just place the disc in the drawer and press *play*. If you want to stop the disc, press *step*. You can also *scan* to jump forward to another section on the disc. Using the control panel is a lot like playing a videotape. You can start (play), stop (step), and fast-forward (scan), but you do not have the ability to input a frame number and search to a specific frame on the disc.

Remote-Control Unit

Another method of controlling a Level I videodisc is with a remote-control unit. In addition to the *step, scan,* and *play* options usually available on a player's front control panel, remote-control units allow users to input a number and access a particular chapter or frame. Chapters on a videodisc are similar to chapters in a book; they help to divide the content into sections. The videodisc chapters are encoded on the disc when it is recorded, and the chapter numbers are provided in printed documentation or on the videodisc jacket. For instance, the jacket or manual of a Level I videodisc may list the following chapters:

Chapter 1: Mammals

Chapter 2: Birds

Chapter 3: Insects

Chapter 4: Reptiles

Chapter 5: Fish

If the remote-control unit is in the chapter mode, you can simply press 3 and *search* to jump immediately to the section on insects. Most videodiscs have between 10 and 20 chapters on each side of the disc.

You can also use the remote-control unit to instantly access a particular frame number. For example, if you know that a picture of a peacock is on frame 23654, you can switch the remote-control unit to the frame mode and press 23654 and *search* to display the peacock. Many of the videodisc programs provide written logs, or lists, of the videodisc frames and their content to facilitate using individual frames for instruction.

In addition to the ability to jump to a chapter or frame, most remote-control units offer other options for Level I delivery. (See fig. 3.5.)

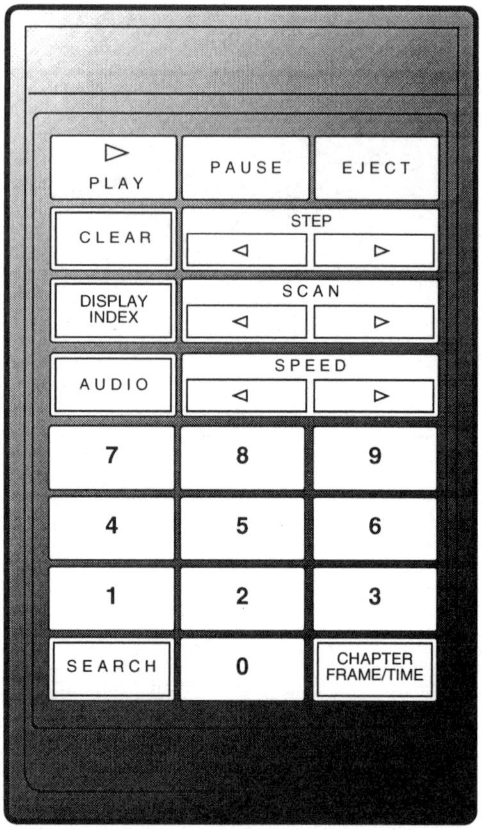

Figure 3.5. Remote-Control Unit.

Index. Two different numbers can be embedded on a CAV disc: frame numbers and chapter numbers. Pressing the *display index* button—a toggle button— displays or erases the chapter number and the frame numbers on the television screen. This is useful for determining locations on the disc or for creating a written log of the disc material. On a CLV disc, time codes are displayed instead of frame numbers.

Chapter frame/time. This button is used to toggle back and forth between the chapter mode and the frame/time mode for searching purposes. When this button is pressed, the monitor indicates whether you are in the chapter or frame/time mode.

Audio. There are at least two audio tracks on each disc, and this button is used to toggle between them. In most cases, it is a four-way toggle. Press it once and you have track 1; twice and you have track 2. Press it three times and you have no audio; four times and you are back in stereo mode. (Note that some discs may also have digital sound tracks, providing a total of four different audio tracks.)

Laser Barcode Reader

An alternative for controlling Level I delivery is the laser barcode reader. A videodisc barcode wand is similar to those used in grocery stores to read a series of black lines that stores the price of an item. Many barcode readers can be operated either with a direct connection to the videodisc player or as a remote-control device. To operate a barcode reader with a direct connection, insert one end of the barcode cable into the plug on the videodisc player. Connect the other end of the cable to the barcode reader. Then hold down the *read* button on the barcode reader as you lightly pass the wand over the barcode. The barcode reader will beep when you have successfully scanned the barcode. (This may require a little practice.)

If the barcode reader is also capable of wireless remote control, it is operated in the same manner but without the cable. Simply scan the barcode, wait for the beep, position yourself in front of the player, and point the reader at the infrared remote sensor on the front panel of the player. Press *send* on the barcode reader and the player will transmit the command.

Barcode readers may offer several other controls in addition to *read* and *send*. For example, the barcode reader in figure 3.6 provides controls for *play, step, scan,* and *audio.*

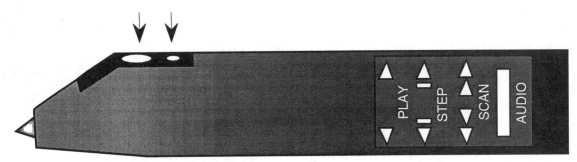

Figure 3.6. Laser Barcode Reader.

Figure 3.7 is an example of generic barcodes that are often supplied with videodiscs. Barcodes can also embed a number to access a particular frame. Many videodisc programs provide books, manuals, or laminated sheets with barcode access to some or all of the frames and chapters on the disc. For example, the *Draw and Color Funny Doodles with Uncle Fred* program provides documentation that has barcode access to each chapter, song, and drawing on the disc. (See fig. 3.8.) Level I videodisc programs with supplemental barcodes have become popular because they are easy for a teacher to implement in a classroom situation.

Play	Step	Video On	Video Off	Audio On	Audio Off

Figure 3.7. Sample Generic Barcodes.

Sea Lion Song

Frame 42157 - 43025

Figure 3.8. Sample Barcode.

Level II

Level II videodiscs have almost disappeared from the school market. They were designed to be used without a computer and included a computer control program that was embedded into the videodisc. For example, the disc might stop on a still frame with a multiple-choice question. If the student answered "3" through the remote-control unit, the control program on the disc would cause the videodisc to display a specific frame for feedback. A major problem with Level II videodiscs is that they can operate only on particular videodisc players—usually the more expensive models. Another issue is that the computer control program that is embedded into the videodisc cannot be changed or revised after the videodisc is recorded.

Level III

Level III videodisc programs include computer software to control the videodisc player—a cable connects the computer to the videodisc player. Level III provides more flexibility than Level I or Level II because a computer program can offer interactivity, such as branches based on keyboard and other student inputs. In addition, the student can choose a term, picture, or link in the software program that automatically displays the corresponding video on the video monitor. Level III programs can also include databases to track student performances and records.

The configuration for Level III delivery is generally the same as for Level I, with the addition of a computer and computer monitor. (See fig. 3.9.) In most cases, two separate monitors are necessary because the video monitor cannot display computer information and the computer monitor cannot display video information. A printer is not required unless the program offers the ability to take notes or print some of the computer information.

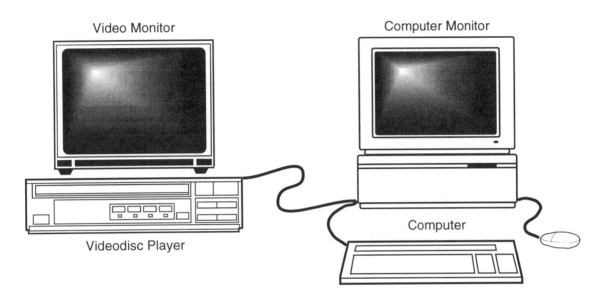

Figure 3.9. Configuration for Level III Interactivity.

An interface cable is required to connect the computer to the videodisc player. These cables are quite inexpensive and can be purchased from videodisc or computer vendors. A software program is also required for Level III delivery. Like other computer software, videodisc software is not interchangeable between Macintosh and MS-DOS/Windows computers. If you are purchasing a Level III program, you must make sure that the software control program is compatible with your computer. The software program contains settings for the baud rate, or speed of transfer, of the videodisc player. Most players have baud-rate settings of 1200 or 4800. Check your videodisc manual for additional information about setting the baud rates and configuring the software.

EDUCATIONAL APPLICATIONS

Many instructional strategies are employed in videodisc programs, including linear movies, tutorials, visual databases, problem-solving programs, simulations, and multimedia libraries. Some discs use only one strategy; others combine a variety of approaches.

Movies and Documentaries

Videodiscs offer a tremendous source of outstanding yet inexpensive movies and documentaries for schools. They can easily replace 16mm film libraries without worries about sprocket holes and rewinding. Even compared with videotape, discs have several advantages. For example, videodiscs do not wear out or degenerate with repeated use. In addition, many educational films, commercial movies, and documentaries are available on videodisc at lower prices than on videotapes. Also, by using the *search* option on the remote-control unit, you can instantly access any location on the disc. Many movies and documentaries are in the linear CLV format and are priced at less than $50.

Examples:

West Side Story (Voyager)

Space Odyssey (Voyager)

King Tut: The Face of Tutankhamen (Lumivision)

Scenic Wonders of America (Lumivision)

John F. Kennedy: A Celebration of His Life and Times (Lumivision)

Tutorials

Some videodisc programs are designed with a tutorial strategy in which new information is introduced and questions or other interactions are included through a software program or barcode activities. With the ability to branch easily to any segment on the disc, a student is not locked into a particular sequence.

Examples:

Minds-on-Science: The Impact of Discovery by Tom Snyder Productions features a videodisc, 28 student workbooks, and a teacher's guide with lesson plans and activities. The program is structured in a problem-solving scenario with tutorial information and research activities. For example, students can watch a video segment about how the brain functions, or they can learn about memory through an activity in which they watch a series of 12 still frames and record the pictures they can remember.

Windows on Math by Optical Data can be used as a supplement to a textbook or as a replacement for a text. The program is available at various grade levels and provides videodiscs, teacher handbooks, barcode guides, blackline masters, a CD-ROM, and activity cards. This program is an excellent way to introduce new mathematical concepts or to reinforce concepts with practice activities.

On Assignment by McDougal Littell and Houghton Mifflin provides 12 mini-tutorials that teach and reinforce thinking and communication skills. In these investigations, the students pitch a new advertisement campaign, produce a news report, take on city hall, and review new rock bands.

STV Atmosphere by National Geographic is a Level III program that contains several linear segments and still images. Each section includes preview questions for introduction and review questions to test students' understanding. Hints are provided for incorrect answers, and reinforcement follows correct answers.

Visual Databases

A *visual database* is a videodisc primarily made up of individual pictures rather than motion sequences. Because there can be up to 54,000 individual frames on a videodisc, visual databases offer access to an enormous amount of visual material. Each frame can be accessed and displayed for a lesson or presentation with either the remote-control unit, the barcode reader, or a computer.

Examples:

Bio Sci II by Videodiscovery contains more than 6,000 photographs of animals, plants, and biomes. The photographs can be accessed either through remote control—a log with barcodes is provided—or through a HyperCard (Macintosh) or LinkWay Live (MS-DOS) stack. Information concerning the classification of plants and animals is also included in the stack. To make the program easy for a teacher to use, the stack provides keyword searching and the ability to save a list of slides for manual or automatic presentation. The book *Bio Sci Elementary* is also available and contains lesson plans with barcodes.

The *Visual Almanac,* distributed by Voyager, provides a wealth of visual images that can be incorporated into classroom lessons. This disc has pictures in a wide range of topics and is an excellent resource for student projects.

Problem-Solving Programs

Excellent problem-solving videodisc programs have been developed that provide authentic learning environments for students. These programs generally present an issue through a video-based scenario. Students then access different parts of the videodisc for clues or research in their decision-making process.

Examples:

Science Sleuths by Videodiscovery includes 25 problem-based activities. For example, in "Twins or Not," students watch and listen to interviews with three people, each claiming to be a long-lost triplet. They can also obtain information to help them analyze blood types, compare fingerprint samples, and investigate DNA structures to determine if one of the three applicants is a legitimate relative. *Science Sleuths Elementary* is a similar program that includes activities for students in grades K-6.

The Adventures of Jasper Woodbury from Optical Data Corporation is an interactive videodisc series consisting of three kits, each with two program episodes. Each episode provides a videodisc-based adventure with information that is required to solve mathematical problems and subproblems. In *Rescue at Boone Creek,* Jasper finds a wounded eagle. His problem is to figure out the fastest way to rescue the eagle. Should he use an ultralight airplane, a truck, or a combination? To answer that question, he must determine the fuel required and the amount of weight that the ultralight can carry—in people and fuel.

Houghton Mifflin produces a language-arts series entitled Channel R. E. A. D. (Reading Enters Another Dimension). Each Level I videodisc in this series focuses on an aspect of literature, such as biographies or personal narratives in a story or mystery format. For example, in *The Case of the Missing Mystery Writer,* the students use their reading and writing skills to help find a famous mystery writer.

Simulations

Simulation programs can be used for problem-solving scenarios or role playing. In some cases, a procedure such as a chemistry experiment may be simulated that may be too dangerous or expensive to perform. In role-playing simulations, the student can make decisions and view the enacted results.

Examples:

The Great Ocean Rescue by Tom Snyder Productions provides a variety of simulations that can be delivered with a remote-control unit, barcode reader, or computer software. This program is designed to be implemented in a classroom environment with one videodisc player. The students work collaboratively and assume the roles of geologists, environmental scientists, marine biologists, or oceanographers to conduct experiments and solve ocean-related ecological problems.

Animal Pathfinders by Scholastic provides interactive visual databases and other information for science education. It also contains the activity "Turtle Mystery," which requires a blend of analysis and thinking skills as the students assume the role of investigators looking into the perils afflicting sea turtles. Creative graphics, sound effects, and animation on a HyperCard stack are coupled with motion sequences from the videodisc to enable students to solve the mystery.

Multimedia Libraries

The best way to describe videodisc programs such as *AIDS* by ABC News Interactive or *A Geographic Perspective on American History (GTV)* by National Geographic is to call them *multimedia libraries*. These applications are not designed to teach—at least not in the customary tutorial or problem-solving fashion. Instead, they offer a wide array of interrelated information in video clips, still frames, sound, maps, text, and graphics.

Examples:

The ABC News Interactive Videodisc series by Glencoe consists of several different multimedia programs, including *AIDS*, *Teenage Sexuality*, and *Tobacco*. Each of these applications provides one or more videodisc sides with HyperCard or LinkWay Live stacks and supporting documentation. These and similar programs contain a wealth of information and features for middle, secondary, and college levels. Areas and sequence of investigation are entirely at the discretion of the students or teachers. For example, in the *Teenage Sexuality* program, students have access to the following:

- Video clips about teens and sex
- Still video frames with images and graphs
- Glossary of terms on videodisc and software
- Computer database of related textual information
- Resource information such as telephone help lines and statistics
- Instant selection of English or Spanish narration
- Closed-caption option

The video report maker is another feature that makes these programs valuable to educators. This feature enables teachers to produce their own presentations or lessons from the materials on the videodisc. Editing tools are used to select the start and stop points for video segments and to access them in the desired sequence. It is also possible to type in a limited amount of text that will appear on top of the video or on a blank screen. In addition, narration can be added to the programs through a digitizing device. Video report makers provide an easy-to-use and powerful tool for designing a lesson or presentation.

A Geographic Perspective on American History (GTV) was developed by National Geographic and LucasFilm. It covers American history from pre-Columbian times to 1990 and contains 1,600 still images, 200 maps, 60 video segments, and complementary textual information. Lesson plans with summaries, background information, and suggested classroom activities are also included. *GTV* is an extremely flexible program that can be used in either a Level I or Level III configuration with a Macintosh, Apple II GS, or MS-DOS computer.

REPURPOSING VIDEODISCS

Videodiscs are generally designed and produced with a particular purpose in mind. Most are created either to teach a specific concept, to provide a database of images and motion, or to entertain. Many videodiscs are designed in conjunction with control programs such as barcodes or HyperCard stacks. For example, long before the video was mastered onto the *AIDS* or *Bio Sci* videodiscs, instructional designers and teachers had determined and outlined how the video could be accessed and delivered with the final software and barcode lessons.

Repurposing refers to creating a control program for an existing videodisc. In other words, the control program is created after the videodisc. A teacher or instructional designer carefully analyzes the content on a videodisc and then determines the sections and sequences that would be appropriate for a certain lesson. A software program or barcode list is then produced to control the videodisc and deliver the lesson in the desired sequence. It is important to note that *any* videodisc can be repurposed whether it is a Level I linear movie that you bought for $25 or a Level III program with extensive software that cost $995.

Benefits of Repurposing a Videodisc

Repurposing videodiscs can provide some outstanding benefits, not the least of which is the challenge to the students' or instructor's creativity.

It saves money. Many educators are wrestling with the dilemma of trying to provide a good variety of quality videodisc programs on a small or nonexistent budget. Questions arise such as, Given a $400 limit to purchase videodisc materials, is it better to buy one program with extensive software and print materials or 16 different linear movies with no support materials? A similar question might be, Without any money for new videodisc materials, how can I better utilize the few videodiscs that are currently available at the school? By buying some Level I discs and repurposing them, you can ease the strain on your budget—or at least stretch what is available. In most cases, Level I videodiscs are less expensive than Level III because Level I does not provide computer software, which is costly to develop.

It enhances the curriculum. By repurposing a videodisc, you can multiply its usefulness and impact on the curriculum. For example, the videodisc *Salamandre: Chateaux of the Loire* from Voyager costs about $50. It focuses on 18 castles in France and is excellent for studying French architecture. However, by repurposing this disc, you could also deliver a lesson on art, history, language, or politics at various grade levels. Even movies such as *Star Wars* can become lessons on special effects or science.

It introduces new technologies. You do not have to be a superprogrammer to repurpose a videodisc. In fact, with the easy-to-use tools that are currently available, no programming experience is necessary. Repurposing a disc acquaints you and your students with some of these tools and gives you a sense of accomplishment with each lesson you create. Repurposing can also increase your understanding and appreciation of the commercial software provided with Level III and barcode programs.

It motivates students. Students can benefit from repurposing discs in two ways. First, they will be the recipients of an enhanced curriculum. Most students are comfortable with television and enjoy the opportunity to view video images and sequences. Second, students can participate in creating their own programs. The authoring tools and templates serve as an excellent introduction to technology for students as well as teachers. Students across the nation are now producing video reports and multimedia presentations.

Procedure for Logging a Disc

The first step in repurposing is to locate a videodisc that can potentially contribute to your curriculum. The disc can be CAV (30 minutes per side with still-frame capability) or CLV (60 minutes per side for linear play) and Level I, II, or III—in other words, any videodisc with appropriate subject content will do. After you have the disc, you need a log, or index, for detailing the frame number of each still and motion sequence you intend to use. If you are lucky, a log will be provided with the disc. For instance, the *Bio Sci II* videodisc by Videodiscovery provides a written list of the frame numbers for each picture. (See fig. 3.10.)

Frame #	Topic
14858	Butterfly
15992	Angelfish, Emperor
16766	Panda, Red
17122	Rose, Prairie
40674-40837	Flamingos, feeding

Figure 3.10. Frame Number Index from *Bio Sci II* Videodisc.

If an index of the frames is not provided with the videodisc, you will have to make one for the parts of the disc you are interested in using. Follow these steps to create a log:

1. Insert a videodisc and press *play* to start the player.

2. Press *step* to stop the player on a frame that is of interest to you.

3. Press *display index* on the remote control to display the frame number. You will probably see a number such as 01 02132. This means you are on frame 2132 in the first chapter. Press *scan* or *play* to advance to another frame and chapter, such as 05 21033 (frame 21033 in chapter 5). Note that some videodiscs do not have chapters; in that case, you may see only a five-digit frame number.

4. If you get a time code when you press *display index* (such as 0:06.31), that means you have a CLV disc. Even though this disc can be repurposed, it is best to use a CAV disc for your first attempt. Find a different disc and start over at step 1.

5. After previewing the entire disc, use the remote-control unit to move through the disc and write down the frame numbers of the sections you want to include in your lesson. Be sure to include enough descriptive information to identify each section. (See fig. 3.11.)

Frame #	Topic	Notes
2988	AIDS Title Screen	Full screen, good for overlay
3120	Ryan White	Still frame with Ryan
3301	Newspaper Headline	Ryan White can return to school
42978-42980	Risky Behavior	Three step frames in Fact File
50133	Bar Chart	AIDS cases reported by year

Figure 3.11. Sample Log for *AIDS* Disc, Side 2.

Selecting Frames Out of Motion Sequences

If the disc is made up of still frames—individual pictures, as on the *Bio Sci* disc—it is relatively easy to find the best frames to use. You can just "step" through the disc or use the index that is provided to find what you want.

If the disc is composed primarily of motion sequences, the task becomes more difficult. For one thing, videodiscs with motion sequences usually provide indexes only for the beginning and ending frames of major sequences. If you want only a frame or a part of the sequence, it will take time and effort to determine the best frame numbers. When you consider that the motion segments play at 30 frames per second and you could stop and "freeze" any one of these frames, you realize that for every minute on the disc, there are 1,800 potential freeze frames! (Note: *Still-frame* refers to displaying a frame that was designed as a static picture; *freeze-frame* refers to displaying a frame that was designed as a part of a motion sequence.)

One problem you may encounter when you stop in a motion sequence is *interfield flicker*. This term refers to a frame that appears to flicker or shake when you stop on it. Interfield flicker occurs because every frame on the disc is actually made up of two fields, each of which displays on the screen every sixtieth of a second when the frame is frozen on the screen. If there was movement between the two fields of a frame, the part that moved appears to flicker back and forth between the two images, making part of the image fuzzy. Figure 3.12 shows the two fields of frame 12345. Note that field 1 shows the dart close to the man's nose. In field 2, he has started to throw the dart. If you stop on this frame (12345) for a freeze frame, the dart will flicker back and forth between the two fields. (See fig. 3.13.)

Figure 3.12. Two Fields of a Motion Video.

Figure 3.13. Example of Interfield Flicker.

Interfield flicker can be a problem whenever there is a large or fast movement on a frame. It is often seen as a hand that shakes or an eyelid that quivers. There is no solution except to "step" forward or back a few frames to try to locate a frame with less movement and, therefore, less flicker.

Another recommendation when selecting still images out of motion sequences is to beware of dissolves and fades. When motion sequences are combined for a master disc, the video producer often dissolves or fades from one shot or sequence to another. Unless you want a special effect, these frames are not good candidates for freeze frames.

A final consideration for motion sequences is that audio is usually attached. That is fine if you want to play the whole segment, but if you want only a part, you must be certain the audio and video coincide and start and stop together. You must also note which audio track you want; remember, there are two tracks that can be played independently or together. To determine which track you want, press *audio* on the remote as the segment is playing. Note on your log the track you will use. In some cases, if the audio does not match or if you are changing the purpose of the segment, you may want to turn the audio off. After you have located all the segments you wish to use in a particular lesson, list the numbers of the frames and motion segments in the desired lesson sequence.

Barcode Generation Programs

One way to repurpose a disc is to use a commercial barcode generator, such as *Bar'n'Coder* by Pioneer. Barcodes are generic. It does not matter which software program or computer you use to create them because all barcodes work with all videodisc players. You can print the barcodes with dot-matrix or laser printers, and you can duplicate them with a copy machine. For more durability, you can even laminate the barcode activities.

When you create your own barcodes, you can electronically "paste" them into a word processor, or you can print them on labels and stick the labels on paper and other objects. For example, barcodes can be placed on a map, a skeleton, or a globe to provide access to pertinent information on a videodisc. Barcodes are easy to create, and barcode activities are easy to use in class. You do not need a computer in the classroom, and the barcodes automatically start and stop the videodisc at the appropriate places.

Figure 3.14 is an example of a barcode lesson. The lesson was created by typing in the name of the lesson, the frame numbers, and descriptions of the frames or segments. The lesson can be used by a teacher or student to present information or to review information.

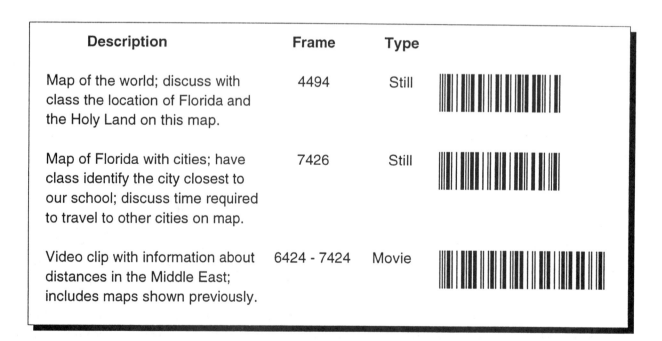

Description	Frame	Type	
Map of the world; discuss with class the location of Florida and the Holy Land on this map.	4494	Still	
Map of Florida with cities; have class identify the city closest to our school; discuss time required to travel to other cities on map.	7426	Still	
Video clip with information about distances in the Middle East; includes maps shown previously.	6424 - 7424	Movie	

Figure 3.14. Barcode Lesson for *In the Holy Land* by ABC News Interactive.

Barcode activities can also be created for individual or small group activities. For example, the barcodes for the student worksheet in figure 3.15 were created with *Bar'n'Coder* and then pasted into *PageMaker*. The barcodes could also be printed on labels and pasted in workbooks or lesson plans.

Description	Frame	Type	
Scan the barcode on your worksheet. Which of the countries on the map were allies of the United States during the Desert Storm Operation?	4496	Still	‖‖‖‖‖‖‖‖‖‖
Scan the barcode on your worksheet. In which state are the cities located that you see on the map?	7415	Still	‖‖‖‖‖‖‖‖‖

Figure 3.15. Barcode Worksheet for *In the Holy Land*.

To use programs such as *Lesson Maker* and *Bar'n'Coder,* you must still preview the disc and log the frames or sequences you wish to use. Again, it is not necessary to use a complete video sequence from the disc. Once you have completed this step, you are ready to enter the information into the program and create the barcodes.

The potential for barcode activities in the curriculum is limited only by your imagination. Students enjoy creating barcodes and can incorporate them into multimedia research reports or other activities.

Hypermedia Programs

The past few years have seen a proliferation of hypermedia programs (such as HyperStudio) that can be used to repurpose videodiscs. These programs are relatively easy to use and provide quick and accurate access to videodisc stills and motion sequences.

To repurpose a videodisc with a hypermedia program, the disc must be logged and the frame numbers for the appropriate segments noted. The frame numbers are then input into the hypermedia program to create a program that can control the videodisc. For more details on hypermedia programs, refer to chapter 6.

CREATING YOUR OWN VIDEODISC

It is possible—and quite easy—for a school to create their own videodisc of such activities as a school performance, talent show, or an art festival.

If you want to produce your own videodisc, you must first create a videotape. The quality of the videotape used to record the source material is important and directly proportional to the quality of the final videodisc. You should, therefore, use the best quality video camera that you can obtain.

The content of the video can include anything you can videotape, including motion, artwork, slides, or photographs. The only limit is that the final videotape cannot exceed 30 minutes in length. There are a few technical aspects you will need to add to the videotape, such as a color test signal and an audio tone. Check with the recording studio for details.

After the master videotape is recorded and edited, you need to note the time code for the chapter and picture stops. A chapter stop is a particular frame on the disc that the player can "jump" to with a chapter search. A picture stop is a frame on the disc where the player will automatically stop and wait for the user to press *play*. Picture stops are often placed on menu screens, where the disc will pause until the user makes a new selection. The production studio will insert the stops as the videodisc is made. Most production houses will allow you up to 50 chapter and picture stops per disc without an additional charge.

When you are ready to record the videodisc, you have two choices.

1. You can create a master videotape and send it to a production studio, in which case the "master" videodisc will cost about $1,800 and each copy will cost between $15 and $18. This is the best approach if you need numerous copies of the disc.

2. You can create a one-of-a-kind check disc for about $250. With this approach, the initial cost is less, but the check disc cannot be used to produce other copies. In other words, the second disc would also cost $250.

(A list of production studios that offer videodisc recording services is included at the end of this chapter.)

SELECTION AND EVALUATION OF VIDEODISC PROGRAMS

There are many videodisc programs on the market, with prices ranging from $25 to more than $1,000. The following items are suggestions for evaluating videodisc programs and selecting the ones most appropriate for your school.

1. *Content.* Begin by considering videodiscs that will support the school's curriculum. If the content is appropriate for interdisciplinary subjects and multiple teachers, it can provide even greater benefit.

2. *Support materials.* Analyze the print materials that are provided with the videodiscs. Lesson plans, student workbooks, and instructor manuals are

valuable assets for the implementation of videodiscs. In many cases, there are more teacher support materials for videodisc programs than there are for comparable CD-ROM programs.

3. *Frame and barcode indexes.* Check for printed logs of videodisc frames and barcode indexes. These features are useful for class presentations or for repurposing a videodisc through barcodes or hypermedia.

4. *Image quality.* Although CD-ROMs are available on a variety of topics, if your lesson requires high-quality images for subjects such as human anatomy, videodiscs may be the best option.

6. *Correlation with textbook.* Some of the major textbook manufacturers have added barcodes to the teachers' editions. Before purchasing a videodisc, check to see if there is one that correlates to other instructional materials.

CONCLUSION

Videodisc technology offers great potential to add new dimensions to classrooms. A single videodisc can incorporate many forms of instructional media—text, charts, graphs, audio, and video motion—into a single medium. The user can randomly search for any frame or chapter, vary the direction of play—forward or reverse—and vary the speed among normal, fast, slow, or still frame.

When the capacities of a videodisc and player are combined with the power of barcodes or a computer, the system becomes a tool for delivering individualized interactive instruction, illustrating lecture material, or providing a multimedia research library. Although new technologies such as Digital Versatile Disc (DVD) are on the horizon and may affect the future of videodiscs, they currently offer substantial benefits for educational environments.

VIDEODISC GLOSSARY

audio track. The narration, sounds, and music that accompany the video on the videodisc. Videodiscs usually have two audio tracks that can be accessed independently or in stereo.

barcode. Small parallel lines that can be read and interpreted by a scanner (barcode reader). Barcodes contain instructions for the videodisc player, such as "play from frame 12345 to frame 23455."

barcode-generation program. A software program that produces printed barcodes for specific frames or chapters.

barcode reader. A penlike wand used to read barcodes from paper. Some barcode readers are connected to the videodisc player with a cable; others use a remote infrared beam as the connection.

Bar'n'Coder. A software program for creating barcodes.

baud rate. The speed at which binary, or computer, data are transmitted. Common baud rates for videodisc players are 1200, 2400, 4800, and 9600. Videodisc players have switches to set the baud rate.

CAV (constant angular velocity). A videodisc format that allows the user to address each frame separately. It can store a maximum of 30 minutes of motion on each side.

chapter. One linear segment of a videodisc. Chapter searches can be done through the remote-control unit, the barcode reader, or a computer.

chapter stop. A preset place on the videodisc that can be accessed by doing a chapter search with a remote-control unit or barcode reader. Chapter stops are generally located at the beginning of linear segments.

check disc. A one-of-a-kind videodisc that can be recorded for about $250.

CLV (constant linear velocity). A videodisc format that can store 60 minutes of motion on each side. This format cannot display an individual frame.

disc. Usually refers to a videodisc or compact disc. Computer diskettes are generally referred to as *disks* (with a *k*), and videodiscs and other optical storage media are referred to as *discs* (with a *c*).

DVD (Digital Versatile Disc). A second generation of CD-ROM technology that can store up to 4.7 gigabytes in one layer—equivalent to two hours of full-screen video.

field. One half of a complete videodisc scanning cycle, or one sixtieth of a second. Two fields make up a complete videodisc frame.

frame. A single, complete picture in a video recording.

frame number or address. Each frame on a videodisc has a unique number between 1 and 54,000. These numbers can be used to access the frame with the remote control, barcode reader, or computer.

freeze-frame. Displaying a single frame that was originally produced as part of a motion sequence.

HyperCard. A Macintosh-based hypermedia program that allows access to a variety of information, including text, audio, and videodisc.

hypermedia program. A software program that provides seamless access to text, graphics, audio, and videodiscs.

HyperStudio. A Macintosh-based hypermedia program that allows access to a variety of information, including text, audio, and videodisc.

interface cable. The cable that connects a computer to a videodisc player.

interfield flicker. The jitter that occurs on a video frame when the two fields do not match perfectly. Interfield flicker usually occurs when there is a large, rapid movement between the fields that constitute a single frame.

IVD (interactive videodisc). Generally refers to Level III interactivity, in which a computer is used to control the videodisc player.

Lesson Maker. A software program for creating barcodes.

Level I interactivity. Interactivity achieved when the videodisc player is controlled through the player, a remote control, or a barcode reader. The player is not connected to a computer.

Level II interactivity. Interactivity achieved when the videodisc contains a control program as well as the video material. The player is not connected to a computer.

Level III interactivity. Interactivity achieved when a computer is used to control the videodisc player.

log. An index created to list the frame numbers for the content of the videodisc.

monitor. A visual display device capable of accepting video and audio signals.

picture stop. A frame on the disc where the videodisc player will automatically stop until the user presses *play* or another command.

remote-control unit. A hand-held device used to control a videodisc player. Some remote-control units are connected to the player with a cable; others communicate using an infrared light beam.

repurposing. Using a videodisc for a purpose other than the one originally intended. Software can be used to adapt a Level I program to a Level III program.

scan. A mode of play in which the player skips over several frames at a time. Scanning can be done in forward or reverse.

search. To find a specific frame number, chapter, or time-code address on a videodisc.

step frame. A function of a videodisc player that moves from one frame to the next whether forward or reverse.

still frame. A single video frame that is presented as a static image, not as part of a moving sequence.

video report makers. Software programs that are usually part of a commercial videodisc program. Video report makers allow users to access the segments on the disc in a different sequence and to alter the start and stop points of motion sequences.

VIDEODISC RESOURCES

Videodisc Catalogs

AIMS Multimedia
9710 DeSoto Avenue
Chatsworth, CA 91311
800-367-2467

CEL Educational Resources
655 Third Avenue
New York, NY 10017
800-235-3339

Coronet/MTI
108 Wilmot Road
Deerfield, IL 60015
800-321-3106

D. C. Heath and Company
2700 N. Richardt Avenue
Indianapolis, IN 46219
800-334-3284

Discovery Channel Interactive
7700 Wisconsin Avenue
Bethesda, MD 20814
800-762-2189

Disney Educational Productions
105 Terry Drive
Newtown, PA 18940
800-295-5010

Emerging Technology Consultants
2819 Hamline Avenue North
Saint Paul, MN 55113
800-395-3973

**Encyclopaedia Britannica
Educational Corporation**
310 S. Michigan Avenue
Chicago, IL 60604
800-554-9862

Fred Lasswell, Inc.
1111 N. Westshore Boulevard, Suite 604
Tampa, FL 33607-4711
813-289-4486

Glencoe
P.O. Box 543
Blacklick, OH 43004
800-334-7344

Health Sciences Consortium
201 Silver Cedar Court
Chapel Hill, NC 27514
919-942-8731

Houghton Mifflin Company
222 Berkeley Street
Boston, MA 02116
800-758-6762

IBM Corporation
4111 Northside Parkway
Atlanta, GA 30327
800-IBM-4EDU

Laserdisc Fan Club
P.O. Box 93103
Long Beach, CA 90809-3103
800-322-2285

Lumivision
877 Federal Boulevard
Denver, CO 80204
800-776-5864

McDougal Littell and Houghton Mifflin
P.O. Box 1667
Evanston, IL 60204
800-323-5435

Minnesota Educational Computing Corporation (MECC)
6160 Summit Drive North
Minneapolis, MN 55430
800-685-6322

National Geographic Society
1145 17th Street NW
Washington, DC 20090
800-368-2728

Optical Data Corporation
30 Technology Drive
Warren, NJ 07059
800-524-2481

Pioneer New Media
2265 E. 220th Street
Long Beach, CA 90810
800-LASER-ON

Scholastic Software
730 Broadway
New York, NY 10003
800-325-6149

Scott Foresman
1900 E. Lake Avenue
Glenview, IL 60025
800-554-4411

Silver Burdett Ginn
P.O. Box 2649
Columbus, OH 43216
800-848-9500

Society for Visual Education, Inc.
1345 Diversey Parkway
Chicago, IL 60614-1299
800-829-1900

Sunburst Software
101 Castleton Street
Pleasantville, NY 10570
800-321-7511

Tom Snyder Productions
80 Coolidge Hill Road
Watertown, MA 02172
800-342-0236

Turner Educational Services
10 N. Main Street
Yardley, PA 19067
800-344-6219

U.S. Laser
3-A Oak Road
Fairfield, NJ 07004
800-USA-DISC

Videodiscovery, Inc.
1700 Westlake Avenue North, Suite 600
Seattle, WA 98109
800-548-3472

Voyager Company
578 Broadway, Suite 406
New York, NY 10012
800-446-2001

Ztek Company
P.O. Box 11768
Lexington, KY 40577
800-247-1603

Videodisc Players

Panasonic Corporation
2 Panasonic Way
Secaucus, NJ 07094
800-524-0864

Pioneer New Media
2265 E. 220th Street
Long Beach, CA 90810
800-LASER-ON

Sony Electronics
1 Sony Drive
Park Ridge, NJ 07656-8003
800-686-SONY (7669)

Repurposing Tools

The following list contains addresses for a selection of barcode makers and hypermedia programs for videodiscs.

Authorware Professional
Macromedia, Inc.
600 Townsend Street, Suite 408
San Francisco, CA 94103
800-945-4051

Bar'n'Coder; BarKoder
Pioneer New Media
2265 E. 220th Street
Long Beach, CA 90810
800-LASER-ON

Digital Chisel
Pierian Spring Software
5200 S.W. Macadam Avenue, Suite 250
Portland, OR 97201
800-472-8578

HyperCard
Apple Computer, Inc.
1 Infinite Loop
Cupertino, CA 95014
800-776-2333

HyperStudio
Roger Wagner Publishers
1050 Pioneer Way
El Cajon, CA 92020
800-497-3778

Lesson Maker
Optical Data Corporation
30 Technology Drive
Warren, NJ 07059
800-524-2481

LinkWay Live
IBM Corporation; K–12 Education
1500 Riveredge Parkway
Atlanta, GA 30328
800-IBM-4EDU

Media Max
Videodiscovery, Inc.
1700 Westlake Avenue North, Suite 600
Seattle, WA 98109
800-548-3472

SuperLink
Alchemedia, Inc.
619 Commercial Avenue
Anacortes, WA 98221
360-299-3289

Multimedia ToolBook
Asymetrix Corporation
110 110th Avenue NE
Belleview, WA 98004
800-448-6543

Voyager VideoStack
Voyager Company
578 Broadway, Suite 406
New York, NY 10012
800-446-2001

Videodisc Production Studios

Call Optical Disc Corporation (800-350-3500) for a mastering bureau near you, or call one of the following companies:

Crawford Communications
535 Plasamour Drive
Atlanta GA 30324
800-831-8027

Imation—3M
1187 Wolters Boulevard
Vadnis Heights, MN 55110
800-336-3636

Laser Disc Recording Center, Inc.
725 Concord Avenue
Cambridge, MA 02138
800-800-9864

Magno Sound & Video
729 7th Avenue
New York NY 10019
212-302-2505

Optimus
161 E. Grand Avenue
Chicago IL 60611
312-321-0880

Pioneer New Media
2265 E. 220nd Street
Long Beach, CA 90810
800-LASER-ON

The Post Group at the Disney/MGM Studio
Lake Buena Vista, FL 32830
407-560-5600

REFERENCE LIST

Fletcher, J. D. (1990). *The effectiveness of interactive videodisc instruction in defense training and education.* Arlington, VA: Institute for Defense Analyses, Science and Technology Division (IDA paper P-2372).

RECOMMENDED READING

Barron, A. E. (1994). Multimedia research reports. In *School library reference services in the 90s: Where we are, where we're heading,* ed. C. Truett, 71–82. New York: Haworth Press.

Barron, A. E., F. Breit, Z. Boulware, and J. Bullock. (1994). *Videodiscs in education: Overview, evaluation, activities. Second edition.* ERIC Document Reproduction Service No. ED384335.

Barron, A., and Z. Boulware. (1993). Tools and techniques for repurposing videodiscs. *Educational Media International* 30(1): 9–13.

Barron, A., and H. Fisher. (1993). Affordable videodisc production: A model for success. *TechTrends* 38(2): 15–21.

Bennett, P. (1995). Videodiscs in schools: Selecting essential players and videodiscs. *Media & Methods* 31(5): 14–16.

Blissett, G. (1993). Are they thinking? Are they learning? A study of the use of interactive video. *Computers and Education* 21(1–2): 31–39.

Bohren, J. L. (1993). *Science learning and interactive videodisc technology.* ERIC Document Reproduction Service No. ED363286.

Cognition and Technology Group at Vanderbilt University. (1993). The Jasper experiment: Using video to furnish real-world problem-solving contexts. *Arithmetic Teacher* 40(8): 474–78.

Cohen, K. (1993). Can multimedia help social studies teachers? Or are videodiscs worth the expense? *Social Studies Review* 32(2): 35–43.

Ekhaml, L. (1993). Caring for your videodiscs, CD-ROM discs, and players. *School Library Media Activities Monthly* 9(6): 39–41.

Fletcher, J. D. (1992). *Cost-effectiveness of interactive courseware.* ERIC Document Reproduction Service No. ED355914.

Fricke, D. (1994). The heart of the school: Interactive video. *MultiMedia Schools* 1(3): 12–15.

Haas, M. E. (1993). "The Great Solar System Rescue": A highly usable videodisc program. *Social Education* 57(1): 11–12.

King, C., and R. Stifter. (1995). Laserdiscs in English and language arts. *Media & Methods* 32(2): 5–12.

Merrill, P. (1996). Staying alive: Laserdisc continues to find work in the digital world. *Multimedia Producer* 2(2): 19–20.

Multimedia and videodisc compendium: 1996 edition (1995). Saint Paul, MN: Emerging Technology Consultants.

Padgett, H. L. (1993). All you need to know about videodiscs: One easy lesson. *Media & Methods* 29(4): 22–23.

Pride, P. (1994). Videodiscs on the cold war and the presidency. *Social Education* 58(1): 48–50.

Reneaux, T. (1993). Videodiscs: A shrinking market. *NewMedia* 3(5): 44.

Rhodes, J. (1995). Achieve picture-perfect interaction with videodiscs. *Multimedia Producer* 1(5): 22–23.

Rittenhouse, R. K. (1993). A technological teaching tool: Interactive video systems. *Perspectives in Education and Deafness* 12(1): 2–6.

Shamp, S. A. (1993). A primer on choosing the medium for multimedia: Videodisc vs. videotape. *T.H.E. Journal* 20(7): 81–86.

Sherwood, S. (1995). Laserdisc lessons for teachers. *Computing Teacher* 22(5): 11–13.

———. (1994). Student laser projects. *Computing Teacher* 22(2): 32–33.

Simsek, A. (1992). The effects of cooperative versus individual videodisc learning on student performance and attitudes. *International Journal of Instructional Media* 19(3): 209–18.

Snepp, L. (1994). Creating a videodisc with fifth graders. *Computing Teacher* 22(2): 28–29.

Thorp, B. (1993). Kids can create videodisc reports. *Computing Teacher* 20(5): 22–23.

Waring, B. (1994). Laserdisc players for multimedia. *NewMedia* 4(4): 37–38.

INTERACTIVE VIDEODISC

An Overview Of

Dr. Ann E. Barron
University of South Florida

Dr. Gary W. Orwig
University of Central Florida

This brochure is an excerpt from:

New Technologies for Education

A Beginner's Guide

Third Edition

To obtain the complete book, contact:

Libraries Unlimited
P.O. Box 6633
Englewood, CO 80155-6633
800-237-6124

Level I Interactivity

Level I interactivity refers to using a videodisc player without a computer connection. The videodisc is controlled through either the control panel on the player, a remote control unit, or a barcode reader. Level I delivery allows users to exercise control over the program without the expense of connecting a computer.

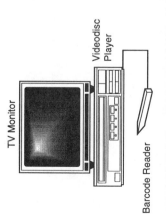

TV Monitor

Videodisc Player

Barcode Reader

Level III Interactivity

Level III interactivity is achieved when a computer is connected to a videodisc player. Level III allows more flexibility because computer programs can provide branches based on keyboard and other student inputs.

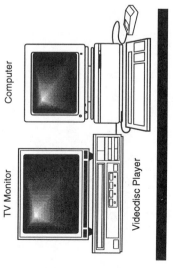

TV Monitor

Computer

Videodisc Player

FEATURE	CAV	CLV
Minutes per Side	30	60
Normal Play	Yes	Yes
Still-Frame	Yes	No
Step-Frame	Yes	No
Multispeed	Yes	No
Scan	Yes	Yes
Frame Search	Yes	No
Time Search	No	Yes
Chapter Search	Yes	Yes

Audio Tracks

The audio on a videodisc is stored in two separate audio tracks that can be turned on or off independently. This provides the potential of having two different languages for the same video content.

Audio will be produced only if the videodisc is playing forward at the standard rate of 30 frames per second. If you are playing the disc faster, slower, or in reverse, there will not be any sound.

Videodisc Formats

Two different formats are used to store the video information on videodiscs—CAV and CLV. On a Constant Angular Velocity (CAV) disc, each circle on the disc holds one individual frame of video. This allows a single frame to be played over and over to produce a still picture. The ability to display a still frame gives the user access to every single frame on the disc. With 30 minutes of motion on each side of the CAV disc, and 30 frames per second, you can access any of the 54,000 still frames.

Every frame on the videodisc has a frame number. To access a particular frame, you can use the remote control unit or computer to input the frame number. Other features of a CAV videodisc are that it can "step" and "play" in forward or reverse.

On a Constant Linear Velocity (CLV) disc, the video frames are stored in a different configuration. Instead of having one frame on each concentric circle, several frames and parts of frames may be on the same circle.

CLV format allows more video to fit on each side of the disc—in fact, twice as much. However, you lose many of the best features of videodiscs, such as the ability to still frame and step frame. CLV discs are used primarily to play movies and programs that are designed to be linear. Instead of frame numbers, most CLV discs have time codes, which are displayed in hours, minutes, and seconds.

Videodisc Frames

Videodiscs are usually 12 inches in diameter. The video material on the disc is produced in exactly the same manner as a videotape. The difference is that after the videotape is edited, it is sent to a mastering studio to produce the videodisc. Once mastered, a videodisc cannot be changed or altered.

Videotapes and videodiscs consist of a series of many frames or pictures. When the tape or disc is in the "play" mode, it moves at a rate of 30 frames per second to create the illusion of motion. The difference between the storage of the frames on a tape and disc is illustrated below.

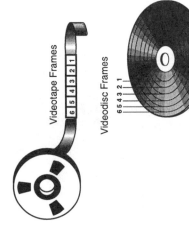

Videotape Frames

6 5 4 3 2 1

Videodisc Frames

6 5 4 3 2 1

On a videodisc, the frames are stored in concentric circles that are read with a laser beam. Each circle represents one or more frames, and the beam can easily jump from one circle to another to provide almost instant access.

4

Digital Audio

A Scenario

Rafael and Bonnie were almost finished with their project—at least with the visual parts. They had created all the graphics and text for the computer screens, and they were ready to add the sounds. They were developing a multimedia research report about Italy and wanted to include some Italian words and music.

Their first task was to find someone who could speak Italian. Luckily, one of Bonnie's neighbors, Mr. Curce, was more than willing to provide some translations. Armed with a tape recorder and microphone, Rafael and Bonnie met with Mr. Curce one evening and recorded his voice on the tape as he translated their script into Italian.

The next day, they connected the tape player to the digital audio card in the computer, opened the recording software program, pressed *play* on the tape recorder, and clicked on the *record* icon in the software program. After the segment was recorded, they opened the sound-editing program and played the recording from the computer file. They noted hearing a short blank area with a hissing sound at the beginning and the end of the audio segment. Using the editing tools in the program, they easily highlighted the parts of the sound wave they did not need, deleted them, and saved the file.

The next task was to integrate the sounds into their PowerPoint presentation. This, too, was quite easy. They only had to access the screen they wanted to be displayed when the audio played and then select *insert . . . sound.* Everything worked great—except that with the sound embedded into the program, the file was very large. Even though they had only recorded 45 seconds of audio, the file was 990K in size.

Now that they had the narration embedded, they decided they also needed some music. Although they could buy a commercial song and record it, their teacher had cautioned them about copyright laws. Instead, they decided to do a quick search on the Internet. Within seconds, they located a World Wide Web site called the Italian Music Homepage (http://www.cilea.it/music/entrance.htm). They searched its contents. Soon they were on another page called the Classical MIDI Archives and clicked on a sonata by an Italian composer.

Within a few seconds, the music was playing on their computer, and it was perfect! After reading through the permission statements to make sure they were not violating any copyrights, Rafael and Bonnie downloaded the file onto their computer. It was unbelievable. The file was only 17K, and it played beautiful music for almost three minutes! Their music teacher had been correct—though they would not tell him. The MIDI files were only a fraction of the size of a sound that was digitized with a microphone.

Music, narration, sound effects, and other audio components have been important tools in education for many generations. Records, tapes, and films have added realism to classroom lessons and have exposed students to a variety of voices, languages, and music. In this chapter, we examine digital formats for recording, storing, and playing audio on a computer. This chapter includes

- An overview of digital audio
- Procedures for digitizing audio
- Educational applications for digital audio
- Advantages and disadvantages of digital audio
- Compact disc-audio technology
- A description of text-to-speech synthesis and voice recognition
- Applications of computerized music
- Configuration and implementation of MIDI technology
- Audio on the Internet
- Resources for further information

INTRODUCTION

Sound, in its natural form, is an analog waveform best described as continuous variations in air pressure. For many years, sounds have been converted to electrical pulses with a microphone and stored on tapes, records, or films. With the advent of microcomputers, techniques have been sought to store sounds on computer disks so that users can access them interactively with a computer program.

There have been several difficulties with recording audio and storing it on a computer. For example, computer diskettes can store information such as audio only in digital form—bits and bytes—not electrical pulses, and when audio is digitized and converted into bits and bytes, an enormous amount of disk storage space is required. Second, for a long time, most computers could not play audio because the hardware and software were too expensive or not available. Today, computers such as Macintosh have built-in digitizing hardware; others require an add-on card (board) or peripheral.

The combination of several factors has recently made realistic computer sound feasible. For one thing, tremendous pressure for better computer-generated sound was applied by the home game market. Consumers wanted a flight simulator that sounded like an airplane and villains and heroes who could talk and sing. This demand fostered the creation of a variety of affordable audio cards and software editing programs.

Another factor in the increased use of digital audio has been the availability and reasonable prices of large storage devices such as CD-ROM and large hard drives. In addition, the formats for sound have been standardized, and compression techniques have been developed that allow sounds to be stored on a computer with reduced storage requirements.

Now that digital audio is feasible, teachers are discovering many ways to incorporate it into instruction. For example, multimedia programs can be created that include the sounds of bird calls, heartbeats, or electronic instruments. Students can also listen to poetry or a foreign language and have the control to repeat each example as many times as they wish. Digital audio has also had a major impact on the teaching and composition of music. With a computer and a software program, students can learn to read, edit, and compose music.

Currently, four primary methods are employed to produce and store computerized sounds: digitized audio, compact disc-audio, text-to-speech synthesis, and MIDI. These methods vary tremendously in quality, cost, applications, and hardware requirements.

Digitized Audio

If you want to record voices or sounds, the best approach is digitized audio. This technology produces extremely realistic sounds, and its educational potential is enormous. Digitized audio is recorded using a digital audio chip in a computer and is stored as files on either a computer disk or a compact disc. The audio files can then be controlled by a computer program, retrieved, and played instantly. The real advantage of this technology for schools is that teachers and students can record their own voices or sounds and store them on a computer disk.

Bringing sound into the digital domain of computer bits and bytes requires a sampling process. At small but discrete time intervals, the computer takes a "snapshot" of the level of the waveform. The result is a digital, stairstep-type representation of sound rather than a continuous analog waveform. (See fig. 4.1.) This process is called *sampling,* and the number of samples taken each second is referred to as the *sampling rate*—the more samples, the better the sound. For example, audio sampled 44,000 times per second (44 kilohertz or kHz) will provide better quality than audio sampled 22,000 times per second (22kHz).

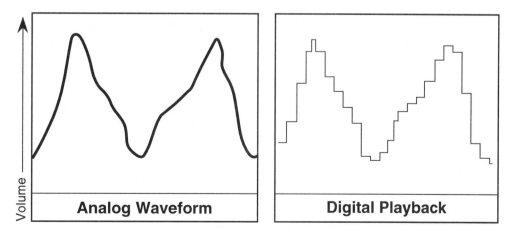

Figure 4.1. Analog and Digital Representation of Sound.

A major decision you must make when recording digital audio files is which sampling rate to use. Most digital audio boards provide at least three alternatives, usually between 11kHz and 44kHz. The selection of a sampling rate is based primarily on two factors: the quality of sound needed and the disk storage space available. The two factors are interrelated because the higher the quality, the more disk space required, and vice versa.

In most cases, the amount of disk storage space available will be a major factor in the sampling rate you choose. One hour of digitized audio requires many megabytes of storage. In fact, 1 megabyte can hold only 22 seconds of sound recorded at 44kHz. Figure 4.2 shows the trade-off involved in sampling rate and storage requirements by listing the amount of audio that fits in 1 megabyte at various sampling rates. Note that even at 11kHz, only 90 seconds of digitized audio will fit on each megabyte of disk space. For most educational applications, a sampling rate of 11kHz is sufficient. If storage space is at a real premium, even 5–8kHz will provide intelligible narration. For music programs, higher quality and, therefore, higher sampling rates are recommended (usually 22kHz or 44kHz).

Sampling rate	Storage for 1 second of sound	Seconds of sound per 1MB storage
44kHz	44 Kilobytes	22 seconds
22kHz	22 Kilobytes	45 seconds
11kHz	11 Kilobytes	90 seconds

Figure 4.2. Storage Requirements for Various Sampling Rates.

MPC Specifications

To record digital audio with an MS-DOS computer, a digital audio card or peripheral must be added to a computer. A few years ago, the MPC (multimedia personal computer) standard was established by multimedia vendors to help define a minimum hardware-software configuration for MS-DOS. In other words, if you have an MPC-compliant setup and you buy software marked with the MPC logo, it should work. After a few years, the MPC standard was enhanced, and an MPC-2 standard was set. (See fig. 4.3.)

The specifications for MPC have had major impacts on digital audio cards. For example, they helped to standardize digital audio cards by requiring that all the cards be compatible with Microsoft Windows. To meet this requirement, the audio cards must save the digital audio files with the extension .WAV. If you create a digital audio file with a SoundBlaster card, you can save it with a file name such as *audio1.WAV*. You can then play that file on any other audio board that complies with MPC specifications.

	MPC (Original)	**MPC-2**
CPU	386	486
Hard Drive	30 MB	160 MB
RAM	2 MB	4 MB
Operating System	MS Windows	MS Windows 3.1
CD-ROM	Single Speed	Double Speed
Audio Card	8-bit; 11-22kHz	16-bit; 11-44kHz
Display	16 Colors	65,536 Colors
Interfaces	Joystick; MIDI	Joystick; MIDI
Peripherals	Mouse, Keyboard	Mouse, Keyboard

Figure 4.3. MPC and MPC-2 Specifications.

The MPC specifications also list a minimum resolution—8 bit or 16 bit—for the audio card. The number of bits of resolution indicates the accuracy with which the digital sample is stored. With 8-bit resolution, there are 256 possible values; with 16-bit sound, there are 65,536 possible values, providing more exact measurement and playback of the sound. If you are recording with a 16-bit card, you have the option to record with 8-bit or 16-bit resolution. Remember that the 16-bit resolution might sound a little better, but it will also require twice as much storage space. The same correlation is true of the sampling rates. All audio cards that comply with MPC-2 standards can record files up to 44kHz. In most cases, however, you can record at a much lower rate to save disk storage space.

Considerations When Purchasing an Audio Card

In addition to the sampling rates and bits of resolution, several other factors are important in the selection of an appropriate digital audio card.

Compression techniques. Some audio cards provide compression techniques that can reduce the file sizes automatically or by selecting a ratio of 4:1, 3:1, or 2:1. These techniques are "lossy"—some of the sound quality will be lost. Narration can generally withstand a degree of compression and remain intelligible; however, music requires top-level dynamics and can suffer at even low compression ratios.

MIDI/joystick interface. The MPC specification requires that soundboards provide external MIDI (Musical Instrument Digital Interface) ports to connect to MIDI devices, such as a MIDI keyboard. Most vendors implement the external ports via a MIDI connector that plugs into a joystick port on the audio card.

Wavetable synthesis. To play or create MIDI files, the soundboard must have special hardware that can interpret the MIDI commands. In the past, the main approach was to use an FM (frequency modulation) synthesis chip on the audio card. An FM synthesizer approximates the audio waveforms of the different instruments; however, FM synthesized music usually sounds gamelike and tinny.

Instead of FM synthesis, many of the current audio boards offer wave-table synthesis to record and play MIDI files. Wave tables store prerecorded samples of actual sounds and musical instruments and play back the notes according to the MIDI instructions. The results vary, depending on the number of instruments and voices stored on the card, but wave-table synthesis is noticeably better quality than FM synthesis.

Inputs and outputs. There are two basic types of inputs on digital audio cards: line level and microphone level. (See fig. 4.4.) The line-level input is used for input from an audiotape or other recorded audio source. Microphone inputs will usually result in more noise and static than line-level input. Additional inputs may include interfaces for MIDI, joysticks, and CD-Audio. Outputs on audio cards can include headphones or speakers. (See fig. 4.5.)

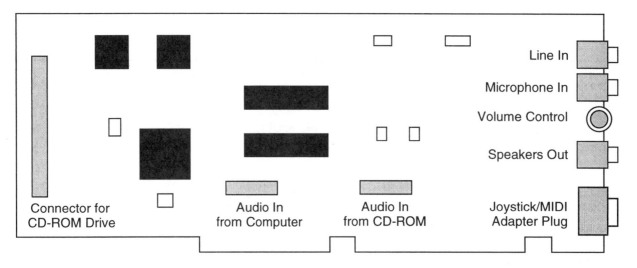

Figure 4.4. Inputs and Outputs on a Digital Audio Card.

CD-ROM interface. Many audio cards include a port to connect a CD-ROM. This eliminates the need to have an additional controller board—and computer slot—for a CD-ROM. Some audio boards provide proprietary interfaces for specific CD-ROM players. The better boards include SCSI or SCSI-2 controllers that will work with many different CD-ROM drives and other peripherals (see chapter 2 for more information about CD-ROM).

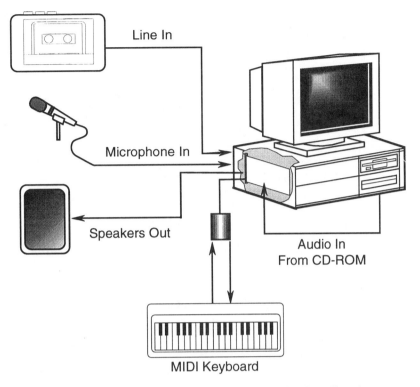

Figure 4.5. Configuration for Digital Audio Card.

Text-to-speech synthesis and voice recognition. Many of the digital audio cards include a speech synthesis component that can translate text into audio output. In addition, they may provide the hardware and software to translate spoken words into computer commands or text.

Editing software. Digitized sounds can be copied, cut, and pasted with sound-editing software just as text can be edited with a word processor. Many of the commercial audio boards provide sound-editing software that displays a graphic representation of the sound files. Look for sound-editing tools that include several levels of zoom to allow editing of specific parts of the sound.

Mixer software. Audio mixer software is included in the purchase of many audio boards, or it can be purchased separately. This software enables you to control levels and mix various files, such as Audio-CD, MIDI, and WAV files, into one output file. Special effects such as fades and inversions are often available in mixer software.

DIGITIZING AUDIO

Audio on
MS-DOS Computers

Digital audio cards for MS-DOS computers must be installed in a slot in the computer. To digitize audio with an audio card, follow this procedure:

1. Insert the audio card into a free computer slot.

2. Install the software program that controls the card.

3. Plug a microphone or tape recorder into the audio input on the card.

4. Select a sampling rate and bits-of-resolution level.

5. Choose *record* on the menu of the digitizing software program.

6. Speak into the microphone, or play the tape recorder.

7. Test the recording with the *play* command. If it is acceptable, save the file to the disk.

Sounds recorded with audio cards can be played back through the software program or, if the software permits, by issuing a *play* command at the system prompt. Almost all the presentation programs and hypermedia programs can play the digital audio files if an audio card is in the computer. (See chapter 6 for more information on hypermedia programs.)

An alternative for recording audio with MS-DOS computers is an *audio peripheral,* such as DigiSpeech. With audio peripherals you do not have to install an audio card in the computer. Instead, you merely attach the unit to the computer's serial port, install the software program, and record the audio. Audio peripherals are advantageous for laptop computers or in situations where you must frequently move the audio unit from one computer to another.

Audio on
Macintosh Computers

The Macintosh computer is a popular platform in education for digitizing audio files. These computers have built-in digital-to-analog converters; therefore, no additional hardware is required to play audio files. That means that audio files recorded on one Macintosh computer can be played on any other Macintosh without adding an audio card or peripheral.

All the Macintosh computers produced in the past few years also provide an internal analog-to-digital converter. These computers have a microphone and can record audio without additional hardware. To record audio with a Macintosh, you can use commercial software such as SoundEdit, obtain shareware programs such as SoundMachine, or you can use the recording features of hypermedia programs such as HyperCard and HyperStudio.

The illustration in figure 4.6 shows the recording component of HyperStudio. To record a sound, follow these steps:

1. Connect a microphone into the microphone port on the computer.

2. Click *record* and speak into the microphone.

3. Click *stop* to end the recording.

4. Test the recording by pressing *play*.

5. Type in a name for the sound and save it.

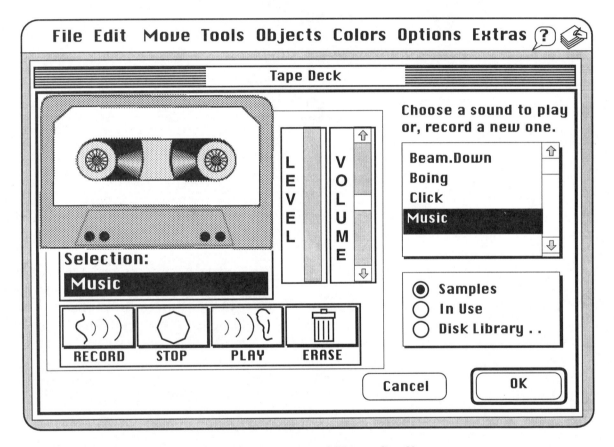

Figure 4.6. Audio Recording Component of HyperStudio.

Editing Sounds

Digitized sounds recorded with either Macintosh or MS-DOS computers can be edited like text in a word processor. With the appropriate software program, sounds can be selected, cut, copied, pasted, and mixed with other sounds. Figure 4.7 on page 92 shows the editing window for a digitized phrase, "New Technologies for Education." The center portion (technologies) has been selected and can now be cut, copied, or deleted. In other words, if you wanted to place the middle of the phrase at the beginning, you would cut it and click at the beginning to paste the segment. Audio editing is a powerful tool that allows you to rearrange sounds or cut out parts you do not need.

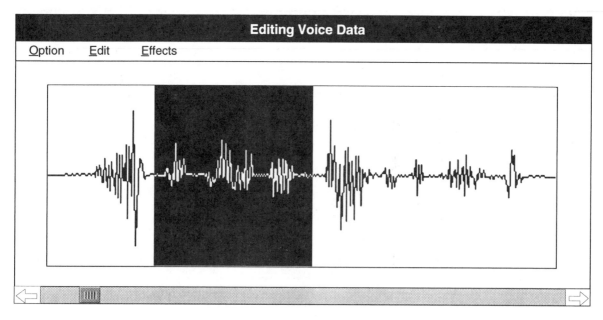

Figure 4.7. Editing Sound.

EDUCATIONAL APPLICATIONS
FOR DIGITAL AUDIO

Digitized audio is an important component of multimedia. Educational applications for digital audio include the following categories (note that programs listed in this section are listed in the Resources section of this chapter).

Computer-based slide shows and presentations. Computers have become effective presentation tools for teachers, administrators, and students. With the addition of audio, the equivalent of a slide-tape show is possible. Multimedia presentation programs such as PowerPoint by Microsoft, Persuasion by Aldus, Compel by Asymetrix, and Harvard Graphics by Software Publishing Corporation have features for easy incorporation of audio files.

Custom hypermedia programs. An exciting application of digital audio is recording your own audio for a computer-based lesson. Audio makes programs come alive and can be used to enhance instruction—especially for nonreaders and students with poor vision. The audio is under computer control and can be accessed instantly. Programs such as HyperCard by Apple Computer and HyperStudio by Roger Wagner provide easy interfaces for digitizing and playing audio.

Audio feedback. Some commercial programs allow learners to record their own voices and then compare their recordings to the correct pronunciation in the digital file. Examples of programs with audio feedback include *Primary Integrated Language Arts Program* by Jostens Learning Corporation, *English Express* by Davidson and Associates, and *Diez Temas* by Encyclopaedia Britannica Educational Corporation.

Audio notes. Many word processors, spreadsheets, and databases allow the users to add sound notations for selected words or phrases. With applications such as this, students or teachers can produce papers or letters that "talk" or provide a spoken glossary.

Repurposing of videodiscs. Repurposing videodiscs can present a problem in that the audio on the disc is tied to the video and cannot be changed. By implementing digital audio, you can use existing video segments and add customized audio to correspond with lesson objectives. Digital audio can also be used in conjunction with still frames on a videodisc.

Speech therapy. Programs such as *SpeechViewer II* by IBM can be used by speech and language therapists to help people with speech impairments. Speech-therapy programs digitize and analyze verbal characteristics such as pitch, loudness, and intonation. They also provide exercises on pronunciation, pitch, and speech timing.

Audio on the Internet. It is quite easy to add audio links to pages on the World Wide Web. You might add a short speech from your principal or play a student composition. (See Audio on the Internet on page 99 for more information.)

ADVANTAGES AND DISADVANTAGES OF DIGITAL AUDIO

Advantages of Digital Audio

Random access. Digital audio can be retrieved and played almost instantly. In most systems the user accesses the audio simply by entering a *play* command followed by the name of the file.

Ease of editing. Audio files are stored with a file name, just like other computer files. Therefore, audio files can be deleted or replaced simply by using file command utilities. Sound-editing programs enable users to cut and paste sounds to edit narration. The process is as easy as using a word processor.

Cost. Moderate-cost, good-quality digital audio cards for MS-DOS computers are becoming more widely available. In addition, Macintosh computers have built-in audio-record and -play capabilities.

Disadvantages of Digital Audio

Large storage requirements. Audio files require a tremendous amount of disk storage space. At 22kHz, a 720K floppy diskette can hold only 30 seconds of audio.

Large memory requirements. Although a Macintosh with one megabyte of random access memory (RAM) can be used to digitize and play audio, the results will be limited. In some cases, audio files must be loaded into RAM before playing. A large amount of RAM is essential, or the files will be limited to a few words each.

Lack of adequate computer speakers. To achieve adequate volume for the audio, external speakers are generally required.

COMPACT DISC-AUDIO

Compact disc-audio (CD-Audio) is the popular consumer format that can store up to 74 minutes of high-quality music on a compact disc. CD-Audio was first developed in 1982. The standard sampling rate for CD-Audio is 44.1kHz—providing high-quality sound.

CD-Audio discs can be played on CD or CD-ROM players. The discs can be controlled by a computer through software programs designed for CD-Audio or by specifying the time code in a hypermedia or authoring program. For example, if you want to create a multimedia program with HyperCard that plays a particular section of Beethoven's Fifth Symphony, you would specify the time code—in minutes, seconds, and frames—at which to start playing and the time code at which to stop. (See chapter 6 for more information on hypermedia and authoring systems.)

Many of the commercial CD-ROM programs discussed in chapter 2 contain some audio in the form of CD-Audio. These CD-ROMs are referred to as mixed mode: Part of the CD-ROM disc stores the text, graphics, and video, and the other part stores the CD-Audio. For example, a multimedia encyclopedia that has pictures of Mozart as well as excerpts of his music would first display the picture, then the laser would travel to the audio part of the disc and play the music that is stored in CD-Audio format.

All the recent CD-ROM players contain built-in digital-to-analog (D/A) converters that can play CD-Audio discs. When a CD-Audio disc is played in a CD-ROM player, the audio can be outputted directly from the CD-ROM player through speakers or headphones. If the computer contains a digital audio card for digitized audio, the CD-Audio can also be sent back through the audio card for playback. This approach simplifies the audio output by playing all the audio—CD-Audio and digitized audio—through one set of speakers.

Advantages of CD-Audio

Quality. CD-Audio is recorded at 44.1kHz, providing top-quality sound.

Durability. CD-Audio is recorded on durable compact discs that are read with a laser beam. The discs do not wear out and are impervious to minor scratches.

Ease of access. The audio is stored by time code—minutes, seconds, frames—on the discs. Most hypermedia and authoring programs can easily access the audio for interactive control.

No impact on RAM or hard drive storage space. If CD-Audio is used to provide the audio components of a multimedia instructional application, it will not be affected by the amount of RAM in the delivery computer and will not require any hard drive storage space.

Disadvantages of CD-Audio

Read only. Audio that is stored on a compact disc cannot be changed or revised.

Limited to 74 minutes. The CD-Audio standard specifies that the audio be recorded at 44.1kHz. With current technology, this limits the amount of audio on each disc to 74 minutes.

Requires CD-ROM player. To play CD-Audio with a computer, a CD-ROM player must be connected.

TEXT-TO-SPEECH SYNTHESIS

The most memory-efficient approach to computerized speech is *text-to-speech synthesis*. In this approach, language is defined as a fixed set of sounds, and computer algorithms are used to translate text into "spoken" output without any recording process. Because text-to-speech synthesis works with a set number of rules to produce sounds, little computer memory or storage space is required.

Text-to-speech sound is ideal for "talking" word processors that can "read" anything that is typed into the computer. The potential vocabulary is unlimited: Any word or group of letters can be spoken by the synthesizer. It simply applies its phonetic rules to pronounce the word.

The disadvantage of the text-to-speech synthesis method is the unnatural and mechanical sound. For instance, problems arise with words such as *live* that do not follow consistent rules of pronunciation. Most computer synthesizers cannot accurately differentiate between the use of *live* in these two sentences: *I live in Florida* and *We are using live bait.* Another problem is that synthesizers do not have the inflections of a voice, which in natural speech "drops off" to indicate the end of a sentence. The robotic sounds produced can be a problem in educational settings, where realistic speech is important for teaching pronunciation and language.

Nevertheless, text-to-speech synthesizers have many applications. The best-quality and most expensive units are found in business. They can be used to read computer documents over telephone lines. For example, an executive might place a telephone call to the office computer to retrieve the latest electronic mail. A text-to-speech synthesizer can answer the telephone and "read" the documents to the executive.

Some commercial multimedia products incorporate text-to-speech synthesis. For example, the *Golden Book Encyclopedia* by Jostens Learning includes a "read" icon that can read the entire text of any page. When this icon is selected, a text-to-speech synthesizer translates the text into audio.

Advantages of Text-to-Speech Synthesis

Very little RAM or storage space needed. Because text-to-speech synthesis works with a set number of rules to produce sounds, little computer memory is required.

Unlimited vocabulary. The potential vocabulary of text-to-speech synthesis is unlimited: Any word or group of letters can be "spoken" by the synthesizer. The computer simply applies the phonetic rules to pronounce the word.

Disadvantages of Text-to-Speech Synthesis

Robotic sound. A major disadvantage of text-to-speech synthesis is the unnatural sound. Synthesizers do not have natural voice inflections, and the words sound mechanical.

Phonetic pronunciations. Another limitation is that the pronunciations are strictly phonetic, and, unfortunately, the English language does not always follow the rules of phonics.

Voice Recognition

Voice recognition is the opposite of text-to-speech synthesis. With voice recognition, computers can interpret spoken words or phrases, respond to them, or convert them to text. For example, you could say "save, close, exit" to leave a word-processing file without touching the keyboard or mouse. Voice recognition is also valuable for doctors who like to dictate their records and for people who do not have the use of their hands.

Voice recognition software is developing rapidly. As the technology is improving, the hardware is becoming less expensive. For example, SoundBlaster audio boards are quite inexpensive, and they include a voice recognition component called VoiceAssist. With VoiceAssist, users can control virtually any Windows application with spoken instructions. The user can define more than 1,000 different commands in each application, and the program can support a total of nearly 30,000 commands for each user. A similar program, PlainTalk, now ships with Power Macintosh computers and provides an interactive voice recognition system that allows users to command Macintosh computers through natural language.

MUSIC

In addition to playing synthesized or digitized voice inputs, many digital audio cards can play synthesized or sampled music. This capability enables teachers to use a computer and keyboard to teach music and composition.

For example, the *Juilliard Music Adventure* is an educational game for ages nine and up that provides an introduction to rhythm, melody, orchestration, form, and musical styles. Using the CD-ROM–based program (Windows or Macintosh), students can even create and play their own music. The music can also be edited to change the tempo, pitch, and rhythm. *Music Ace* by Harmonic Vision is designed to operate on an MS-DOS computer with a mouse. Without requiring a MIDI connection, it provides challenging games and 24 self-paced tutorials on note reading, key signatures, major scales, and so on.

With *MiBAC Music Lessons,* students can use an on-screen keyboard or attach a MIDI keyboard for lessons targeted at various skill levels. A "Show Me" option gives students the chance to see and hear a musical sequence before playing it. *Musicware Piano, Musicshop,* and *MusicTime* all require a MIDI keyboard for beginning through second-year piano lessons. The programs provide inexpensive, interactive approaches to music education.

Musical Instrument Digital Interface (MIDI)

A *synthesizer* is a musical instrument or device that generates sound electronically. Synthesizers can produce the sounds of many different things—from bells and guitars to drums and electric pianos. Synthesizers have existed in various forms since the 1940s, but most of them spoke different "languages" and could not communicate with one another to play, sequence, or mix music.

In 1982 and 1983, several manufacturers of synthesizers got together and agreed on a hardware standard for their instruments. The agreement led to the development of the MIDI (Musical Instrument Digital Interface) specification. Since then, many electronic instruments have been manufactured to conform to the MIDI standard so musical signals can easily be communicated among all synthesizers.

MIDI Applications

The MIDI specification allows computers to control musical instruments through a MIDI interface and MIDI software. It is important to note that MIDI music is *not* sampled and digitized like digital audio files. Instead, MIDI contains information *about* the sound, not the sounds themselves. Similar to sheet music, MIDI files provide the instructions on how to produce the music. The computer then interprets the MIDI instructions and produces the music using the sounds that are embedded in the sound card or sound module.

The configuration for the Macintosh includes MIDI software, a MIDI interface box, speakers, and one or more MIDI instruments. (See fig. 4.8.) The same MIDI keyboard can be connected to an MS-DOS computer with MS-DOS software and interface. In either configuration, the piano keyboard can be used to input the musical information to the computer software and to output the recorded songs if the keyboard contains a synthesizer and speakers.

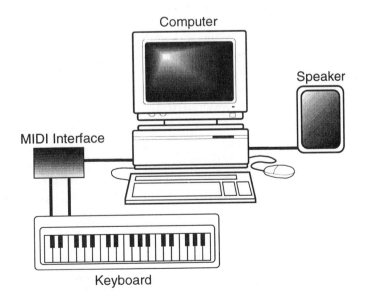

Figure 4.8. Configuration for Macintosh MIDI.

An advantage of MIDI technology is that it can produce complex music. For example, it can play the sounds for stringed instruments, woodwinds, brass, and percussion simultaneously. To produce a MIDI composition, one uses sequencing software that captures everything that was played. The sequencer records the musical information, not the actual sound. It can record and play back several parts or instruments in perfect synchronization—sort of like an old-fashioned player-piano roll. After the musical information is loaded into the computer, it can be edited or revised in relation to its rhythm, meter, tone, and many other parameters. With MIDI sequencing software, you can experiment with harmonies, record different parts, and play them back as a complete arrangement.

Many kinds of extremely powerful and complex music software are available for MIDI. The programs range from presequenced MIDI songs to complex composition software that allows you to score, edit, and print sheet music. Programs such as *Cakewalk, Musicshop,* and *MusicTime* can serve as excellent means for students to compose and edit music with MIDI.

Advantages of MIDI

Small file size. MIDI files are a fraction of the size of digital audio files. Many computer games store music in MIDI files rather than digital audio to conserve disk space.

Compatibility. The MIDI standard provides for the interchange of files among all MIDI synthesizers, sound modules, and sound cards.

Editing. MIDI software enables you to "edit an orchestra" by changing the parameters of the notes and the instruments.

Disadvantages of MIDI

Cannot create narration. Although MIDI technology is great for creating sound effects and music, it is not appropriate for human voices and narration.

Playback may be unpredictable. Unless a new standard called General MIDI is used, MIDI files may sound markedly different when played back through different sound synthesizers and sound cards.

Musical talent is recommended. Creating or editing MIDI music requires a certain degree of musical talent. For those of us who are not musically endowed, MIDI files can be obtained via bulletin boards, the Internet, or CD-ROM collections.

AUDIO ON THE INTERNET

The Internet is a great repository for the storage and transfer of audio files. Using file-transfer techniques, you can easily locate audio files on a remote computer, transfer them to your own computer, and play the files. This is a great way to find thousands of shareware and public-domain audio files in digitized audio and MIDI formats. (See chapter 8 for more information about the Internet.)

With the recent explosion of the World Wide Web, audio has become increasingly common on the Internet. In addition to transferring audio files to play at a later time, you can embed audio links within documents. For example, with *LiveAudio* by Netscape, any link to an audio file stored in a common format, including MIDI, WAV, or AU, will automatically play the sound.

One consideration with playing audio files directly from the Internet is that many of the files are quite large, and they may require considerable time to transfer over the Internet before they can begin to play. With a relatively slow connection, such as a 14,400bps (bits per second) modem, it is conceivable that you may have to wait several minutes for a 45-second audio file to transfer to your computer before it will begin to play.

One solution to the long transfer-wait time has been developed by Progressive Networks. The solution, *RealAudio,* allows the audio file to be streamed over the Internet and play as it transfers. In other words, when you click on a *RealAudio* file link that is embedded in a World Wide Web page, the audio file begins to play almost immediately and will continue to play as it transfers. In this manner, you can listen to radio stations or concerts on the other side of the world, or you can hear a "live" presidential address with only a short delay while the file is digitized.

CONCLUSION

The goal of making the computer talk and play music has been achieved. Educators can easily use text-to-speech synthesis, MIDI, CD-Audio, and digital audio to include sound in their presentations, lessons, and computer programs. With computer-controlled sounds and music, no time is ever lost in rewinding a tape to find the correct starting point or in trying to place a phonograph needle on the right record groove. Random access to sounds, voice, and music is at the heart of multimedia instruction and presentations.

DIGITAL AUDIO GLOSSARY

analog recording. A method of recording in which the waveform of the recorded signal resembles the waveform of the original signal.

.AU. A common audio format for files that are linked to World Wide Web pages. These files will play on Macintosh, Windows, or UNIX computers.

audio chip. A computer chip that can produce sounds. Macintosh has built-in audio chips.

CD-Audio. High-quality audio stored on a compact disc in a linear format.

CD-ROM (Compact Disc–Read Only Memory). An optical storage device capable of storing approximately 650 megabytes of digital data (see chapter 2).

channel. The paths over which MIDI information travels. MIDI can send data on as many as 16 channels with a single MIDI cable.

compression. Reducing data for more efficient storage and transmission. Compression saves disk space, but it also reduces the quality of the playback. Compression ratios of 2:1, 3:1, or 4:1 are often available for digitizing audio.

decibel. A relative unit to measure the ratio of two sound intensities.

digital recording. A method of recording in which samples of the original analog signal are encoded as bits and bytes.

dynamic range. The difference between the loudest sound and the softest sound. Dynamic range is measured in decibels.

8-bit. An 8-bit audio card stores one of 256 values for each sample of sound.

frequency. The number of times per second that a sound source vibrates. Frequency is expressed in hertz (Hz) or kilohertz (kHz).

General MIDI. A MIDI standard that assigns each instrument a unique identification number.

hertz (Hz). Unit of measurement of frequency; numerically equal to cycles per second.

HyperSound. A HyperCard stack that enables the user to record, store, and play sounds with a MacRecorder.

kilohertz (kHz). Unit of measurement of frequency; equal to 1,000 hertz.

LiveAudio. An audio plug-in player that is built for the Netscape browser and allows computers to play files stored in many file formats.

MacRecorder. A hand-held sound-input device distributed by Macromedia that has a built-in microphone, external microphone jack, and line-in jack to digitize sound and record it on a Macintosh computer.

MIDI (Musical Instrument Digital Interface). A standard for communicating musical information among computers and musical devices.

mixed-mode CD-ROM. Compact discs that contain computer data and CD-Audio tracks. The computer data is generally recorded on the inner tracks of the disc, and the audio is recorded on the outer tracks.

MPC (multimedia personal computer). A standard that specifies hardware and software requirements for multimedia personal computers in the MS-DOS environment. The standard includes memory requirements, CD-ROM performance, display adapter, operating system, and so on.

RealAudio. A compression and transfer technique that allows audio files to play over the Internet as they are transferring.

resolution. The number of bits used to store sounds; 16-bit audio cards have higher resolution and produce a richer sound than 8-bit audio cards.

sampling rate. The number of intervals per second used to capture a sound when it is digitized. Sampling rate affects sound quality; the higher the sampling rate, the better the sound quality.

sequencer. A device that records MIDI events and data.

16-bit. A 16-bit audio card stores one of 65,536 values for each sample of sound.

sound module. A peripheral for MIDI that uses an electronic synthesizer to generate the sounds of musical instruments.

synthesizer. A musical instrument or device that generates sound electronically.

text-to-speech synthesis. Sounds created by applying computer algorithms to text to produce "spoken" words.

upgrade kit. Components needed to upgrade older MS-DOS computers to meet the MPC standards.

voice recognition. The ability of computer hardware and software to interpret spoken words. The computer can react to commands or transfer the words to text.

.WAV. The extension, or last three letters, for sound files saved in Microsoft wave format. To be compatible with the MPC standards, all audio files must be stored with this format.

waveform. The shape of a sound depicted graphically as amplitude over time.

wave-table synthesis. Wave tables store prerecorded samples of actual sounds and musical instruments on digital audio boards for MIDI playback.

DIGITAL AUDIO RESOURCES

Programs Referenced in Text

Cakewalk Music Software
P.O. Box 760
Watertown, MA 02272-0760
800-234-1171

Compel
Asymetrix Corporation
110 110th Avenue, NE
Bellevue, WA 98004
800-448-6543

Diez Temas
Encyclopaedia Britannica Educational
Corporation
310 S. Michigan Avenue
Chicago, IL 60604
800-554-9862

English Express
Davidson and Associates
19840 Pioneer Avenue
Torrance, CA 90503
800-545-7677

Harvard Graphics
Software Publishing Corporation
P.O. Box 62900
El Dorado, CA 95762
800-336-8360

HyperCard
Apple Computer, Inc.
1 Infinite Loop
Cupertino, CA 95014
800-776-2333

HyperStudio
Roger Wagner Publishers
1050 Pioneer Way
El Cajon, CA 92020
800-497-3778

Jostens Learning Corporation
7878 N. 16th Street
Phoenix, AZ 85020
800-422-4339

Juilliard Music Adventure
Theatrix Interactive
1250 45th Street
Emeryville, CA 94608
800-955-TRIX

LiveAudio
Netscape Communications
Corporation
415-937-3777
http://home.netscape.com

MiBAC Music Lessons
MiBAC Music Software
P.O. Box 468
Northfield, MN 55057
507-645-5851

Music Ace
Harmonic Vision
906 University Place
Evanston, IL 60201
800-644-4994

Musicshop
Opcode Systems, Inc.
3641 Haven Drive
Menlo Park, CA 94025
800-557-2633

MusicTime
Passport Design, Inc.
100 Stone Pine Road
Half Moon Bay, CA 94019
800-443-3210

Musicware Piano
Musicware
8654 154th Avenue NE
Redmond, WA 98052
800-99-PIANO

Persuasion
Aldus Corporation
1585 Charleston Road
Mountain View, CA 94039
800-833-6687

PlainTalk
Apple Computer, Inc.
1 Infinite Loop
Cupertino, CA 95014
800-776-2333

Primary Integrated Language Arts Program
Jostens Learning Corporation
6170 Cornerstone Court East
San Diego, CA 92121-3710
800-521-8538

RealAudio
Progressive Networks
800-230-5975
http://www.realaudio.com

SoundEdit
Macromedia
600 Townsend Street
San Francisco, CA 94103
800-945-4051

SoundMachine
ANUTECH
The Australian National University
Canberra, ACT 0200
Australia
61-6-249-5111

SpeechViewer II
IBM Corporation
4111 Northside Parkway
Atlanta, GA 30327
800-IBM-4EDU

Stickybear Music
Optimum Resource, Inc.
5 Hiltech Lane
Hilton Head Island, SC 29926
800-327-1473

VoiceAssist
Creative Labs
1901 McCarthy Boulevard
Milpitas, CA 95035
800-998-1000

Digital Audio Hardware
and Software Companies

Adaptec (AudioEdge)
691 S. Milpitas Boulevard
Milpitas, CA 95035
800-934-2766

AITech (Audio Show)
47971 Fremont Boulevard
Fremont, CA 94538
800-882-8184

Alpha Systems Lab (Cyber Audio)
2361 McGaw Avenue
Irvine, CA 92714
800-576-4275

Antex Electronics (Z1)
16100 S. Figueroa Street
Gardena, CA 90248
800-338-4231

Aztech Labs (Sound Galaxy)
46707 Fremont Boulevard
Fremont, CA 94538
800-886-8859

Best Data Products (Soniq Sound)
21800 Nordhoff
Chatsworth, CA 91311
818-773-9600

Cardinal Technologies (Digital Sound)
1827 Freedom Road
Lancaster, PA 17601
800-775-0899

Creative Labs (SoundBlaster)
1901 McCarthy Boulevard
Milpitas, CA 95035
800-998-1000

Diamond Computer (SonicSound)
1130 E. Arques Avenue
Sunnyvale, CA 94086
408-325-7000

Digidesign, Inc. (Sound Designer/ Pro Tools)
1360 Willow Road
Menlo Park, CA 94025
800-333-2137

DSP Solutions (DigiSpeech)
2464 Embarcadero Way
Palo Alto, CA 94303
415-919-4000

Ensoniq (Soundscape)
155 Great Valley Parkway
Malvern, PA 19355
800-776-8637

IBM (Audiovation)
4111 Northside Parkway
Atlanta, GA 30327
800-IBM-4EDU

Logitech, Inc. (Sound Man)
6505 Kaiser Drive
Fremont, CA 94555
800-231-7717

Macromedia (Sound Edit/Deck)
600 Townsend Street
San Francisco, CA 94103
800-945-4051

Media Magic (DSP 16)
10300 Metric Boulevard
Austin, TX 78758
800-624-8654

Microsoft Corporation (Windows Sound System)
1 Microsoft Way
Redmond, WA 98052
800-426-9400

Midisoft Corporation (Sound Impression)
P.O. Box 1000
Bellevue, WA 98009
800-776-6434

Omni Labs (Audio Master)
777 South Street Road 7
Margate, FL 33068
800-706-3342

Orchid Technology (NuSound PnP)
45365 Northport Loop West
Fremont, CA 94538
800-767-2443

Passport Design (Alchemy)
1151 Triton Drive
Foster City, CA 94404
415-726-0280

Reveal Computer Products, Inc. (SoundFX)
6045 Variel Avenue
Woodland Hills, CA 91367
800-326-2222

Roland (RAP-10)
7200 Dominion Circle
Los Angeles, CA 90040
213-685-5141

Sonic Foundry (Sound Forge)
100 S. Baldwin
Madison, WI 53703
800-577-6642

Turtle Beach Systems
5690 Stewart Avenue
Fremont, CA 94538
510-624-6200

Voyetra Technologies (Audio View)
5 Odel Plaza
Yonkers, NY 10701
800-233-9377

Wildcat Canyon Software (Autoscore)
1563 Solano, Suite 264
Berkeley, CA 94707
800-336-0989

RECOMMENDED READING

Anderton, C. (1996). Digital audio software for multimedia. *NewMedia* 6(2): 55–61.

Anzovin, S. (1995). Listen up: Multimedia speakers come of age. *CD-ROM Today* 3(1): 58–63.

Barron, A. E. (1995). Digital audio in multimedia. *Educational Media International* 32(4), 190–93.

Barron, A. E., and M. L. Kysilka. (1993). The effectiveness of digital audio in computer-based training. *Journal of Research on Computing in Education* 25(3): 277–89.

Burger, J. (1995). Audio workshop: Rappin' on a shoestring. *NewMedia* 5(6): 94–95.

Danz, T. (1995). Making beautiful music together. *Multimedia Producer* 1(6): 10–12.

Fritz, M. (1995). A new audio arsenal: MIDI sound and Windows 95. *CD-ROM Professional* 8(8): 28–30.

Lee, L. (1995). More audio on demand. *NewMedia* 5(12): 22.

———. (1995). Self-powered speakers. *NewMedia* 5(6): 69–71.

Lehrman, P. D. (1995). 16-bit Mac sound editors for multimedia authoring. *NewMedia* 5(1): 90–97.

Liberman, A. (1996). Sounding off: Multimedia speakers. *Multimedia World* 3(3): 71–81.

Perkins, C. (1996). The trouble with audio. *Multimedia World* 3(2): 90–100.

Sirota, W. (1996). Orchestrating your digital music studio. *Multimedia World* 3(6): 82–93.

Swaine, M. (1995). Interface the music. *MacUser* 11(9): 125.

Trubitt, R. (1995). Audio to go: PCMCIA sound cards. *NewMedia* 5(8): 91–95.

———. (1996). Head to head: Four digital audio workstations. *NewMedia* 6(4): 47–57.

Trubitt, R., and T. Tully. (1996). Getting real with RealAudio. *NewMedia* 6(6): 56–57.

Tully, T. (1995). Audio editing software. *NewMedia* 5(6): 63–67.

———. (1995). Sound cards. *NewMedia* 5(6): 53–61.

DIGITAL AUDIO

An Overview Of

Dr. Ann E. Barron
University of South Florida

Dr. Gary W. Orwig
University of Central Florida

This brochure is an excerpt from:

New Technologies for Education

A Beginner's Guide

Third Edition

To obtain the complete book, contact:

Libraries Unlimited
P.O. Box 6633
Englewood, CO 80155-6633
800-237-6124

MIDI

MIDI stands for Musical Instrument Digital Interface. It is an international standard that allows a wide variety of musical instruments (such as electronic keyboards) to be connected to computers.

The configuration for MIDI includes a computer, a MIDI instrument, and a MIDI interface box.

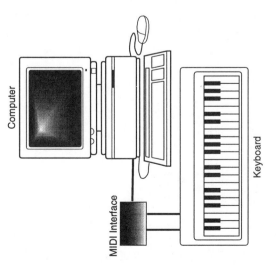

Computer

MIDI Interface

Keyboard

The MIDI keyboard, sound module, or other MIDI instrument can be connected to either Macintosh or MS-DOS computers. Software programs for MIDI allow you to compose, sequence, edit, record, and save music. Commercial MIDI files can be purchased, and MIDI files are available on the Internet.

- *Random Access.* Digital audio files can be retrieved and played instantly. In most systems, to access the audio, the user simply enters a "play" command followed by the name of the file.

- *Ease of Editing.* Audio files are stored with a file or resource name, and they can be deleted, replaced, or copied relatively easily. Editing tools, usually included in the software, allow users to cut and paste sounds.

- *Cost.* Good-quality audio cards are now available for MS-DOS computers at very reasonable prices. Macintosh computers have built-in audio record and playback capabilities.

- *Large Storage Requirements.* Audio files require a tremendous amount of disk storage space.

- *Large Memory Requirements.* In many cases, the audio is loaded into RAM before it is recorded or played. Therefore at least 2 megabytes of RAM are recommended.

- *Lack of Adequate Computer Speakers.* To achieve adequate volume for the audio, additional external speakers are generally required for computers.

MS-DOS Configuration

To use digital audio with an MS-DOS computer, a digital audio card or peripheral must be added to the computer. Audio cards have a variety of inputs and outputs.

When purchasing an audio card, be sure that software is included to control the digitization and playback processes.

Macintosh Configuration

All Macintosh computers have built-in digital-to-analog converters; therefore, no additional hardware is required to play audio files. Newer Macintosh computers also have a microphone and the built-in capability to record audio files. If a Macintosh does not have a microphone attachment, an external sound digitizer, such as the MacRecorder, is required to record the audio.

Sampling Rates

Audio is digitized by recording it through a microphone, converting it into computer data, and storing it on a disk. Some computers have recording capabilities and allow the microphone to be attached directly to them. Other computers require internal audio cards or external recording devices.

The recording process is referred to as "sampling," and several thousand samples (snapshots) of the sounds are taken each second. The sampling rate is expressed in kilohertz (kHz). The larger the sampling rate, the better the sound quality, but more disk space will be required to store the sound. For example, 180 seconds of audio sampled at 5kHz will fit on one megabyte; whereas, if the audio is sampled at 22kHz, a megabyte can only store 45 seconds.

Sampling rate	Seconds of sound per 1MB storage
44kHz	22 seconds
22kHz	45 seconds
11kHz	90 seconds
5kHz	180 seconds

For most educational applications, a sampling rate of 8-12kHz is sufficient. When recording music, higher quality, and higher sampling rates are recommended.

5

Digital Images and Video

A Scenario

Lorna, Maria, and Rodney were well into the process of collecting materials for their class project: a multimedia critique of the negative campaign techniques used in the presidential primaries. In particular, they wanted to present a summary of the opinions of fellow students regarding these campaign tactics.

Rodney enjoyed working with video, so he recorded several campaign commercials on his home videocassette recorder. After clearing some copyright concerns with the media specialist and their teacher, the team evaluated the commercials and decided to select short segments from four of them. Rodney used the media center equipment to digitize these short clips and save them on a computer that had a large hard drive just for student projects. Even though he made the clips as short as possible, he still needed more than 200 megabytes of the hard drive space.

The team members originally wanted to collect digital video reactions of students to the commercials, but they soon realized that their workstation would not be able to store more than two or three additional video samples. Instead, they decided to take a digital snapshot of each student, then use the audio digitizer to record the student reactions to the commercials.

Lorna was great at public relations, so she scouted out "clients" during lunch period and ushered them into the media center. There Maria was waiting to take each student's picture with an Apple QuickTake digital camera. Then she helped each student view the video clips and record their responses. Within three lunch periods, they were able to photograph and record 15 students.

Next, the team reviewed their collected data. It was easy to transfer the digital images in the camera to the computer. Lorna had been careful to keep a log of each student, so it was also easy to keep track of who was saying what. There were some interesting comments about the commercials, but there was also quite a bit of duplication that could be discarded to make more space on the hard drive.

Using a multimedia editing program, they created their final project. It had a title page that showed a still image from each of the commercials. When one of the images was "clicked," that video clip played. Following the video clip, a page with a number of miniature pictures of students appeared. When one of those was clicked, a larger picture of that student appeared, and his or her comments were played.

The team was careful to make sure that each student who was interviewed appeared in a couple of the comment screens, but they did edit out about half of the total audio because it was fairly redundant and simply took up too much space on the hard drive. They also found that they had room for either large pictures of the students with a reduced amount of coloration, or they could have smaller pictures with the best coloration. They liked the big pictures better, so they decided to use them.

The team worked hard after school for a couple of days, and they finished in time. When it was time to demonstrate their project, they wheeled the multimedia computer into their classroom, explained the issues of negative campaign tactics that concerned them, then invited students in the class to explore the opinions of their classmates.

The project was such a success that the media specialist let them move the computer into the hall during lunch periods so that other students could see and hear the opinions of their classmates. After a few days, however, interest declined. The project was finished, and the discussion had run its course.

The media specialist encouraged the team to save the project pages, still images, and audio comments onto a recordable CD for possible use in later projects or portfolios, but she explained that the campaign video clips had served their purpose, and the principles of "fair use" instructed that they should be deleted. After lengthy discussions about writing for permission to keep the video segments, the team also came to an agreement that the odds would not be good for getting written permission to keep the video.

The project ended with a quiet little ceremony in the media center. After copying all the still images and audio comments to a recordable CD, they clicked on the folder icon for their project. After hitting the delete key and working through the "Are you sure?" messages, they watched as their former project became available hard drive space for the next student team project.

Videodiscs can provide random access to video still or motion segments, but connecting a player to a computer to play interactive video programs involves equipment, cables, and software. This can make an interactive video workstation complex, difficult to manage, and expensive. The trend is to convert the video to a digital form that is directly accessible by a computer. Increased interactivity and decreased equipment costs are primary reasons for this trend toward digital storage of images and video. In this chapter, we differentiate between analog and digital formats, in addition to providing techniques for digitizing images and video. Technologies that focus on digital video, such as QuickTime, Video for Windows, and Digital Versatile Disc, are also outlined and described. This chapter includes

- A description of digital-image formats
- An overview of scanning techniques for images
- Advantages and disadvantages of scanned images
- An overview of still video and digital cameras
- Advantages and disadvantages of still video cameras
- Techniques for digitizing motion video
- Alternatives for image compression
- Configuration and applications for QuickTime and Video for Windows
- An overview of Digital Versatile Disc (DVD)
- Resources for further information

INTRODUCTION

As the resolution and number of available colors on computer display systems have increased, images have become increasingly prevalent in computer programs. However, to draw complex computer-generated images, a professional graphic artist and a sophisticated computer graphics program are required. Even then, it is often difficult to produce images with the required realism. For example, a photograph-like image of a person is difficult to draw from "scratch" on a computer.

Digitizing techniques simplify the process by enabling individuals to capture still images and motion segments and incorporate them into a computer program from hard paper copies, cameras, videotapes, videodiscs, or other sources. After these images are stored in the computer, they can be enhanced, resized, or repositioned. They can also become a part of a computer slide show, an interactive lesson, a desktop-publishing project, or a page on the World Wide Web.

WHAT IS ANALOG? WHAT IS DIGITAL?

The discussion of images on computers is complicated enough, and the constant reference to "analog" and "digital" terminology can create even greater confusion. Analog images are the traditional images we have dealt with over the years. Regardless of whether we are looking at a photograph, a motion picture, a regular over-the-air television program, or a standard VHS videotape, we are looking at visual information that is represented in analog form. An analog image has a continuous nature to it. The colors in a photograph appear to be made up of unlimited hues, colors, and shading. The details in the images are limited only by the reproduction processes that are used to produce them. If they are video images, the electronic signals that create them vary continuously through a range of voltages.

Digital images, however, are reduced to a finite set of numeric values that describe their coloration and their resolution. Because computers deal directly with numeric values, they can store and manipulate digital representations of pictures much as they would store or manipulate the values in a database or a spreadsheet. Once an image is in a digital form, a computer needs no additional equipment, such as a videodisc player, to display it.

SCANNING IMAGES

Some images begin as true digital images. For example, computer drawing, painting, and drafting programs all create image files that are digital from their inception. In addition, new digital cameras, such as the Apple QuickTake, create digital images. However, there are many times when you may want to convert an image from its original analog "paper" form into a digital form. To digitize a paper-based image, a scanner is used.

Digital-image scanners are computer peripherals that are used to convert print materials into a digital image on a computer. Scanners can capture and convert any image—a photograph, line art, or text—into a graphics file in a cost-effective and efficient manner. Capturing images with a scanner makes it possible to incorporate complex drawings into multimedia projects.

The typical scanning process is similar to copying a piece of paper on a photocopy machine. The difference is that instead of producing a copy on paper, the image is transferred to the computer screen. After a computer image is produced, it can be modified or enhanced with a computer graphics or "paint" program. Depending on the type of scanner you have and the production requirements, scanners can produce graphics in black and white, shades of gray, or a wide range of colors. The enhanced image can then be imported into a computer program or saved as a graphics file.

The resolution of a scanner is measured in dots per inch (dpi), which is equivalent to pixels (picture elements) in the final digitized image. In other words, if a picture is scanned at 100 dots per inch, it will have 100 by 100 "dots" of picture information collected from each square inch of picture surface. If the picture is 6 inches wide and 4 inches high, then a computer system must be capable of displaying at least 600 pixels horizontally and 400 pixels vertically to show the entire picture on the screen.

When materials are scanned, the computer "sees" them as one image made up of many pixels. (It is often referred to as a bit-mapped, or "paint," image.) The computer does not recognize the individual lines, shapes, or letters in the image as it would with a vector or "draw" image.

If your goal is to scan text and, for spell-checking and editing purposes, to have the computer recognize it as text characters, you will need optical character recognition (OCR) software. Many different OCR software programs are available; however, the accuracy of the scanned textual information varies. Some OCR programs are limited by the number of fonts or type styles they can decipher; therefore, they can recognize only a portion of the text you scan in. The additional cost of OCR software with a high accuracy rate should be contrasted with the time required for error checking with a less expensive package.

Configuration for Scanning

Scanners come in many shapes and sizes, and the cost ranges from about $40 for a small hand-held scanner to thousands of dollars for a high-resolution color scanner with OCR software. Many scanners are *flatbed scanners,* which look and operate like copy machines: The item is placed on the bed, a light passes under it, and a computer image is produced. (See fig. 5.1.) Scanners for Macintosh computers usually connect to the SCSI (Small Computer Systems Interface) port on the back of the Macintosh through a cable. Some MS-DOS computers also have a SCSI port; if not, an additional card must generally be installed into the computer.

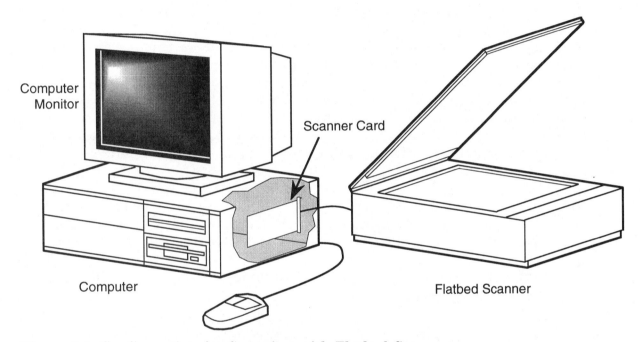

Figure 5.1. Configuration for Scanning with Flatbed Scanner.

The configuration for scanning includes

- A computer
- A computer monitor
- A scanner
- An interface cable
- A scanning card installed in the computer (if necessary)
- Scanning software

Computer software is needed to acquire, or import, the scanned image. Many different settings are usually available in the software for contrast, brightness, and resolution. The resolution you choose is determined by the output you desire. If the scanned image is to be printed on a laser printer, 300 dots per inch (dpi) are appropriate. However, if you are going to incorporate the graphic into a computer program, then a resolution of 100 dpi or less is sufficient because most computer screens will then display an image approximately the same size as the original. Scanning at a higher resolution for display on a computer screen might be a waste of disk storage space.

Scanners require large amounts of random access memory (RAM) to capture the images and large amounts of storage space to save the images. The best technique is to scan only the area of the graphic that is required. Many programs offer a "preview" option that allows you to view the image and adjust the contrast, brightness, and so forth before saving it to disk.

Advantages of Scanned Images

Reduced development time. When artwork is available for scanning, a graphic artist can reduce development time by 25 percent to 50 percent. Even though the images may require some cleanup with the computer's graphics program, scanning the images is still faster than creating them from scratch.

Increased quality of graphics. Scanning technology allows the user to capture complex graphics, such as photographs, that would be difficult or impossible to create in a computer graphics program. Depending on the resolution and the number of colors, extremely realistic and high-quality graphics can be produced with a scanner.

No typing to capture text. Another advantage of scanned images is the elimination of the need to reenter text. OCR scanners read printed words from a page into a text file that can be edited with a word-processing program.

Cost. Scanners can be purchased for reasonable prices, with hand-held scanners selling for as low as $40.

Disadvantages of Scanned Images

Accuracy. OCR scanners achieve various levels of accuracy depending on the font and typeface scanned. If the software cannot scan with a high degree of accuracy, you may spend more time cleaning up the file than you saved by scanning it.

Memory requirements. Computers must have a large RAM capacity to scan in large graphics.

Storage requirements. After the image is scanned, a large amount of disk space is required to store it. The file size of each image may be several megabytes.

Cost. Even though hand-held scanners can be purchased for a reasonable price, they are difficult to use properly. Flatbed scanners are much easier to use, but when high-resolution graphics and text recognition are requirements, these scanners can cost thousands of dollars.

Copyright restrictions. Although virtually any hard copy can be scanned, you must be careful to respect the intellectual rights of others and obtain permission to scan any copyrighted materials.

STILL VIDEO AND DIGITAL CAMERAS

Scanners are great if you have a photograph to copy, but what if you still need to take the picture? In that case, the best solution may be to use a still video camera. Still video cameras are designed to take pictures that can be stored on a computer without using photographic film or a scanner. Many schools are using digital cameras extensively to take pictures for newsletters and multimedia projects.

The first generation of still video cameras (such as the out-of-production XapShot by Canon) were analog cameras. That means that even though they stored the images on a small floppy diskette, the images could not be imported directly into a computer. Instead, they produced analog video images that could be displayed on a television monitor or digitized through a board for computer input. (See fig. 5.2.) In many cases, a digitizing board was included in the purchase of a still video camera. After the image was saved on the computer drive, it could be modified with a computer graphics package, incorporated into a computer program or document, or stored for later use.

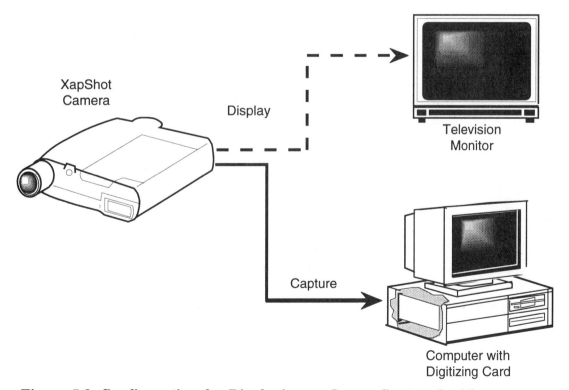

Figure 5.2. Configuration for Displaying an Image Captured with an Analog Camera.

QuickTake, a small camera sold by Apple Computer, is an example of the newer generation of true digital cameras. That means that the photos do not have to be digitized through a digitizing board but can be downloaded from the camera directly into a computer through the serial port. (See fig. 5.3.) This camera does not usually store the pictures on floppy diskettes. It stores the pictures in the camera until they are downloaded to a computer. Many other companies, such as Casio, Chinon, Epson, Ricoh, and Sony, also produce digital cameras (see the Resource list at the end of the chapter for a list of companies).

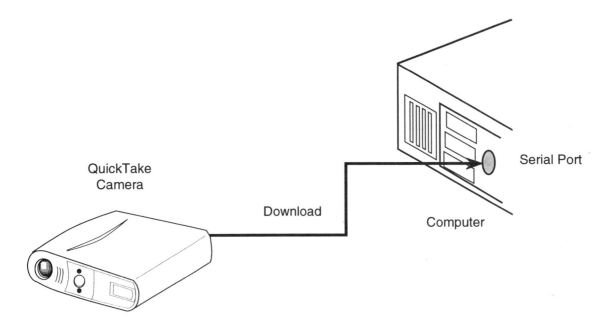

Figure 5.3. Configuration for Downloading Images Made with a Digital Camera.

Advantages of Still Video Cameras

Save time. Still video cameras save time because you do not have to take film to the corner store for development. There is no traditional film processing involved. Instead, the pictures can be accessed instantly and saved on the computer.

Save money. In addition to saving the film processing time, you also save the film processing expenses. With still video cameras, you can simply delete the pictures and start recording again.

Encourage experimentation. Students and teachers are more likely to experiment and try to get just the right picture when they realize that there is little or no expense involved.

Disadvantages of Still Video Cameras

Reduced quality. The resolution, or quality, of the still video cameras is not nearly as good as the quality of photographs or slides. If high-quality photos are necessary, you may want to develop film and scan the photographs with a scanner or use a 35mm camera to take the pictures and record them on a Photo CD.

Cost of camera. Although the cost of the still video cameras has decreased, they average about $600 each.

Portability of camera. Some of the cameras do not have diskettes or other means to store and remove the photographs from the camera. For example, the QuickTake can save 32 standard-resolution pictures, but these must be downloaded to a computer. A problem may arise if you want to take the QuickTake on a field trip and you do not have a portable computer. You would be limited to a total of 32 pictures.

DIGITIZING MOTION VIDEO

The still video and digital cameras, such as the QuickTake, are designed to capture single images. If you want to capture a motion video segment and save it on a computer, it must be shot with a motion camera and converted to digital form.

Conventional video sources such as television and videotape produce an analog form of video. Analog video uses technologies that have been in existence for decades, but there are two clear limitations to this form of video. First, computers cannot work directly with the video. Second, analog video is degraded by any process of duplication. In other words, each time a copy is made, the video signal and images get worse.

Although computers can be used to control analog video devices such as videodisc players or videocassette players, computers cannot directly store or manipulate the images that are created by such devices. For a computer to store or manipulate a video image or motion segment, the video must be converted to a digital form. Once in digital form, the computer can treat the digital information as if it were any other file of data.

When video is digitized, it is processed through a special card added to a computer. Video-digitizing cards, or peripherals, convert the electronic signals of the analog video into digital bits of information for each pixel, or picture element, of the computer screen. The conversion process makes it possible to use a camera, videotape, videodisc, or broadcast television as a computer-input device and, once it has been converted to digital form, to display the video on a standard computer monitor. (See fig. 5.4 on page 116.)

Digitizing video requires

- A computer
- A computer monitor
- A digitizing card or peripheral
- An input source for video, such as a video camera, VCR, videodisc, or television
- Digitizing software

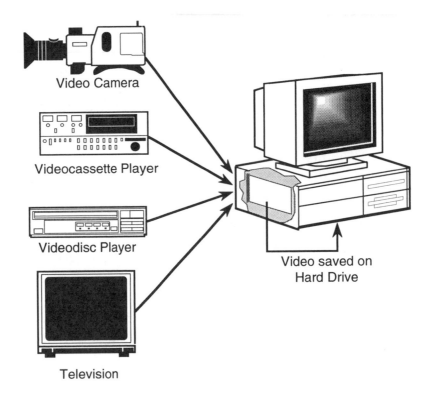

Video Camera

Videocassette Player

Videodisc Player

Video saved on
Hard Drive

Television

Figure 5.4. Configuration for Video Digitizing.

The software used in conjunction with the digitizing cards generally allows the user to set various levels of brightness, contrast, and colors. Higher-resolution color digitizations yield a better picture, but the picture also requires much more storage space. Experimentation is usually the name of the game: Try different levels of brightness, color, and so on, and save the file only after you are happy with the combination. To digitize video with a digitizing card, follow this procedure:

1. Insert the video-digitizing card into a free slot of the computer—unless the computer is an A/V model, which has a built-in digitizer.

2. Install the software program that can control the card.

3. Connect a video source—camera, videotape, or videodisc—to the video input on the card.

4. If you are also recording audio, connect an audio source—microphone, tape recorder, or videodisc—to the audio input on the computer.

5. Set the parameters for recording on the software program: number of colors, size of video image, compression method, and so on.

6. Choose *record* on the menu of the digitizing software program.

7. Select *stop* when you have recorded the segment you want.

8. Test the recording with the *play* command. If it is acceptable, save the file to the computer disk.

This procedure can be used to capture a video segment or a single image. Single frames can be "grabbed" from the video and stored as graphics images, or files, thus providing color illustrations for reports or other applications. (Be sure to keep copyright limitations in mind!)

After the video segments or single images are captured, editing software such as Adobe Premier can be used to edit the sequence, add special transitions, and construct a movie.

Video File Constraints

If you are capturing video segments, you will discover quickly that the files generated by digitizing motion video can be huge. For example, 10 seconds (300 frames) of full screen (640 by 480 pixels), true color (24 bits per pixel), motion images would require the transfer and processing of 276 megabytes of data! As a result, compromises in image size, coloration, and other factors are essential if any reasonable amount of video is to be displayed in digital form. Factors that influence the size of the file include:

Size of video window. There are three basic image sizes used for digital video, although other sizes are possible. A full screen on a computer display that is set for digitized video is usually 640 pixels by 480 pixels. (See fig. 5.5.) One-quarter of a screen is 320 pixels by 240 pixels, and a $\frac{1}{16}$ of a screen is 160 pixels by 120 pixels. The file sizes are also proportional. An image saved in full screen will result in a file that is four times larger than one for a quarter screen.

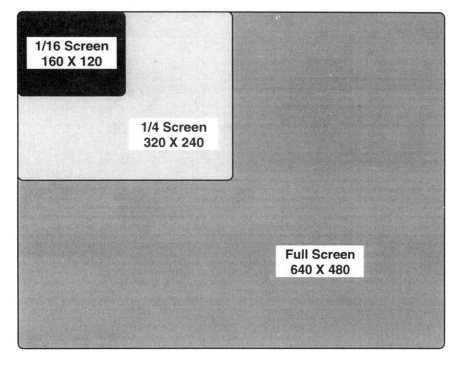

Figure 5.5. Alternate Sizes for Digital Video Windows.

Frame rate. When a computer displays digital motion images, it displays a sequence of still images, much like motion-picture film or videotape. If the computer has the processing speed to show the images at 30 frames per second (fps), then the motion appears to be natural and is referred to as "full motion." If fewer images are displayed each second, then the motion may appear to be jerky. At slow display rates, such as two or three frames per second, the illusion of motion disappears.

If the file size of a video segment is too large, you may want to reduce the frame rate and capture the video at less than full motion. Frame rates of 10 to 15 frames per second are common with digital video. The reduction in the frame rate will result in a corresponding reduction in file size. For example, if a segment is captured at 30 fps, it will be twice as large as a segment captured at 15 fps.

Number of colors. When you capture video, you can choose to digitize in black and white—actually gray scale—or with a different number of colors. The more colors you use, the larger the file size will be.

The number of colors used to capture an image is often referred to as the color depth, because it denotes the number of bits of color for each pixel. The chart in figure 5.6 outlines the number of colors in different color depths. For example, a 24-bit color file will be three times larger than an 8-bit color file.

	16.7 Million Colors (24 bits)	256 Colors (8 bits)	16 Colors (4 bits)
Full screen; 30 fps	27.0 MB	9.0 MB	4.5 MB
Full screen; 15 fps	13.5 MB	4.5 MB	2.25 MB
1/4 screen; 30 fps	6.8 MB	2.3 MB	1.15 MB
1/4 screen; 15 fps	3.4 MB	1.1 MB	.55 MB

Figure 5.6. A Comparison of File Sizes as They Relate to One Second of Motion Digital Video.

IMAGE COMPRESSION

Even with techniques such as reducing the frame rate and screen size, most video files are still too large. The rapid growth of inexpensive, large-capacity hard drives and recordable CD-ROMs has not completely solved the problem of large image files. Large files present problems that go beyond storage. For example, local area networks (LANs) have limits on how much data they can transport at any instant in time. A large image or video file being retrieved from a file server can slow or even stop all other LAN activities. Wide Area Networks (WANs) and telecommunications via modems have even greater limitations. The transmission of a large file can take minutes, or even hours, in some situations.

Because large image files tend to create problems with storage and transmission of computer data, computer scientists have found ways to reduce the size of files. Digital video files can be compressed by using either of two families of techniques. One type, called lossless compression, preserves every bit of the original information in an image. In other words, the image can be completely restored to its original form.

A second type of compression is called lossy. Using this approach, an image file can be "shrunk" to much smaller sizes than with lossless compression, but some information is lost in the process. When the image is displayed after lossy compression, some detail and coloration will be missing. As one might expect, the greater the compression, the greater the loss of information.

Lossless Compression

One of the oldest methods of lossless compression takes advantage of the tendency for pixels in some parts of an image to be identical. Called Run Length Encoding, or RLE, this method simply counts adjacent identical pixels. For example, a portion of a picture taken outdoors might be blue sky. It is possible that a number of adjacent pixels in this part of the picture would be exactly the same color. These pixels might be represented as follows (Brown and Shepherd 1995):

...BBBBBBBBBBWBBBBBB...

...BBBBBBBBBWWWBBBBB...

...BBBBBBBBBWWWWBBBB...

...BBBBBBBBBBBWBBBBB...

In this example, the Bs represent a single color of blue and the Ws represent a white cloud in the sky. In reality, every color is actually assigned a unique number in the computer, but letters are easier to imagine in this example. Using RLE, this portion of the picture might be reduced to:

...10B1W6B...

...9B3W5B...

...9B4W4B...

...11B1W5B...

The information contained in 68 bytes in the top example is reduced to 26 bytes in the compressed form. RLE simply counts the number of adjacent identical bytes and numbers them. This is effective in pictures that use large areas of just a few colors. However, if small areas of millions of colors are present, then RLE might actually produce a file that is larger than the original.

Lossy Compression

If you are willing to sacrifice information to reduce image file size, then a variety of techniques are possible. Some tend to simplify colors in areas where many close shadings of color are mixed together. For example, let us assume that three similar colors are assigned the numbers 121, 122, 123. These might be three similar shades of blue found in a picture of the sky. The binary digits that represent these numbers are:

121	111001
122	111010
123	111011

Notice that only the last two binary digits vary. If the computer is instructed to reduce its precision by "dropping" the last two digits of color information from every pixel, then the file required to store the image becomes smaller. However, these three shades of blue will become one shade of blue, and the prior shading is "lost" in the compressed file.

Far more complex algorithms perform sophisticated analyses of images prior to compression in an effort to create the minimum file size and still preserve as much of the original information as possible. Perhaps the best known compression technique in use today is the JPEG process defined as a nonproprietary standard by the Joint Photographic Expert Group. It combines lossless and lossy techniques of compression to still images through a complex process that allows individuals to select the image quality that they would like to preserve.

Motion-Image Compression

The JPEG process has also been used to compress motion images. Called Motion JPEG, the process individually evaluates and compresses each image of a motion sequence. Although Motion JPEG can reduce the size of a motion-image file, the process was designed for still images and does not always produce satisfactory results. Another nonproprietary standard, MPEG, has recently been released. Developed by the Moving Picture Expert Group, this algorithm takes a different approach. In addition to compressing the data within a single image, or intra-image data, consecutive images are also examined. When there are only a few changes from one image to the next in the motion sequence, such as in a clip of a person talking, then only the differences between the consecutive images, or inter-image data, are compressed. Thus, the second image of the motion sequence can be reconstructed by modifying only what has changed to the first image.

This process of inter-image compression adds a whole new dimension to the compression of motion images. The result is image files that can be hundreds of times smaller than the original. A variety of such compression techniques is in use right now. Although MPEG is getting attention because it is an open standard that is available for anyone to adopt, proprietary standards also exist. For example, QuickTime (Apple), Video for Windows (Microsoft), Indeo (Intel), and Cinepak (Radius) are examples of software techniques used to compress and decompress digital motion-image files.

Image compression, whether for still or motion images, makes it possible for computers and networks to handle the massive file sizes generated by our increasing use of multimedia. Techniques will continue to be refined over the next few years, so many consumers are taking a cautious approach to purchasing expensive hardware-based systems that might rapidly become outdated.

QUICKTIME AND VIDEO FOR WINDOWS

After the video has been captured and compressed, it must be saved in a format that can be recognized on your computer. Several techniques have been developed that store digital video on a computer drive. These techniques generally rely on compression to reduce the video files to a manageable size for storage and display. QuickTime (QT) is a format developed by Apple Computer, Inc. to enable color-compatible Macintosh computers and Windows-capable computers to create, edit, and play digitized video movies. A similar technology, called Video for Windows (VFW) by Microsoft, has been developed to display motion images on Windows-capable computers.

A digitizing board is required to capture video for QT and VFW movies, but no additional hardware is required on the computers that play the movies. The video is compressed when it is recorded and decompressed when it is played back. The movies can be pasted or imported into a variety of computer applications such as word processors, spreadsheets, and hypermedia programs.

Because no additional hardware is used to play back the images, the quality of the image and apparent motion depend upon the power of the computer and its display system. Most QT and VFW movies play in a small window on a monitor—about $\frac{1}{4}$ of the screen or less—at about 15 frames per second. Depending on the speed of the computer, some versions can play up to 30 frames per second and cover the entire screen of the monitor. For example, a movie on a high-end Macintosh might run fine on the full screen, but a movie on a Mac LC may appear smoother if it is sized to a portion of the screen. Likewise, if a movie is recorded at 30 fps on a Pentium, it may be able to play at only 15 fps on a 386 computer.

Applications for QuickTime and Video for Windows

Digital movies enhance many existing educational applications and have led to the development of several new ones. For example, almost all the electronic encyclopedias now incorporate movies, and countless multimedia programs on CD-ROM include movie segments (see chapter 2 for more information on CD-ROM programs).

QuickTime and Video for Windows are also having an effect on low-cost video editing. With the use of relatively inexpensive capture boards and software, video clips can now be edited on a desktop computer. Editing software programs such as Adobe Premier provide a wealth of editing options and special effects. Many video-clip libraries are also available for editing and incorporation into final productions.

Configuration for QuickTime
and Video for Windows

The QuickTime file format operates on any color-compatible Macintosh with at least 2 megabytes of RAM and System 6.07 or above. QuickTime for Windows requires a 386-level computer or above with at least 4 megabytes of RAM, an audio card, and Windows 3.1 or above. Video for Windows has similar requirements. The only additional requirement for delivery of video clips are some systems files. The QuickTime file, called QuickTime Startup Document, is included with the purchase of system software from Apple Computer, and the files for QuickTime for Windows and Video for Windows are available on electronic bulletin boards and the Internet.

Advantages of QuickTime
and Video for Windows

Inexpensive. The file needed to run a QuickTime movie is distributed by Apple Computer with its system software. The file must be placed in the system folder. The QuickTime for Windows and Video for Windows files are distributed with many applications or may be obtained from online services.

Do not require delivery hardware. The best feature of QuickTime and Video for Windows is that no additional hardware is necessary for delivery.

Synchronize video and audio. When digital movies are recorded, the audio and video can be recorded together, so they remain in synchronization.

Extend computer interface for video. Because QT and VFW are recognized file formats, the movies can be cut and pasted between applications as easily as graphics and text.

Disadvantages of QuickTime
and Video for Windows

Small pictures. Although QT and VFW can provide full-screen movies, in many cases the movies display best in a small area of the screen because the computer is too slow or the file sizes are too large for full-screen movies.

Large amounts of RAM needed. Several megabytes of RAM are recommended to play digital movies.

Large storage requirements. Even though video is compressed when it is stored, the file size is still enormous. A high-density diskette can hold only a few seconds of digital movies; therefore, most movies are distributed on CD-ROM.

Less than 30-frames-per-second playback. Most digital movies display at about 15 frames per second, which results in a slightly choppy appearance.

DIGITAL VERSATILE DISC (DVD)

Digitized motion video has evolved over the last few years, but it still has one major problem. High-quality, full-screen video with 30 frames per second creates tremendous amounts of data. Although standard CD-ROM drives have greatly increased their speed, and thus their ability to transfer data at higher rates, the CD-ROMs have been limited to approximately 650 megabytes of data. This represents a large amount of information, but it still can provide only about one hour of fairly low-quality full-screen video when using the current state-of-the-art digital video techniques.

A group of commercial leaders in compact disc technologies—Toshiba, Matsushita, Sony, Philips, Time Warner, Pioneer, JVC, Hitachi, and Mitsubishi Electric—have agreed on a standard for the next generation of compact disc. Called the Digital Versatile Disc, or DVD, it has the outward appearance of standard compact discs. However, only the physical dimensions have been maintained in the new generation. The DVD will store 4.7 gigabytes of data in its standard form, and an enhanced form will store two layers of data for a higher capacity of 8.5 gigabytes of data. If the higher-capacity disc is single-sided, both layers of data can be accessed from one side by refocusing the laser beam in the new DVD drive. (See fig. 5.7.)

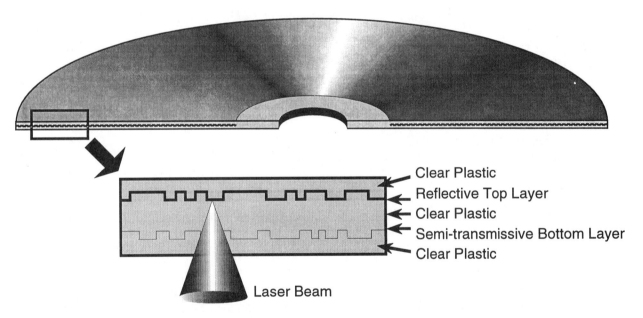

Figure 5.7. Cutaway Section of a DVD.

The DVD video standards call for data compression using the MPEG2 standard. When this standard is applied to appropriate original video material, the result is a highly compressed video that can be played back with exceptional quality that far exceeds that of current analog sources, such as videodisc. DVD has the capability of delivering approximately 2 hours and 13 minutes of video on a single-sided, single-layer DVD disc. In addition to the high-quality video, a DVD disc can provide up to three languages in discrete surround sound, along with captions or subtitles in four other languages.

Despite all the DVD's features, it is still an emerging technology, and it has competition. Only time will tell if the DVD will eventually replace the VHS cassette tape as a movie delivery medium, much as the CD-Audio disc replaced the LP phonograph record. Although current specifications for DVD discs have been demonstrated in read-only form, the specifications also cover write-once and erasable forms. If inexpensive record-and-erase machines become available, then DVD might replace current VHS tape machines.

CONCLUSION

When video is digitized, it can be duplicated without any loss of quality. In addition, you can modify and enhance the images with a computer. Many emerging technologies use video in digital form, and numerous applications are becoming available for educators. The chart in figure 5.8 provides a comparison and summary of several video technologies presented in this chapter.

	Videodisc	QuickTime	Video for Windows	DVD	Analog Camera	Digital Camera
Manufacturer	Various	Apple	Microsoft	Various	Canon (XapShot)	Various
Analog/Digital	Analog	Digital	Digital	Digital	Analog	Digital
Media	Videodisc	CD-ROM, Hard Drive	CD-ROM, Hard Drive	Compact Disc	2 Inch Disk	Stored in Camera
Typical Size Video Window	Full Screen	1/4 Screen	1/4 Screen	Full Screen	Full Screen	Full Screen
Motion/Still	Motion/Still	Motion/Still	Motion/Still	Motion/Still	Still	Still

Figure 5.8. Comparison of Video Technologies.

DIGITAL IMAGES
AND VIDEO GLOSSARY

analog video. Video that is stored as an electrical signal with a continuous scale. Videotape and videodisc generally store analog video.

aspect ratio. The width-to-height ratio of an image. Changing the aspect ratio can make images appear out of proportion.

authoring systems. Software that is used to create computer-based training. Such software contains program components to manage the instructional process.

bit-mapped image. A computer image that is stored as individual pixels, rather than graphic formulas.

capture. The process of collecting and saving text or image data. When an analog source such as a videodisc is used as a source to record a digital image on a computer, it is said to be captured.

CD-Audio (Compact Disc–Audio). A popular format for high-fidelity digital music. Each compact disc can store 74 minutes of sound with no degradation of quality during playback.

CD-i (Compact Disc–Interactive). A system specification for an interactive audio, video, and computer system based on compact disc as the storage medium. CD-i uses an integrated player and is focused at the consumer market.

CD-ROM (Compact Disc–Read Only Memory). A prerecorded, nonerasable disc that stores approximately 650 megabytes of digital data.

Cinepak. A technique produced by Radius for software-only compression. It requires considerable compression time but results in high quality.

coloration. The number of distinct colors that can be presented on a computer screen at one time. In bit-mapped images, this is related to the number of bits allocated to each pixel. For example, 4 bits results in 16 colors; 24 bits, 16.7 million colors.

compression. Technique used to store files with fewer bits; therefore, less disk storage space is required. Lossless compression preserves all image qualities, while lossy compression sacrifices some image quality for greater compression ratios.

digital camera. A camera that records images in true digital form. The images are usually downloaded directly into a computer through its serial port.

digital video. Video that is stored in bits and bytes on a computer. It can be manipulated and displayed on a computer screen.

digitizing. The process of converting an analog signal into a digital signal.

disc. Usually refers to a videodisc or compact disc. Computer diskettes are generally referred to as *disks* (with a *k*), and videodiscs and other optical storage media are referred to as *discs* (with a *c*).

DVD (Digital Versatile Disc). A second generation of the original CD-ROM format. It provides up to two layers of digital information on a single-sided compact disc. It stores up to 4.7 gigabytes for one layer; 8.5 gigabytes for two layers. Advanced digital video and audio features are specified.

8-bit. An 8-bit video display card can display 256 different colors for each pixel.

4-bit. A 4-bit video display card can display 16 different colors for each pixel.

fractal compression. A technique that uses mathematics to analyze similarities in images and create algorithms for compression. It results in extremely large compression ratios.

frame. One complete video picture.

frame grabber. A device that converts a single analog video frame into digital format to store on a hard drive.

frame rate. The number of video frames displayed each second.

full-motion video. Video frames displayed at 30 frames per second.

hypermedia program. A software program that provides seamless access to text, graphics, audio, and video.

image. A graphic, picture, or one frame of video.

Indeo. A software technique created by Intel to compress and decompress video.

JPEG (Joint Photographic Expert Group). An organization that has developed an international standard for compression and decompression of still images.

lossless compression. Compression programs that retain all the information in the original file.

lossy compression. Compression programs that discard some information during the reduction process.

MPEG (Moving Picture Expert Group). Working parties for standardization of motion-video compression. MPEG1 is used for linear video movies on compact discs, MPEG2 is designed for broadcast-quality digital video, and MPEG3 is being developed for high-definition TV.

MPEG2. A digital video standard designed for broadcast video.

NTSC (National Television Systems Committee). The U.S. standard for motion video of 525 horizontal lines per frame at 30 frames per second.

OCR (optical character recognition). Software that enables a scanner to recognize individual letters or words. Text that is scanned with OCR software can be imported and manipulated by a word-processing program.

optical media. Media read with a laser beam. CD-ROM and videodisc technologies use optical media.

overlay. A computer-generated graphic placed on top of a video display.

pixel. A single dot or point of an image on a computer screen. Pixel is a contraction of the words *picture element.*

QuickTake. A camera marketed by Apple Computer that takes digital pictures that can be transferred directly to a computer through the modem port.

QuickTime. A file format that allows Macintosh computers to compress and play digitized video movies.

raster. The horizontal lines of light that make up an image on a standard computer screen. The number of pixels in each raster and the total number of raster lines dictate the screen's resolution, such as 640 by 480.

resolution. The sharpness or clarity of a computer screen. Displays with more lines and pixels of information have better resolution.

scanner. A hardware peripheral that takes a "picture" of an item and transfers the image to a computer.

SCSI (Small Computer Systems Interface). A standard for connecting external devices, including scanners, to a computer.

16-bit. A 16-bit video display card can display one of 65,536 different colors for each pixel.

still video camera. A camera that captures pictures without using film.

24-bit. A 24-bit video display card can display 16.7 million different colors for each pixel, and it is often referred to as true color.

vector image. A computer image that is constructed from graphic formulas. Usually images such as charts that are produced of lines, boxes, and circles are vector images.

VFW (Video for Windows). A file format that allows MS-DOS computers to compress and play digitized video movies.

XapShot. A still video camera (no longer in production) that stores photographs on a small diskette. The pictures are analog and can be displayed on a television monitor. They can also be captured on the computer through a digitizing card.

DIGITAL IMAGES AND VIDEO RESOURCES

Scanners

AGFA
1 Ramland Road
Orangeburg, NY 10962-2693
800-685-4271

Apple Computer, Inc.
1 Infinite Loop
Cupertino, CA 95014
800-776-2333

Chinon America
615 Hawaii Avenue
Torrance, CA 90503
800-441-0222

Connectix Corporation (QuickCam)
2655 Campus Drive
San Mateo, CA 94403
800-950-5880

Envisions Solutions
47400 Seabridge Drive
Freemont, CA 94538
800-365-7226

Epson America, Inc.
20770 Madrona Avenue
Torrance, CA 90503
800-922-8911

Hewlett-Packard
3000 Hanover Street
Palo Alto, CA 94303
800-722-6538

Howtek, Inc.
21 Park Avenue
Hudson, NH 03051
603-882-5200

Logitech, Inc.
6505 Kaiser Drive
Fremont, CA 94555
800-231-7717

Microtek Lab, Inc.
3715 Doolittle Drive
Redondo Beach, CA 90278
800-654-4160

Our Business Machines
12901 Ramona Boulevard, Suite J
Irwindale, CA 91706
800-433-1435

Panasonic
2 Panasonic Way
Secaucus, NJ 07094
800-524-0864

Pentax Technologies Corporation
100 Technology Drive
Broomfield, CO 80021
800-543-6144

Sharp Electronics Corporation
Sharp Plaza, MS1
Mahwah, NJ 07430-2135
800-237-4277

Umax Technologies
3353 Gateway Boulevard
Fremont, CA 94538
800-562-0311

Visioneer
2860 W. Bayshore Road
Palo Alto, CA 94303
800-787-7007

Video Digitizers

**Advanced Digital Imaging
(Digital Magic)**
22 Rocky Knole
Urbane, CA 92612
714-779-7772

**AITech International (WaveWatcher
TV-II)**
47971 Fremont Boulevard
Fremont, CA 94538
510-226-8960

**ATI Technologies (Video Basic,
Video-IT!)**
33 Commerce Valley Drive East
Thornhill, Ontario L3T 7N6
Canada
905-882-2600

Cardinal Technologies (SNAPplus)
1827 Freedom Road
Lancaster, PA 17601
717-293-3049

CEI (Video Clipper)
210A Twin Dolphin Drive
Redwood City, CA 94065
415-591-6617

**Computer Friends, Inc. (ColorSnap
PC PRO)**
14250 N.W. Science Park Drive
Portland, OR 97229
800-547-3303

Connectix Corporation
2655 Campus Drive
San Mateo, CA 94403
800-950-5880

**Creative Labs (Video Blaster;
Video Spigot)**
1523 Semoran Plaza
Stillwater, OK 74075
800-998-1000

**Diamond Computer Systems, Inc.
(VideoStar)**
1130 E. Arques Avenue
Sunnyvale, CA 94086
408-325-7000

**Digital Processing Systems
(Perception)**
11 Spiral Drive
Florence, KY 41042
606-371-5533

Digital Vision (ComputerEyes/RT)
270 Bridge Street
Dedham, MA 02026
800-346-0090

**FAST Electronic U.S. (Movie
Machine Pro)**
393 Vintage Park Drive, Suite 140
Foster City, CA 94404
800-248-3278

**Hauppauge Computer Works
(Win/TV)**
91 Cabot Court
Hauppauge, NY 11788
800-443-6284

IEV International (ProMotion)
3855 S. 500 West, Suite O
Salt Lake City, UT 84115
800-438-6161

**In-Motion Technologies Inc.
(Picture Perfect Pro)**
1940 Colony Street
Mountain View, CA 94043
415-968-6363

Intel (Smart Video Recorder)
5200 N.E. Elam Young Parkway
Hillsborough, OR 97124-6497
800-538-3373

Intelligent Resources (Video Explorer)
3030 S. Creek Lane
Arlington, IL 60005
847-670-9388

JJ&K Enterprises (MR RAM GRAB)
5012 Whishett Avenue
Valley Village, CA 91607
818-985-9407

Logitech, Inc. (MovieMan)
6505 Kaiser Drive
Fremont, CA 94555
800-231-7717

Matrox Electronic Systems (Marvel)
1025 Stregis Boulevard
Dorval, Quebec H9P 2T4
Canada
800-810-2550

Miro Computer Products (DC20)
955 Commercial Street
Palo Alto, CA 94303
800-249-6476

New Media Graphics (Super Video Windows)
780 Boston Road
Billerica, MA 01821
416-248-4473

Omnicomp Graphics (M&M Pro)
1734 W. Sam Houston Parkway
Houston, TX 77043
713-464-2990

Optibase (MPEG VideoPro)
5000 Quorum Drive, Suite 700
Dallas, TX 75240
800-451-5101

Optivision (OptiVideo MPEG Encoder)
3450 Hillview Avenue
Palo Alto, CA 94304
415-855-0200

Orchid (Vidiola)
45365 Northport Loop West
Fremont, CA 94538
800-767-2443

Quadrant (Q-Motion)
269 Great Valley Parkway
Malvern, PA 19355
800-700-0362

RasterOps (MediaTime)
2500 Walsh Avenue
Santa Clara, CA 95051
800-729-2656

Sigma Designs (RealMagic)
46501 Landing Parkway
Fremont, CA 94538
800-845-8086

Truevision (Targa)
7340 Shadeland Station
Indianapolis, IN 46256
800-522-8783

Video Labs, Inc. (VideoShot)
10925 Bren Road East
Minneapolis, MN 55343
800-467-7157

Videomail (DigiTV)
568-4 Weddell Drive
Sunnyvale, CA 94089
408-747-0223

Xing Technology (XingIt!)
1540 W. Branch Street
Auroyal Grande, CA 93420
800-294-6448

Still Video and Digital Cameras

Apple Computer, Inc. (QuickTake)
1 Infinite Loop
Cupertino, CA 95014-6299
800-776-2333

Canon U.S.A., Inc. (XapShot)
1 Canon Plaza
Lake Success, NY 11042
800-828-4040

Cardinal Technologies, Inc.
1827 Freedom Road
Lancaster, PA 17601
717-293-3000

Casio Computer Company (QV-10)
570 Mount Pleasant Avenue
Dover, NJ 07801
800-962-2746

Chinon America, Inc. (ES-3000)
615 Hawaii Avenue
Torrance, CA 90503
800-441-0222

Connectix Corporation
2655 Campus Drive
San Mateo, CA 94403
800-950-5880

**Eastman Kodak Company
(DC 40; DC 50)**
Electronic Photography Division
Rochester, NY 14650
800-235-6325

Epson America, Inc. (Photo PC)
20770 Madrona Avenue
Torrence, CA 90503
800-289-3776

Logitech, Inc., (Fotoman Pixtura)
6506 Kaiser Drive
Freemont, CA 94555
800-231-7717

Ricoh Corporation (RDC-1)
475 Lillard Drive
Sparks, NV 89434
800-225-1899

Sharp Electronics, Inc.
Sharp Plaza
Mahwah, NJ 07430
800-BE-SHARP

**Sony Corporation of America
(DKC-1D1)**
Still Image Systems
1 Sony Drive
Park Ridge, NJ 07656
800-472-SONY

Video Editing Software

Adobe Software, Inc. (Adobe Premier)
1585 Charleston Road
P.O. Box 7900
Mountain View, CA 94039-7900
800-833-6687

Apple Computer, Inc. (QuickTime)
1 Infinite Loop
Cupertino, CA 95014-6299
800-776-2333

Asymetrix (Digital Video Producer)
110 110th Avenue NE
Bellevue, WA 98004
800-448-6543

ATI Technologies (MediaMerge)
33 Commerce Valley Drive
Thornhill, Ontario L3T 7N6
Canada
416-882-2600

Avid Technology (VideoShop)
Metropolitan Technology Park
1 Park West
Tewksbury, MA 01876
800-949-AVID

Microsoft Corporation
1 Microsoft Way
Redmond, CA 98052
800-425-9400

Neil Media (Video Graffiti)
2010 Stockbridge Avenue
Redwood City, CA 94061
415-369-6345

Radius, Inc.
215 Moffett Park
Sunnyvale, CA 94089
408-541-6100

VideoFusion (VideoFusion)
1722 Indian Wood Circle, Suite H
Maumee, OH 43537
800-638-5253

DIGITAL VERSATILE DISC RESOURCES

This technology is new and rapidly evolving. The most current news is from Internet sources such as the following:

DVD Information Page
http://www.unik.no/%7Erobert/hifi/dvd/

First DVD Home Page
http://www1.usa1.com/~philk/dvd/

Interactive Multimedia Association
http://www.ima.org/forums/imf/
dvd/faq.html

Philips
http://www.philips.com/pkm/laseroptics/
dvd

Sony
http://www.sel.sony.com/SEL/
consumer/dvd/feat.html

Toshiba
http://www.toshiba.com/tacp/SD/

REFERENCE LIST

Brown, C. W., and B. J. Shepherd. (1995). *Graphics file formats: Reference and guide.* Greenwich, CT: Manning Publishing.

RECOMMENDED READING

Barron, A. E. (1995). An overview of digital video. *Journal of Computing in Higher Education* 7(1): 69–84.

Barron, A. E., and G. W. Orwig. (1995). *Multimedia technologies for training: An introduction.* Englewood, CO: Libraries Unlimited.

Beale, D., and G. Orwig. (1995). What is digital; what is not? Everything you wanted to know about digital and analog, but were afraid to ask. *Educational Media International* 32(4): 186–89.

Berger, M. (1995). Video capture boards: A resource directory. *Multimedia Producer* 1(1): 33–35.

Biedny, D., and N. Moody. (1995). Windows video goes frame-to-frame against the Mac. *New Media* 5(12): 53–58.

DeVoe, D. (1996). Vendors show off future digital video storage technology. *Infoworld* 18(3): 28–29.

Doyle, B. (1995). Mac still king of nonlinear video. *New Media* 5(7): 61–68.

English, D. (1996). Trickle-down video: In-house editing and MPEG target the middle class. *Multimedia Producer* 2(2): 13–14.

Gillmor, S. (1995). Budget video editing. *PC Graphics and Video* 4(1): 18–24.

Gregor, A. (1995). Multimedia video: The next step. *CD-ROM Today* 3(1): 54–56.

Halfhill, T. R. (1995). QuickTime VR: A new worldview. *CD-ROM Today* 3(1): 128.

Harcourt, J. (1995). Take a digital test drive. *Photo Electronic Imaging* 38(6): 34–36.

Huber, R. F. (1996). Scanners turn documents into digital data. *PC Novice* 7(4): 46–48.

LeBlanc, T. (1996). Demystifying the magic of PC video. *PC Novice* 7(4): 30–33.

Menn, E. (1995). The wide angle on digital cameras. *Multimedia World* 3(1): 110–19.

Molinari, C., and R. S. Tannenbaum. (1995). Applications of optical scanners in an academic center. *T.H.E. Journal* 22(8): 60–63.

Murie, M. (1995). Digital cameras: Fun, fast for on-screen work. *New Media* 5(12): 61–64.

O'Conovan, E. (1996). Picture this: Digital photography and desktop video come of age. *Technology and Learning* 16(7): 24–28.

Orwig, G. (1995). Digital Images: Getting the pictures onto the screen. *Educational Media International* 32(4): 194–99.

Ozer, J. (1996). Software MPEG decoders rev up. *New Media* 6(2): 50–52.

——. (1996). Software video Codecs: The search for quality. *New Media* 6(2): 46–49.

Pearson, L. (1995). The changing face of video editing. *Presentations: Technology and techniques for better communications* 9(6): 74–78.

Popko, R. (1996). Turn your PC into a desktop video studio. *Multimedia World* 3(5): 76–83.

Rodriguez, N., M. Banckaert, and M. Lavacry. Digital video for multimedia: Two approaches (MPEG). *Educational Media International* 32(4): 200–207.

Roth, C. (1995). MPEG cards smooth video pixels. *New Media* 5(4): 41–44.

Sauer, J., and B. Doyle. (1996). Windows digital video cards ride the PCI bus. *New Media* 6(6): 45–54.

Seiter, C. (1996). Scan. *Multimedia World* 3(7): 75–78.

Skipton, C. (1996). Digital camera prices drop. *New Media* 6(2): 18.

Stern, J., and R. Lettieri. (1995). A QuickTake on QuickTime. *Multimedia Producer* 1(1): 44–45.

Swanson, C. (1996). How to get the most out of photo CD. *Photo Electronic Imaging* 39(2): 10–11.

Worthington, P. (1995). Catching Codecs: Image compression. *Multimedia Producer* 1(7): 19–20.

——. (1996). One-click wonders: Low-cost digital cameras are here, but do they offer too little, too late? *Multimedia Producer* 2(1): 13–14.

DIGITAL VIDEO TECHNOLOGIES

An Overview Of

Dr. Ann E. Barron
University of South Florida

Dr. Gary W. Orwig
University of Central Florida

This brochure is an excerpt from:

New Technologies for Education

A Beginner's Guide

Third Edition

To obtain the complete book, contact:

Libraries Unlimited
P.O. Box 6633
Englewood, CO 80155-6633
800-237-6124

Advantages

• *Manipulation.* By transferring images from analog to digital formats, they become controllable by a computer. They can be resized, recolored, or duplicated without expensive analog video editing equipment.

• *Duplication.* Each time an analog format (such as a videotape) is duplicated, the quality decreases and the imperfections increase. In contrast, digital files can be reproduced without any loss of quality.

• *Interactivity.* Digital formats also allow users to interact with images by changing the program flow and features.

• *Portability.* Analog videodisc systems generally require a videodisc player and two monitors. With digital formats, the computer monitor can display both the digital video images and the computer graphics.

Disadvantages

• *Storage space.* One frame on an analog videodisc can require more than 3/4 of a megabyte to store in digital form (uncompressed). To keep the size of the computer files reasonable, images and sounds are often compressed and recorded at a reduced quality level.

• *Transfer rates.* Data transfer rates of large digital data files make it difficult to display full motion video at the normal rate of 30 frames per second on a computer screen.

Digital Cameras

Digital cameras can be used to take still pictures, which are then stored in the camera until they are downloaded into a computer. After they are downloaded, the pictures can be imported into software programs, such as HyperStudio or PageMaker, for hypermedia projects or newsletters.

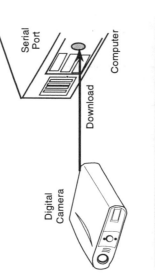

Digital Camera

Download

Serial Port

Computer

Digital Versatile Disc

Digital Versatile Disc, or DVD, has the outward appearance of standard compact discs. However, DVD will store 4.7 gigabytes of data in its standard form, and an enhanced form will store two layers of data for a higher capacity of 8.5 gigabytes of data. The higher capacity disc will still be single-sided, with both layers of data being accessed from one side by refocusing the laser beam in the new DVD drive.

QuickTime

QuickTime is a format developed by Apple Computer Inc. to enable Macintosh computers to compress and play digitized video movies. A digitizing board is required to capture video for a QuickTime movie, but any color-compatible Macintosh computer can play the movies without additional hardware.

The video is automatically compressed when it is recorded and decompressed when it is played back. The movies can be pasted or imported into a variety of Macintosh applications.

Video For Windows

Video for Windows was developed by Microsoft Corporation to enable MS-DOS computers to play digital video movies.

A digitizing card is required to capture the video; however, you can play Video for Windows movies on any MS-DOS computer (386 or better) that has Microsoft Windows and a digital audio card. The software files that are required are available from Microsoft Corporation, or they may be obtained from some electronic bulletin boards.

Digitizing Video

When video is digitized, it must be processed through a special card added to a computer. Video digitizing cards (or peripherals) convert the electronic signals of the analog video into digital bits of information for each pixel of the computer screen. The conversion process makes it possible to use a camera, videotape, videodisc, or television as a computer input device for digital video. The digital video can then be saved as a computer file on the hard drive.

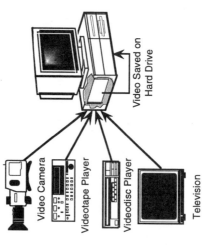

Video Camera

Videotape Player

Videodisc Player

Television

Video Saved on Hard Drive

The software used in conjunction with the digitizing cards generally allows the user to set various levels of brightness, contrast, and colors. Higher resolution color digitizations yield a better picture, but the picture also requires much more storage space.

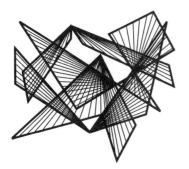

6

Presentation and Hypermedia Programs

A Scenario

Paula had really enjoyed her junior year—especially the work with the yearbook staff. It was a great feeling to see all their efforts turn into a finished product that she and her classmates would cherish for years. The staff was planning one last meeting in May to celebrate the end of the year, and Mr. Turner had asked Paula to give a short presentation.

Paula had been waiting for just such an opportunity. As the photographer for the yearbook, she had many pictures that were not printed in the yearbook—funny pictures, such as Charlie making "rabbit ears" behind the principal's head and Ms. Jones wearing shoes that were two different colors. She also had serious pictures, such as the shots from the awards banquet yesterday and of the damage from the tornado that skirted town last week.

Before she started, Paula debated the relative merits of using PowerPoint or HyperStudio for the presentation. They were both easy to use and could be run on either the Macintosh or Windows computer. Plus they could both integrate the graphics, sounds, and digital video clips that she wanted to present. The main advantage that HyperStudio offered was the ability to click on different parts of the screen for menu branches and interactivity. Because this was planned as a short slide show type presentation, and she only had two hours to create the final product, Paula decided that PowerPoint would be a good choice.

Paul first selected a template, or background, for the presentation. PowerPoint has many preformatted backgrounds that are designed for presentations, and she selected one with balloons and confetti on the edges to symbolize the end-of-year celebration. Then she entered the text that she needed on each screen. Because the text color and size are also preformatted, this task took only a few minutes.

Finally, Paula added the graphics she had scanned, the audio she had digitized, and the digital video clips she had saved. She knew that the movie she shot of the staff working until 3:00 AM on the night the yearbook proofs were due would bring back a lot of memories to everyone.

Paula's presentation was a big hit at the meeting. Everyone enjoyed the outtakes from the yearbook. Even the principal laughed—although it is probably a good thing that Charlie is graduating next week. In addition, a serious question was raised after the presentation: Would it be possible to do an electronic yearbook next year? For a fraction of the cost of producing a printed version, a CD-ROM could be produced and filled with pictures, sounds, and digital movies. But how would students be able to have their friends sign it? Paula and the other staff members who were returning in the fall agreed that they would discuss it again in August.

Presentation and hypermedia programs provide the ability to access text, graphics, sound, video, and animation in unique and exciting ways. Many students, teachers, media specialists, and administrators are taking advantage of this new technology to enhance their research reports, presentations, and lessons.

There are a number of affordable presentation programs and hypermedia development programs on the market. This chapter focuses on two that are of special interest to educators: PowerPoint and HyperStudio. Both are cross-platform—meaning they work on Macintosh and Windows computers—inexpensive, relatively easy to use, and can include text, graphics, audio, and video. A brief overview of other programs, such as HyperCard, Digital Chisel, Multimedia ToolBook, Authorware, and LinkWay Live is also provided. This chapter includes

- An introduction to the educational uses of presentation and hypermedia programs

- An introduction to presentation programs

- An overview of PowerPoint

- An introduction to hypermedia

- An overview of HyperStudio

- Procedures for creating a HyperStudio stack

- A brief discussion of other hypermedia programs

- Advantages and disadvantages of hypermedia

- Tips and techniques for creating hypermedia applications

- Resources for further information

PRESENTATION AND HYPERMEDIA PROGRAMS IN EDUCATION

Research reports and presentations in education no longer consist solely of five double-spaced pages with three references. Instead, students are being encouraged to conduct their research with technology and to produce reports that integrate various media. Likewise, teachers can combine video, audio, text, and graphics to enhance their classroom presentations.

Two of the major development tools that students and teachers can use to produce multimedia reports are presentation programs, such as PowerPoint, and hypermedia programs, such as HyperStudio and HyperCard. There are many benefits for teachers and students that can be achieved by integrating technology into presentations and lessons.

Benefits for Teachers

Computer slide shows. Rather than static overheads or slides, electronic presentations offer the advantages of last-minute changes, dynamic input from the students, and special transitional effects. A projection system that is connected to the computer is necessary to project an electronic slide show for a large group.

Instructional materials. An *authoring system* is a computer program designed specifically to create computer-based instruction. HyperCard, HyperStudio, and similar programs have revolutionized authoring systems because they are inexpensive and easy to use. For example, to create a multiple-choice question, you can place an invisible button over each possible answer. When a student clicks on an incorrect answer, the student activates the button, which may provide feedback about the incorrect answer or another chance to answer the question. If the student clicks on the correct answer, the button provides positive feedback or instructs the program to go on to the next question. This type of interaction is relatively easy to create with hypermedia programs.

Handout materials. Most of the presentation and hypermedia programs offer excellent options for creating handouts. For example, the Print Stack feature of HyperCard allows developers to print between 1 and 32 computer screens on the same sheet of paper. In PowerPoint, you can print up to six screens on each piece of paper for handouts.

Increased familiarity with commercial hypermedia programs. Many commercial educational programs are being written with hypermedia development programs. For example, the software for the *AIDS* and *Bio Sci II* interactive videodisc programs was written in HyperCard, and the *Mammals* CD-ROM was developed in LinkWay Live. If teachers are comfortable with hypermedia development, they can navigate more easily through the commercial software.

Benefits for Students

Encourages creativity. Students generally enjoy working with technology and are motivated by the range of possibilities for electronic presentations. Using new methods and tools can inspire creativity by challenging students to produce relevant information that integrates various media elements.

Promotes critical-thinking skills. Presentation and hypermedia programs encourage students to analyze and evaluate information in many forms, sequence the information, and synthesize the materials into the final products. Activities that construct both internal knowledge and external products are powerful learning tools.

Encourages cooperation and collaboration. Many electronic projects are constructed in groups; students learn how to work together toward a common goal. In addition, most presentation and hypermedia programs allow developers to distribute their programs freely without an additional license fee. This distribution freedom has resulted in increased collaboration and sharing of resources between distant classes. For example, there are many projects and presentations freely available on the Internet that were created by students and teachers using HyperCard, HyperStudio, LinkWay Live, and PowerPoint.

Enhances presentation skills. Students are often required or encouraged to present their final electronic projects to the class or a group of peers. Thus, they have an opportunity to practice their presentation skills.

INTRODUCTION TO PRESENTATION PROGRAMS

Presentation software is used to create electronic versions of slide shows. The presentations are generally linear in format, with one slide following the other when the user clicks the mouse or presses a key. Class lectures and multimedia reports are easy for teachers and students to develop with presentation software.

There are many popular presentation software programs, including PowerPoint by Microsoft Corporation, Action! by Macromedia, and Harvard Graphics by Software Publishing Corporation. All are inexpensive, easy to learn, and easy to use and can incorporate multimedia elements such as graphics, digital video, and digital audio. They also have a variety of predesigned templates with colorful backgrounds and preformatted fonts to make the presentation look professional.

PRESENTATION DEVELOPMENT PROGRAMS

PowerPoint by Microsoft is a presentation program that is designed for creating electronic slide shows. In other words, it produces the slides for a presentation that can be used in a linear fashion, moving from one slide to the next, as a speaker elaborates on the bullets or other information on the slides.

Overview of PowerPoint

One of the best features of PowerPoint is that it is almost 100 percent cross-platform. That means that you can create a presentation on a Macintosh, save it on a disk that is formatted for MS-DOS, and then run the presentation on a Windows computer. Although there may be minor differences in the fonts used on the two systems, most of the colors, graphics, and text will look and act exactly as they did on the Macintosh. The program is equally flexible in the other direction: You can create on a Windows computer and then run or edit the program on a Macintosh.

Step 1. Decide on the Look of the Presentation

PowerPoint supplies several background templates that are specifically designed for optimal use as black-and-white overheads, color overheads, on-screen presentations, or 35mm slides. By using one of the templates, you can save time and produce a presentation with a profession style.

The templates determine the text fonts and sizes, background colors and patterns, and arrangement of information on the screen. They vary in the amount of information that can be placed on each slide. It is a good idea to decide on the template before you start to prepare materials.

Step 2. Create Slides with Text and Graphics

With PowerPoint, you can create the slides for your presentation in Slide View or Outline View. Slide View works best if you have a lot of graphics and different layouts. To create a slide in Slide View, simply click in the title box to type a title and click in the body to type in the bullets. (See fig. 6.1 on page 140.) When you are ready for a new slide, select *insert . . . new slide*, and a new slide will appear with the same background template. Graphics can be added with the *insert* options. PowerPoint supplies a wealth of clip-art images, or graphics can be imported from other programs.

Outline View is probably the fastest way to create slides for a presentation and is easy if you do not have many graphics. Basically, you enter the Outline View and type in your titles and bullets. (See fig. 6.2 on page 140.) The slides will automatically be created for you with the template that you selected.

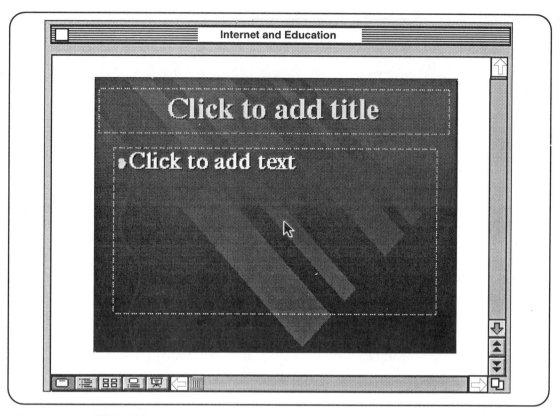

Figure 6.1. Slide View.

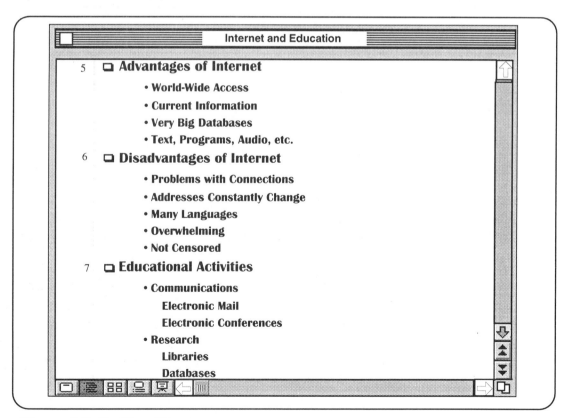

Figure 6.2. Outline View.

Step 3. Sequence the Presentation

Quite often slides are not created in the exact order in which they are to be shown. After all the slides are created, however, their sequence can be adjusted as needed by using an electronic slide table, a feature that allows a group of slides to be viewed in miniature. (See fig. 6.3.) The order of presentation can be altered by using a mouse to click and drag slides into their new positions.

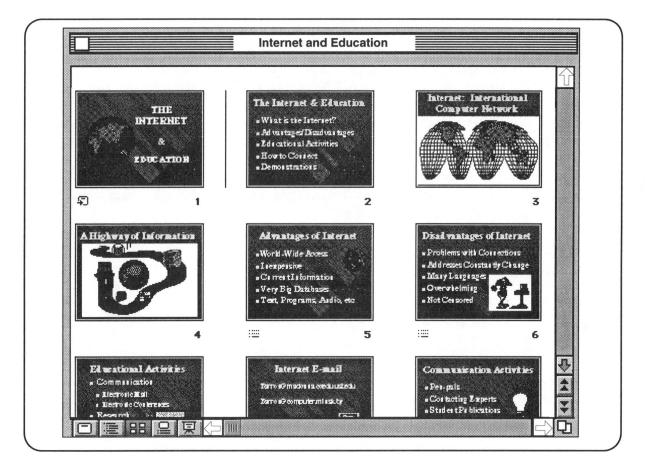

Figure 6.3. Slide Sorter.

Step 4. Add Special Effects

One of the strengths of presentation software is the ability to create dynamic transitions between slides. Rather than having one image simply replace another, the new image can "push" the old one off the screen, "wipe" onto the screen, or evolve out of some geometric pattern.

In PowerPoint, you can integrate Transitions and Builds. Transitions are special effects such as dissolves or wipes that occur between slides. Builds are techniques for using progressive disclosure of the bullets on a slide. Special effects have become common in electronic presentations; however, to maintain a professional image, you should be conservative in their use.

Step 5. Add Multimedia Elements

If a multimedia computer is used to create and deliver a presentation, then sound and digitized video can be added. With PowerPoint, you can simply use the *insert . . . object* options to integrate digital audio, MIDI music, digital video, or animation. Each of these elements can be linked to a screen, with instructions to play as soon as the screen is displayed, to play after a specified number of seconds, or to play when it is clicked.

Step 6. Prepare for Delivery

PowerPoint, like most of the other presentation software, provides a separate run-time program, or viewer, for delivery of the show. The viewer enables you to show the presentation on a computer that does not have the PowerPoint program. For example, if you were going to give a speech at the district office but were unsure whether they had PowerPoint on the computer you were going to use, you could take a copy of your presentation, along with a copy of the PowerPoint Viewer, and load it on the computer.

Viewer programs do not allow you or anyone else to make changes in the presentation, but you can freely distribute the viewer to others. However, if you are planning to develop a presentation that will be sold, you should clarify your distribution rights with the publisher of the presentation software.

Step 7. Print Your Slides

PowerPoint offers many options for printing your slides:

Slides. If you want to print overhead transparencies, this option will print full-size slides.

NotesPages. Sometimes speakers like to have a picture of each slide, along with their notes, on paper. NotesPages will print each slide at the top of a page with notes—which the audience will not see—on the bottom of the page.

Handouts. PowerPoint can print handouts of the presentation with two, four, or six miniature slides per page. This is a great way to save paper and provide written documentation for your audience.

Outline View. You can also print the outline of the presentation for quick reference.

INTRODUCTION TO HYPERMEDIA PROGRAMS

With hypermedia programs, information stored as text, graphics, audio, video, or animation can be accessed in associative, nonlinear ways. For example, the opening screen of a hypermedia application might contain a graphic of a cat. Invisible buttons, or areas, on the graphic could be activated, allowing students to investigate further the anatomy of the cat. If a student clicked on the cat's ear, another screen would instantly appear with a close-up of the ear. Additional buttons on the close-up screen could allow access to graphics illustrating the detailed structure of cats' ears, audio files demonstrating the frequency range of cats' hearing, or a movie clip about how cats' ears react to various sounds.

Hypermedia applications enable students to make their own choices and follow their own paths. Consequently, one student might explore all the information about ears while another concentrates on other areas of the cat, such as the eyes or whiskers.

Although the concept of hypermedia has existed for many years, technical advances in computers and software have only recently made it a reality for educators. In addition to an increase in commercial applications with a hypermedia interface, there are several development programs on the market, such as HyperCard, HyperStudio, LinkWay Live, and Multimedia ToolBook.

HYPERMEDIA DEVELOPMENT PROGRAMS

It is difficult to describe hypermedia development programs, partly because of their unique structure. Most hypermedia development tools are based on a *stack* metaphor, such as a stack of index or playing cards. In HyperStudio and HyperCard, a file is referred to as a *stack,* and each computer screen is called a *card.* In LinkWay Live, files are called *folders,* and each computer screen is a *page.* In either case, each screen can contain a variety of objects, including text objects, buttons, and graphics. (See fig. 6.4.)

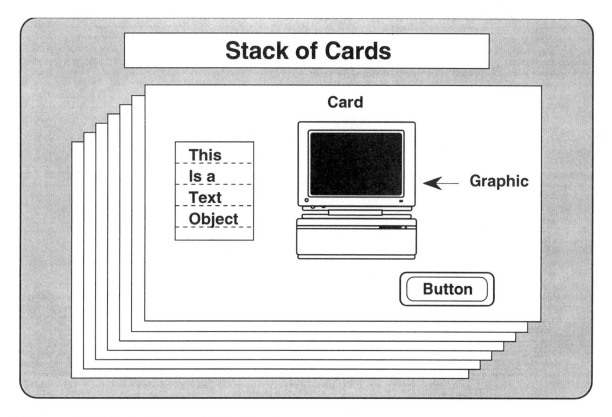

Figure 6.4. Basic Hypermedia Structure.

Text items are similar to miniature word-processing blocks and are designed to contain text. *Buttons* are designated areas of the screens that can initiate an action, such as moving or branching to another card, playing an audio file, or accessing a segment on a videodisc. Graphics can be created with paint tools within the hypermedia program, or they can be imported from clip art or other graphics programs.

A valuable feature in most hypermedia programs is the *run-time* file. The run-time file—often called a player—can be used to deliver or run a stack without owning or using the hypermedia program. In other words, if you want to create a HyperStudio stack about pollution, you must buy or legally own a copy of the HyperStudio program. After you create your pollution stack, however, you may want to give it to someone else—or load it on 20 computers. You cannot legally provide the HyperStudio program with your pollution stack; however, you can distribute your stack with a copy of the HyperStudio Player. The HyperStudio Player enables your pollution stack to run, but the stack cannot be changed. In most cases, if you are distributing stacks for educational purposes and not for profit, you can include the player programs without paying additional fees.

OVERVIEW OF HYPERSTUDIO

HyperStudio from Roger Wagner Publishers is a popular hypermedia program. The Macintosh version requires a hard drive and 2 to 4 megabytes of RAM, and the Windows version requires 256 colors on a Windows-compatible computer.

The basic structure of HyperStudio is made up of stacks and cards. Each card can contain text objects, buttons, and graphics. A series of pull-down menus and dialog windows is used to develop applications. HyperStudio supports color and includes an array of colorful clip art. It is an impressive package that also provides built-in links to videodisc, CD-Audio, QuickTime movies, and digitized audio. A testing function that can track correct and incorrect answers is also available.

CREATING A
HYPERSTUDIO STACK

The best way to understand the unique structure of hypermedia programs is to create a small stack. The following procedure covers the steps for creating a stack with two cards. The first card of the stack contains a title and a graphic of the French flag. The second card contains a graphic of a European map with information about France. A *return* button provides the option of returning to the first card, and a hidden button on the map plays a QuickTime movie. (See fig. 6.5.)

Step 1. Creating a New Stack

First, follow the installation procedure to install the program. After it is installed, click twice on the HyperStudio program icon to start HyperStudio. When HyperStudio opens, there are two ways to start a new stack: You can click on *New Stack* or use the File pull-down menu and select *New Stack*.

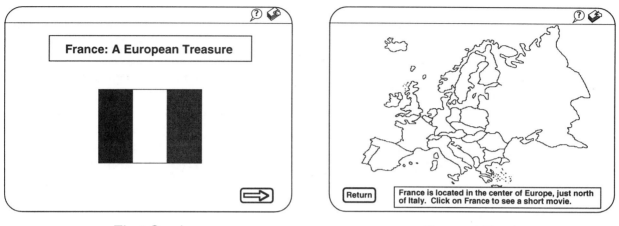

First Card   Second Card

Figure 6.5. Sample Small Stack.

HyperStudio has a feature that can help lead you through the creation of HyperStudio programs. Helpful hints and reminders may appear as you create your stack. Just read the dialog boxes, and click *OK* when you are ready to proceed. If you want to turn these helpful hints on or off, they are accessed under the Edit menu—select *Preferences* and click on the checkbox for *I'm an experienced HyperStudio user* to turn them off. (See fig. 6.6.)

File Edit Move Tools Objects Colors Options Extras

Preferences

┌─ **Stack Preferences** ──────────────────
│ **Stack password:** [▉▉▉▉▉▉▉▉▉▉▉▉]
│ ☐ **Lock stack**
│ ☐ **Show card number with stack name**
│ ☐ **Turn on Automatic Timers & HyperLinks**
│ ☐ **Automatically save stack**
│ ☐ **Presentation mode...**
│ ☐ **Ignore extra mouse clicks**
└──────────────────────────────────

┌─ **Program preferences** ────────────────
│ ☐ **I'm an experienced HyperStudio user**
│ **E-mail address:** [   ]
└──────────────────────────────────

[**Cancel**]   [**OK**]

Figure 6.6. Selecting Preferences in HyperStudio.

Step 2. Creating a Graphic

A relatively powerful graphics program is embedded in HyperStudio. When the Tools menu is selected, the toolbox appears. (See fig. 6.7.) Except for the top three rows, all the tools are paint tools. The tools in HyperStudio are similar to common paint programs such as SuperPaint. The selection tools—rectangle, circle, and lasso in the third row—are used to move or change existing graphics. They can also be used in combination with other keys to stretch and shrink graphics.

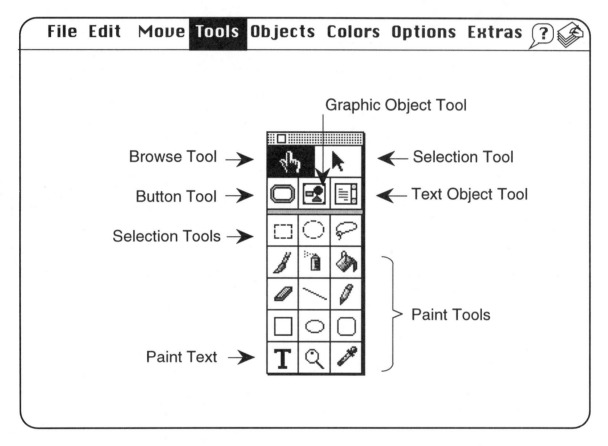

Figure 6.7. HyperStudio Toolbox.

The Tools menu in HyperStudio is a "tear-off" menu. That means that the tools can be moved to another part of the screen, and they will remain in view for easy use. (See fig. 6.8.) To move the tools, click on *Tools* and hold the mouse button down while dragging the tools to another part of the screen. After the Tools are on the screen, use the solid rectangle in the sixth row to create a graphic of the French flag and use the paint bucket to spill red and blue paint into the rectangles. (See fig. 6.8.)

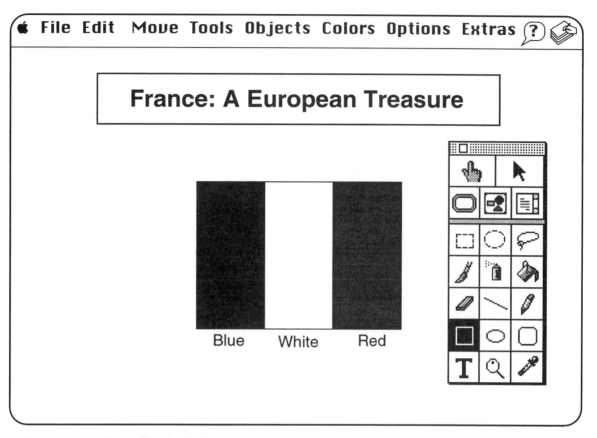

Figure 6.8. First Card of Stack.

Step 3. Creating a Text Object

HyperStudio uses the term "Text object" to refer to areas on the screen that act like miniature word processors. These text areas have word wrap and can be edited and resized (other programs may refer to these areas as fields). On the Objects menu, select *Add a Text Object,* click OK if the instruction box appears, and a dotted rectangle will show up in the center of the screen. This rectangle is the area designated for your text. You can move it by dragging the cursor—a four-headed arrow—in the center of the box, or you can resize it by dragging one of the lines. (When the cursor is on top of a line, it turns into a two-headed arrow.)

When you are satisfied with the size and location of the rectangle—move it to the top of the screen to use it for the title—click anywhere on the screen outside of the rectangle. At that point, a Text Appearance box appears. This dialog window allows you to name the field and set many of its attributes. For this example, there should be an X by the *Draw frame* option. (See fig. 6.9 on page 148.)

Next, click on *Style* in the lower-left corner of the window to access the Text Style menu. You will have a variety of fonts to choose from, depending on the fonts loaded on your computer. (For this example, select *Helvetica . . . Bold . . . Size 18 . . . Center alignment.*) Click *OK* to return to the card.

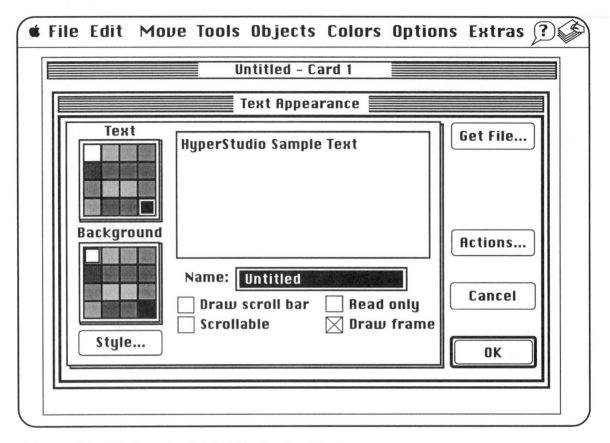

Figure 6.9. Window to Set Attributes for Text.

The final step is to enter the text in the field. The cursor should already be blinking in the Text Appearance box. If it is, simply type the text: in this case, *France: A European Treasure*. If the cursor is not blinking in the Text object, click inside the rectangle and it should appear.

If you discover that your text is not the right size or location, you can edit it by selecting the arrow icon in the toolbox upper-right corner. With this arrow, you can edit almost anything on your screens by double-clicking on the object. After you are done editing, be sure to select the hand (browse) icon in the toolbox in the upper-left corner to continue.

Step 4. Creating Another Card

The next step is to create the second card in the stack. Choose *Edit . . . New Card* in the menu bar, and a new blank card will appear. On this card, we will use one of the graphic backgrounds that is provided with HyperStudio. Choose *Import Background* from the File menu and select the *Disk file* option. Locate the HS Art folder and click to open. Next, scroll down until you find *Europe* and double-click. The graphic will be imported into your card. (See fig. 6.10.) Repeat step 3 to create an instructional text item with information about France, similar to the one in figure 6.10.

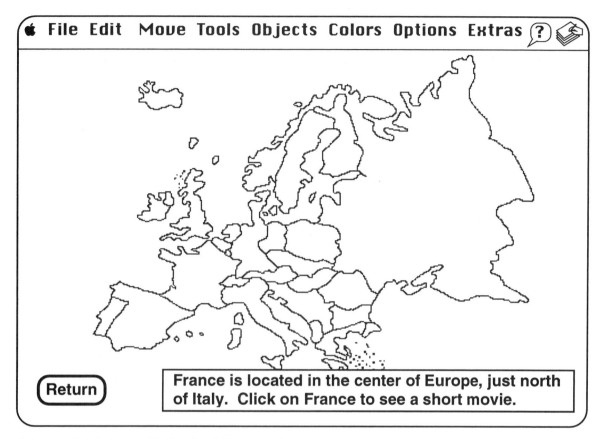

File Edit Move Tools Objects Colors Options Extras

Return

France is located in the center of Europe, just north of Italy. Click on France to see a short movie.

Figure 6.10. Second Card of the Stack.

Step 5. Creating a Button

Buttons are used to initiate actions such as branching to another card. For example, to allow the user to return to the first card from the second card, a return button can be added to the second card. The procedure is similar to that for creating a Text object:

1. Choose *Add a Button* from the Objects menu.

2. Name the button Return. Click on the rounded rectangle (top-right under Type) and on *Show Name* and *Highlight* as illustrated in figure 6.11 on page 150.

3. Click on *OK* and position the button that appears.

4. Click anywhere on the screen outside of the button and the button Actions menu will appear.

5. Select *Previous card* for Places To Go.

6. A dialog box with many transitions will appear. Scroll through the choices and select *Dissolve*. Set the Speed at Medium and click *OK*.

If all worked well, the new button should take you to the first card when it is clicked. If it does not work or if you want to move it, select the arrow icon in the toolbox and double-click on the button.

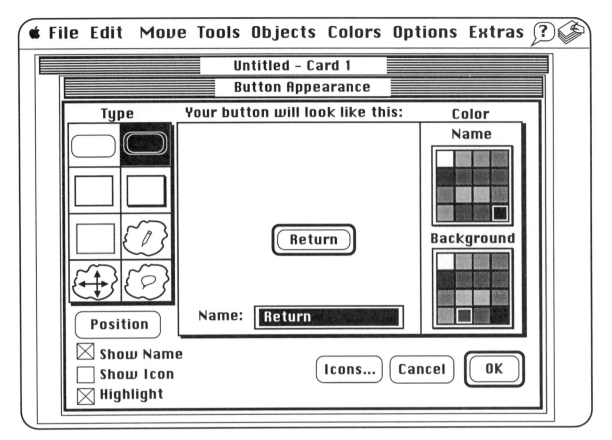

Figure 6.11. Creating a Button.

Follow the same procedure outlined in this step to create a button on the first card. In this case, do not place an X on *Show Name* in the Button Appearance window. Instead, select *Icons* and find a forward arrow. (See fig. 6.11.) On the Button Actions menu, select *Next card* for Places To Go, and select a transition of your choice.

Step 6. Creating an Invisible Button with a QuickTime Movie

You should now be back on the second card, the one with the European map. If you are not on the correct card, you can use the Move menu to move from card to card. We will now create an invisible button on top of France so that when it is clicked, a short QuickTime movie plays.

Begin by selecting *Add a Button* from the Objects menu. This time, select the button in the lower-left corner with the two arrows for Type. Do not highlight the *Show Name* option. (See fig. 6.11.) Click *OK* and you will return to the screen with Europe. At this point, you must click inside of France, and it will automatically make the entire area a hot spot or button. This technique is valuable for activating irregular shapes.

When the Button Actions window appears, select *None of the above* for Places To Go and *Play a movie or video* for Things To Do. (See fig. 6.12.) You will see the following question: *Where do you want to get your movie?* If you are using a Macintosh, select *Disk file (QuickTime movies)*. If you are using a PC, select *movie*.

A standard dialog box will appear, and you can select a movie from the hard drive, or CD-ROM. HyperStudio provides a few movies in the *QuickTime Movies* folder (Macintosh) or *hstudio* directory (Windows). You can also obtain numerous movies through clip-art programs, bulletin boards, or the Internet. (See chapter 5 for more information about making your own movies.)

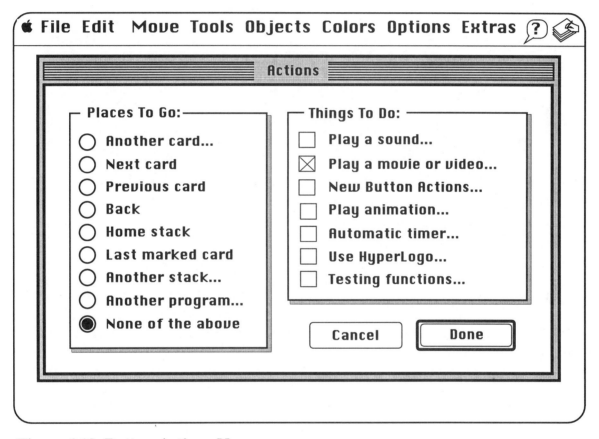

Figure 6.12. Button Actions Menu.

After you have located and selected a movie, it will appear on your screen. Move it to the desired location and resize it if you wish. When you click outside the movie rectangle, the QuickTime Movies dialog box appears. (See fig. 6.13.) There are several options on this menu that you can experiment with. For now, select *Erase when done.* That means that when you click on *France,* this movie will play. When it finishes, it will disappear. Click *OK* and then *Done* to return to your program and test your new button.

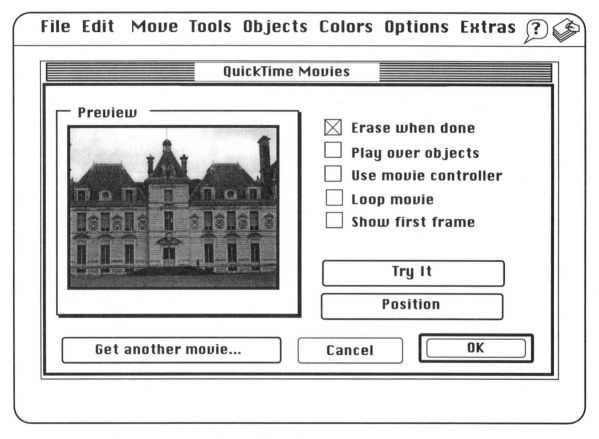

Figure 6.13. QuickTime Movies Dialog Box.

Step 7. Printing a Stack

If you want a printout of a stack, choose *Print* from the File menu. HyperStudio will print cards in various sizes, from one to four cards per page depending on the size. For example, figure 6.14 provides a four-card stack with quick reference information for HyperStudio. These printouts can be handy for distributing a hard-copy version of your presentations or reports.

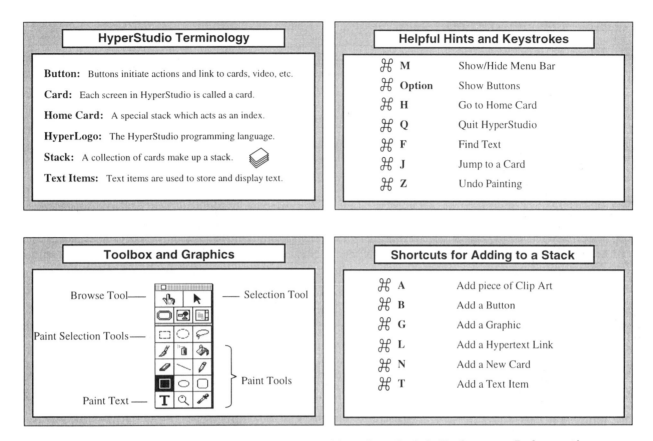

Figure 6.14. Four-Card HyperStudio Stack Showing Quick Reference Information.

OTHER HYPERMEDIA PROGRAMS

In the past few years, the availability of hypermedia development programs has increased tremendously. Although the basic structure of the majority of the programs is similar, the features, price, and system requirements vary significantly. In addition to HyperStudio, popular programs for education include HyperCard (Macintosh), Digital Chisel (Macintosh), Multimedia ToolBook (Windows), LinkWay Live and SuperLink (MS-DOS and Windows), and Authorware (Macintosh and Windows). Additional hypermedia and presentation programs are listed in this chapter's Resource section with complete contact information.

HyperCard

HyperCard was produced by Apple Computer in 1987 and quickly started a revolution in educational hypermedia. One of the reasons for HyperCard's popularity was that the complete program was originally included with the purchase of a Macintosh. (Only the HyperCard Player is currently provided free with new computers.)

The basic structure of HyperCard is similar to HyperStudio: stacks and cards. Each card contains two layers—foreground and background—and each layer contains one or more of the following object components: text fields, buttons, and graphics. In a field, a variety of text fonts and styles can be entered, edited, stored, and retrieved. Buttons provide most of the hypermedia aspects of HyperCard. They are used to initiate movement to another card, access a videodisc player, or play a sound. Graphics in HyperCard can be created and modified with the internal paint tools, or they can be imported. HyperCard contains a sophisticated scripting language called HyperTalk.

Digital Chisel

Digital Chisel is distributed by Pierian Spring Software. The program may be purchased in single copies, lab packs, or by site license. Digital Chisel runs on a Macintosh computer with at least 4 megabytes of RAM. A CD-ROM drive is recommended to access the abundant resources of templates, images, and sounds in the Digital Chisel library.

Projects created with Digital Chisel can contain text, graphics, digital movies, sounds, animation, and interactive questions—all without a scripting language. Several templates are included with the program that enable teachers to create lessons with true-false, matching, multiple-choice, short-answer, and essay questions. An internal database automatically tracks the answers and generates a score for the students.

Multimedia ToolBook

Multimedia ToolBook by Asymetrix is a powerful hypermedia development program for the Windows environment. Multimedia ToolBook's structure is similar to HyperCard's and HyperStudio's. Each screen is made up of cards, buttons, fields, and graphics. Multimedia ToolBook has many colors and patterns and allows easy access to videodisc, sounds, and CD-Audio. In Multimedia ToolBook, the graphics can also act as buttons; that is, graphics can contain scripts that initiate actions or access a videodisc player.

Multimedia ToolBook includes a robust scripting language and some powerful tools, such as the *Record* option, which can generate the script for a series of actions. The increased availability of Microsoft Windows and its multimedia extensions are helping to make Multimedia ToolBook a popular and powerful development tool.

LinkWay Live and SuperLink

LinkWay Live is a popular hypermedia program for MS-DOS computers, and SuperLink is a similar program that is designed to run under Microsoft Windows. Both of these programs were originally developed by Washington Computer Services; LinkWay Live is now produced by IBM, and SuperLink is available through Alchemedia, Inc.

Both LinkWay Live and SuperLink are inexpensive and easy to learn and can incorporate a variety of media elements, such as audio, video, and graphics. The basic structure of the programs consists of pages (screens) and folders (files).

Authorware

Authorware Professional is a powerful hypermedia program that does not require the use of a scripting or programming language. Instead, the program is constructed with the use of icons that define the program flow and media elements. Authorware can be used to create applications ranging from simple slide shows to complex training programs that include record-keeping features. Authorware Professional is available in Macintosh and Windows versions and is one of the few programs that is truly cross-platform. Projects created on a Macintosh can be converted to the Windows platform and vice versa.

Authorware Academic is an adaptation of Macromedia's Authorware Professional. It provides all of the features of the Professional model but limits each program to the creation of up to 500 icons per file—more than enough for many applications. The scaled-down price of this program provides access to a powerful authoring tool at an affordable price for education.

Director

Macromedia Director is a sophisticated multimedia and animation development program. It has several levels of complexity, from an easy-to-create presentation to a complicated scripting language (Lingo). The basic structure used in Director is that of a time line. Each element—graphic, text, sound, animation, video—is placed along the multitrack time line for display in the appropriate sequence.

Director was one of the first authoring programs that had the capability for delivery over the World Wide Web. By distributing a free Shockwave file, or plug-in, to World Wide Web users, Macromedia enabled Director to run from within Netscape and other Internet browsers (see chapter 8 for more information about the World Wide Web).

ADVANTAGES AND DISADVANTAGES OF HYPERMEDIA

Hypermedia is a wonderful tool for education; however, it is not necessarily appropriate for every teacher and every application. This section outlines a few of the advantages and disadvantages of hypermedia in education.

Advantages of Hypermedia

Inexpensive. In comparison with similar computer software, hypermedia programs are quite inexpensive. The majority of hypermedia programs range from $100 to $300, with discounts for educators and students. In many cases, the price also includes the rights to distribute the stacks.

Easy to learn. Sophisticated hypermedia programs can be created with Text items, buttons, and graphic objects, without a scripting component. With only a few hours invested, teachers and students can create lessons and presentations.

Easy to store. Slide shows in the past consisted of a slide projector, carousel, and numerous slides. The slides were often difficult to store and took many hours to rearrange and organize. Computer-based slide shows created with hypermedia are easy to store and modify.

Easy to link. Hypermedia programs offer easy links to graphics, sound, videodisc, digital movies, and CD-Audio. (For more information on these technologies, see the appropriate chapters in this text.)

Fun. Teachers now have the power to create exciting interactive programs. In most cases, this endeavor is enjoyable and rewarding for both students and teachers.

Disadvantages of Hypermedia

Confusing. Poorly designed hypermedia programs can easily turn into hyper-chaos when the user has too many choices and gets lost. Research is continuing to help determine the optimal number of selections, or buttons, per screen and the best methods to promote learning in a hypermedia environment.

Complex at the scripting level. Although the object level with its buttons, graphics, and so on is relatively easy to learn, novices can quickly get lost and frustrated with scripting languages. For example, HyperCard contains HyperTalk, which is just as complex as the BASIC language, with loops, variables, and other sophisticated programming elements.

Difficult to project. Hypermedia can be used for interactive, dynamic computer presentations. The problem is that most schools do not have the equipment to project the presentations. Although liquid crystal display (LCD) technology for projection is rapidly advancing, most of the sophisticated units are still too expensive for schools.

Platform-specific. Most hypermedia programs are restricted to one platform. Multimedia ToolBook, for example, requires an MS-DOS computer with Microsoft Windows to run the program. It will not work in DOS or on a Macintosh.

TIPS AND TECHNIQUES FOR CREATING PROGRAMS WITH HYPERMEDIA AND PRESENTATION SOFTWARE

Although most hypermedia and presentation programs appear user friendly, their complexity can make them quite frustrating. Following are some tips and techniques for development.

1. *Get comfortable with the computer first.* Many hours of frustration can be saved if you practice with a word processor and a graphics program before trying hypermedia and presentation software. It is also wise to be comfortable with a mouse and operating procedures such as copying files.

2. *Begin with presentation programs.* Presentation programs are easier to master than hypermedia, and they can serve as a good introduction for novices. If you have access to a presentation program, practice creating a few slide presentations before you try hypermedia.

3. *Start small.* Nothing is as easy as it looks. To minimize the frustration of learning the structure of a presentation or hypermedia package, first attempt a small program.

4. *Design for baseline hardware.* Programs should be developed on the same minimum hardware needed to deliver them because animation, sound, and graphics are affected by the hardware. In other words, if you intend to deliver or present the program on a Macintosh computer with 2 megabytes of RAM, you should develop it on the same hardware platform.

5. *Use a consistent template.* Whether you are using a template that was provided with the program or creating your own, it is best to be consistent. The program will be easier for the audience to follow if the title is always the same size, the feedback, if any, is located in the same place, and the buttons are uniform.

6. *Follow basic design guidelines.* Because of the wealth of options available in development programs—fonts, colors, animation, icons, transitions—it is easy to get carried away and try to use all of them. Basic instructional design guidelines, such as amount of text on a screen and number of colors incorporated, should be followed.

7. *Learn the shortcuts.* Many presentation and hypermedia programs have keyboard shortcuts. These can save precious time and are well worth the effort to memorize and use. (Some of the most valuable shortcuts in HyperStudio are included in figure 6.14 on page 153.)

8. *Catalog and use clip art.* Although you can create artwork in most programs, many of the graphics will probably be imported from commercial clip-art programs. To save valuable time, catalog the clip art and create a hard-copy reference sheet with file names and locations.

9. *Test all presentations.* It is important to test the program before presenting it. Depending on the type of projection unit, you may find that colors that look great on a computer monitor are washed out when they are projected on a large screen.

10. *Buy a book.* Many excellent books are available for learning presentation packages and hypermedia programs. Look for one that includes step-by-step instructions, lots of examples and exercises, and plenty of illustrations.

CONCLUSION

Many commercial programs are incorporating a hypermedia interface to allow students to access information through a variety of media in associative, nonlinear paths. In addition, several inexpensive development programs are available that enable teachers and students to create presentations and hypermedia applications that can be used for electronic slide shows, student projects, or interactive instruction.

A final word of caution: Be careful. These programs are addictive. You will soon find that the hours just slip away as you make "just one more card" or try "just one more technique." The fun has just begun!

HYPERMEDIA GLOSSARY

authoring system. A computer program designed specifically to create computer-based instruction.

background layer. Many hypermedia cards, or pages, are made up of two layers: the background and the foreground. For example, the background layer of HyperCard can be shared by many cards to enhance consistency and minimize duplication of buttons, graphics, and so on.

base page. The background layer in a LinkWay Live folder. The objects and colors on a base page are shared by all pages in the folder.

branch. To move from one location of a program to another. For example, if a button initiates a videodisc sequence, it is said to branch to video.

browse. In hypermedia, refers to use of a completed hypermedia stack. Usually the browse level of use does not allow the user to alter the stack or delete any objects.

button. An object in hypermedia used to initiate an action, such as a branch to another card or a videodisc sequence.

card. The basic entity of HyperCard and HyperStudio and the equivalent to one screen of information.

clip art. Graphics that are commercially distributed for use in product development.

color graphics adapter (CGA). An IBM resolution mode that supports only four colors in the graphics mode.

command key. Key on the Macintosh keyboard that has a propeller-shaped symbol and sometimes an *open Apple* instruction.

dialog box. A window that asks a question or allows users to input information.

enhanced graphics adapter (EGA). A graphics-display adapter for MS-DOS computers that can display 16 colors simultaneously with a resolution of 640 by 350. EGA adapters have better resolution than CGA, but less resolution than VGA.

field. An object in hypermedia that is designed to hold textual information.

folder. A group of pages in the same LinkWay Live file, usually based on the same theme.

foreground layer. In most hypermedia programs, screens are made up of two layers: the background and the foreground. The foreground layer is unique to each screen and cannot be shared. Generally the foreground layer is viewed as being transparent, and any objects on the background layer will show through the foreground layer.

Home Stack. A special card that acts as an index to other cards in HyperCard. A Home Stack must be available for HyperCard to run.

hypermedia programs. Programs that deliver information through multiple connected pathways. Hypermedia allows students to branch seamlessly among text, graphics, audio, and video.

HyperTalk. The language that is built into HyperCard. HyperTalk is similar to the BASIC programming language. It allows HyperCard developers to write more complex commands, or scripts.

icon. A symbol that provides a visual representation of an action or other information. An icon of an arrow is often used to denote directional movement in hypermedia.

link. A connection from one place or medium to another. For example, buttons contain the linking information between cards.

liquid crystal display (LCD) panel. A panel that connects to a computer to display the computer screen when the LCD panel is placed on top of an overhead projector.

MCGA (Multicolor/Graphics Array). One of the graphics modes available in LinkWay Live. It supports up to 256 colors with a resolution of 200 by 320.

message box. A window in HyperCard that allows the developer to communicate with the HyperCard program. Commands typed into the message box are executed immediately.

multimedia. A type of program that combines more than one media type for dissemination of information. For ex-

ample, a multimedia program may include text, audio, graphics, animation, and video.

objects. In hypermedia, generally refers to elements that are placed on the screen, such as buttons, fields, and graphics. Objects are components that can be manipulated and can contain links to other objects.

page. In a LinkWay Live folder, page refers to one screen of information.

presentation program. Software programs designed to create electronic slide shows. In most cases, the slide shows are linear in structure.

resolution. The number of dots or pixels that can be displayed on a computer screen. Higher resolutions create sharper images.

run-time. A file used to run a hypermedia stack. It can generally be distributed without charge.

scripting language. A set of commands that are included in some icon- and menu-based development systems. The scripting language allows complex computer instructions to be created.

scripts. A series of commands written in a language embedded in a hypermedia program.

slide show (electronic). Computer screens designed in a sequence for projection purposes. Many hypermedia programs provide transitional effects such as dissolves or wipes for these sequences.

stack. A group of cards in the same HyperCard or HyperStudio file, usually based on the same theme.

SVGA (Super Video Graphics Array). A computer resolution mode that displays at least 256 colors with a resolution of 640 by 480.

toolbox. The menu component in hypermedia programs that contains tools to create graphics.

transition. Visual effects, such as dissolves or wipes, that take place as a program moves from one image or screen of information to the next.

user level. The amount of modification a user is allowed to make to a stack. In HyperCard, there are five levels of user control, ranging from one (browsing only) to five (full edit and delete options).

VGA (Video Graphics Array). An IBM resolution mode that displays up to 16 colors with a resolution of 640 by 480.

window. An area on a computer screen that displays text, graphics, messages, or documents.

PRESENTATION AND HYPERMEDIA RESOURCES

Action!
Macromedia
600 Townsend Street
San Francisco, CA 94103
800-288-4797

Adobe Persuasion
Adobe Systems, Inc
Mountain View, CA 94039
800-833-6687

Apple Media Tool
Apple Computer, Inc.
1 Infinite Loop
Cupertino, CA 95014
800-776-2333

Astound!
Gold Disk, Inc.
3160 W. Bayshore Road
Palo Alto, CA 94303
800-465-3375

Authorware Academic
Prentice-Hall
1 Lake Street
Upper Saddle River, NJ 07458
800-887-9998

Authorware Professional
Macromedia, Inc.
600 Townsend Street, Suite 408
San Francisco, CA 94103
800-945-4061
http://www.macromedia.com

Compel
Asymetrix Corporation
110 110th Avenue NE
Bellevue, WA 98004
800-448-6543

DemoShield
Stirling Technologies, Inc.
1100 Woodfield Road
Schaumburg, IL 60173
800-374-4353

Digital Chisel
Pierian Spring Software
5200 S.W. Macadam Avenue, Suite 250
Portland, OR 97201
800-472-8578

Director
Macromedia, Inc.
600 Townsend Street, Suite 408
San Francisco, CA 94103
800-945-4061
http://www.macromedia.com

Freelance Graphics
Lotus Development Corporation
400 River Park Drive
Cambridge, MA 01864
800-343-5414

Harvard Graphics for Windows
Software Publishing Corporation
P.O. Box 62900
El Dorado, CA 95762
800-336-8360

HyperBook
3160 W. Bayshore Road
Palo Alto, CA 94303
800-465-3375

HyperCard
Apple Computer, Inc.
1 Infinite Loop
Cupertino, CA 95014
800-776-2333

HyperScreen
Scholastic Software
P.O. Box 7502
Jefferson City, MO 65102
800-541-5513

HyperStudio
Roger Wagner Publishers
1050 Pioneer Way
El Cajon, CA 92020
800-497-3778

HyperWriter
Ntergaid
60 Commerce Park
Milford, CT 06460
800-254-9737

Icon Author
Aimtech Corporation
20 Trafalgar Square
Nashua, NH 03063
800-289-2884

LinkWay Live
IBM Corp.; K-12 Education
1500 Riveredge Parkway
Atlanta, GA 30328
800-IBM-4EDU

Media Text
Wings for Learning
101 Castleton Street
Pleasantville, NY 10570
800-321-7511

mPower
Multimedia Design Corporation
8720 Red Oak Boulevard
Charlotte, NC 28217
800-921-9493

Multimedia ToolBook
Asymetrix Corporation
110 110th Avenue NE
Bellevue, WA 98004
800-448-6543

Multimedia Workshop
Davidson & Associates
P.O. Box 2961
Torrance, CA 90509
800-545-7677

Persuasion
Aldus Corporation
1585 Charleston Road
Mountain View, CA 94039
800-833-6687

PowerPoint
Microsoft Corporation
1 Microsoft Way
Redmond, WA 98052
800-426-9400
http://www.microsoft.com

Quest .
Allen Communication, Inc.
5 Triad Center
Salt Lake City, UT 84180
800-325-7850

StoryWorks
Teachers' Idea and Information
Exchange
P.O. Box 6229
Lincoln, NE 68505
402-483-6987

SuperCard
Allegiant Technologies, Inc.
9740 Scranton Road
San Diego, CA 92121
800-255-8258

SuperLink
Alchemedia, Inc.
P.O. Box 298
Anacortes, WA 98221
360-299-3289

Visual Basic
Microsoft Corporation
1 Microsoft Way
Redmond, WA 98052
800-426-9400
http://www.microsoft.com

RECOMMENDED READING

Barron, A. E. (1994). Multimedia research reports. *Reference Librarian* 44: 71–82.

Belk, R., and M. Marra. (1994). Problem solving in HyperStudio: Strategies and tips. *Computing Teacher* 22(3): 65.

Boling, D., L. Johnson, and S. Kirkley. (1994). A quick and dirty dozen: Guidelines for using icons. *HyperNEXUS* 4(3): 5–7.

Bush, V. (1945). As we may think. *Atlantic Monthly* 176(1): 101–8.

Cury, J. O. (1996). PowerPoint and Astound: Online. *Multimedia World* 3(7): 42.

Delrossi, R. A. (1996). Learn the lingo. *Byte* (March): 85–90.

Desmond, M. (1996). Quiet! Director 5.0 takes the stage. *Multimedia World* 3(5): 16–17.

Dunham, K. (1995). Helping students design HyperCard stacks. *Learning and Leading with Technology* 23(2): 6–9.

Epstein, B. A. (1995). Director facilitates cross-platform development. *Multimedia Producer* 1(2): 43–47.

Holzberg, C. S. (1994). Hypermedia projects that work. *Technology and Learning* 14(4): 32–36.

Joss, M. W. (1996). Multimedia presents: A look at high-powered interactive presentation software. *CD-ROM Professional* 9(1): 62–72.

Kennedy, L. K. (1995). HyperCard and oral presentation. *Computing Teacher.* 22(6): 15–16.

Low, L. (1995). Aldus Persuasion 3.0. *PC Graphics & Video* 4(1): 58–61.

McArdle, T. (1995). Multimedia as a presentation tool. *Media & Methods* 32(2): 78.

Milone, M. N. (1995). Electronic portfolios: Who's doing them and how? *Technology and Learning* 16(2): 28–36.

——. (1996). Kids as multimedia authors. *Technology and Learning* 16(5): 22–28.

Multimedia authoring products. (1995). *Syllabus* 9(3): 48–52.

Paull, S. (1995). The authoring buzz. *Multimedia Producer* 1(10): 41–46.

Peterson, S. (1996). Multimedia authoring tools. *PC Graphics & Video* 5(5): 52–56.

Taub, E. (1996). Digital Chisel 2.0 and HyperStudio 3.0: Educational-authoring tools go to the head of the class. *MacUser* 12(1): 50–52.

Tuttle, H. G. (1995). Dos and Don'ts of multimedia presentations. *MultiMedia Schools* 2(5): 29–31.

HYPERMEDIA DEVELOPMENT

An Overview Of

Dr. Ann E. Barron
University of South Florida

Dr. Gary W. Orwig
University of Central Florida

This brochure is an excerpt from:

New Technologies for Education

A Beginner's Guide

Third Edition

To obtain the complete book, contact:

Libraries Unlimited
P.O. Box 6633
Englewood, CO 80155-6633
800-237-6124

Multimedia

In most cases, the ability to link to different media is built into hypermedia development tools. When a hypermedia program is used to access a variety of different media, it is called multimedia.

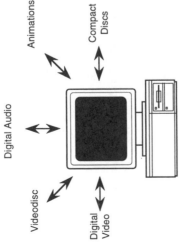

Digital Audio

Animations

Videodisc

Compact Discs

Digital Video

To access a videodisc from a hypermedia program, a command is generally entered into a button with the frame number or chapter number. When the button is clicked, the designated video will play (usually on a separate video monitor).

To incorporate digital audio or video, the audio or video files must be recorded and stored on a computer disk. The files can then be played by specifying the file name. Audio can be accessed from compact discs by designating the time code.

Many of the hypermedia programs can also include links to the World Wide Web.

Hypermedia Structure

Hypermedia development programs are software tools that enable you to link graphics, text, audio, and video into an instructional lesson. Most of the tools for hypermedia are based on a screen and object format. Each screen can contain a variety of objects, including text objects, buttons, and graphics.

Screen (Card or Page)

This is a Text Object

Button

Graphic

Fields are similar to miniature word processing blocks and are designed to contain text. Most programs offer a variety of styles for fields, such as scrolling, rectangular, and transparent.

Buttons are designated areas of the screens that can initiate an action, such as moving or branching to another screen. Buttons can also control videodisc players, play audio files, access audio on a compact disc, or start animation sequences.

Graphics can be created in the hypermedia program, or they can be imported from clip art or other applications.

Hypermedia Programs

HyperCard

HyperCard was developed by Apple Computer and operates on Macintosh computers. It contains a powerful scripting language, called HyperTalk.

HyperStudio

HyperStudio is produced by Roger Wagner Publishers and operates on Macintosh and Windows computers. It features color and built-in support for videodisc, QuickTime, the World Wide Web, and digitized audio.

LinkWay Live!

LinkWay Live is distributed by IBM. One of the major advantages of LinkWay Live over other hypermedia programs for MS-DOS computers is that it can run on a wide variety of hardware platforms.

Multimedia ToolBook

Multimedia ToolBook is produced by Asymetrix. It operates on computers with Microsoft Windows and offers color, multimedia, and scripting.

Authorware/Director

Authorware and Director are produced by Macromedia. They operate on Macintosh and Windows computers and offer full multimedia features.

Advantages

- *Inexpensive.* Hypermedia programs are quite inexpensive. The majority of the programs are priced in a range from $100 to $300.

- *Easy to Learn.* Hypermedia development tools do not require programming skills, and many students and teachers have found it relatively easy to create lessons and presentations.

- *Multimedia.* Most hypermedia programs offer links to graphics, sound, videodisc, compact discs, and the Web.

- *Fun.* In most cases, teachers and students find hypermedia development to be an enjoyable and rewarding endeavor.

Disadvantages

- *Confusion.* Poorly designed hypermedia lessons can easily turn into chaos, where the user has too many choices and gets lost.

- *May Require Projection Equipment.* Interactive, dynamic presentations are easy to create with hypermedia, but many schools do not have projection equipment for large groups.

- *Scripting is Difficult.* Although it is quite easy to create buttons and text objects, the scripting languages can be complex.

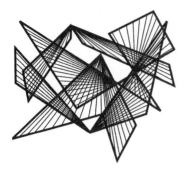

7

Local Area Networks

A Scenario

Central High School is more than 60 years old. It probably would have been less expensive to tear it down and start over, but about eight years ago the members of the community made the decision to renovate the old school and to blend in a new wing to accommodate the growth in the community. Now the original building looks like it did 50 years ago, with large, friendly hallways and restored hardwood trim. The classrooms are comfortable and bright, and the old auditorium is the best in the state. While the look is of an earlier generation, all the county electrical, fire, and disability access codes have been met. Many members of the community walk through the old section of the school and recall fond memories of the Central High of their teenage years.

The new wing is constructed to modern standards. The halls are more narrow, the ceilings are lower, and the windows are smaller. Although the total square footage is similar to that of the old section, there is 20 percent more classroom space. The classrooms are designed for efficient instruction. Lighting is easy to control, and drop-down projection screens are built into the ceiling. Cable television, telephone, and computer connections are available at the front of each room. Two large computer labs are also part of the new wing.

The labs and new classrooms are all connected by a local area network (LAN) that has two file servers. One stores all the software that is used for instruction, while the other stores administrative software that helps teachers with attendance, scheduling, and E-mail. The LAN distributes the software from the appropriate file server to the computer that requests it. Management and security programs protect software from unauthorized use. The technology coordinator for the school has found that the LAN makes it easy to manage the licenses for the software. It is also easy to update software because only the file server needs to have the updated version installed.

But there is a problem. The old section of the school has great "personality" but little technology, while the new section has little personality but great technology. Over the last few years, technology has become important in the school curriculum. Seven years ago, the planners had great foresight by putting in the two computer labs in the new wing. It was almost as an afterthought that they added the conduits for the telephone, cable TV, and computer LAN connections for each new classroom. The cost was so trivial that they put the conduit and cable in place, although they felt that computer cables and telephone cables into each classroom might never really be needed.

The classrooms in the old building, however, were another story. Getting the same conduit and cables to those classrooms would have cost almost 10 times what it cost in the new construction. In addition, there were some areas where the conduit could not go inside the walls; it would have been necessary to place it outside, marring the appearance of the polished hardwood trim. The community design group decided that the cost was an unnecessary expense because the two new labs would be available to all students.

The computer labs have been a tremendous success. The school district has an active in-service education program, and many teachers learned ways to use the labs with their students. Soon, students were using computer technologies as part of their papers and projects. The media center added several rolling multimedia computer carts so that students could demonstrate projects in the classrooms. Within two years after the new wing was completed, the LAN connections were activated in the new classrooms so that students and faculty could tap into the work that took place in the labs. Each classroom has a workstation that is used mainly by the teacher for attendance, E-mail, and some planning. It is now commonplace for a group of students to wheel a cart into a classroom, tap into the LAN, and demonstrate the project that they have completed for a particular assignment.

For the last several years there has been increasing friction between teachers in the new wing and teachers in the old building. The old building is still "technology challenged," and there is no funding available for the expensive wiring of the old building. Teachers in the old building have no workstations in their classrooms, so they must go to the faculty work area in the new wing to take care of E-mail and attendance records. Window blinds have been added and projection screens have been mounted, but the computer carts still have major limitations when they are used in the old building. Because the computers cannot access the LAN, there are limits on how projects and software are demonstrated. In fact, some software is licensed for use on the LAN only, so it cannot be installed on the cart computers.

Finally, a solution has arrived. A wireless LAN capable of covering the entire old building has been installed. Two of the cart computers have been equipped with the wireless LAN adapters, and they can be used in any of the old classrooms. Although there is insufficient funding at the present to equip every classroom with faculty workstations, two workstations have been added to mini-work areas on each floor of the old building. The district even purchased wireless LAN adapters for a couple of faculty who use their personal notebook computers at school. These teachers are proud to demonstrate their ability to access the LAN from anywhere in the old building—even while they are walking in the hallways.

The wireless LAN is not perfect, though. It is slower than the hardwired LAN, and multimedia presentations are not quite as smooth. There is also some interference in the two classrooms near the elevator, but that problem has pretty much been resolved by repositioning the wireless LAN antennae. The community is still working on plans to fund the hardwiring of the old building, but for the time being, the wireless LAN is an affordable and acceptable solution to the technology access problem in the original building.

Local area networks (LANs) connect desktop computers. This makes it easy to share files and to send messages back and forth. However, possibly the most important contribution that a LAN makes to a school is simplified software management. Because most LANs centralize software onto specialized computers that are called file servers, software can be installed or updated by simply working with the file server. In this chapter we will cover the following topics:

- An overview of LANs

- Educational applications for a LAN

- Basic hardware components of a LAN

- Examples of software that works with LANs

- Implementation of a LAN

- Advantages and disadvantages of a LAN

- Resources for further information

INTRODUCTION

In a typical local area network (LAN), one computer is designated as the *file server*. This computer contains one or more large hard disk drives that store all the programs used on the LAN and run the software that makes the entire system work. All the other computers connected to the LAN are called *workstations*. (See fig. 7.1 on page 168.) A student working on one of these computers can use the programs on the hard drive of the file server as easily as if the files were stored on a drive in the student's workstation.

With most networks, a special network interface card is installed in each workstation to allow it to be connected to the LAN. One exception is the Apple Macintosh computer and associated printers. They already contain the needed interfaces for a proprietary LAN system called AppleTalk.

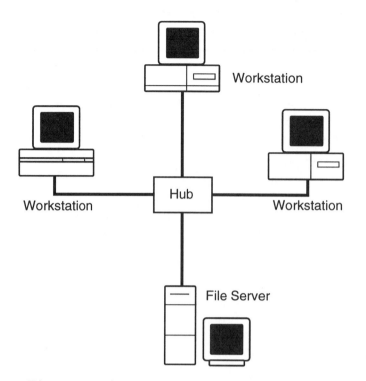

Figure 7.1. Components of a LAN.

It is common to refer to any group of connected computers as a LAN. In some cases, however, the connections are too specialized to qualify the system as a LAN. For example, a group of computers can be connected to a single laser printer, allowing any computer in the group to use that printer. However, the computers cannot share files among themselves, as is the case in a real LAN. Although LANs vary widely in size, shape, and function, they do share several common characteristics:

Proximity of computers. The computers connected to a LAN are usually within the same room or building. In some cases, a LAN might be distributed among several buildings, as on a college campus. Rarely are LAN computers more than a mile apart.

Shared files. A LAN allows computers connected to it to share files. This means that a word-processing task started by one person can be finished by someone else at another location on the LAN.

Speed. When compared to alternatives, a LAN offers a more rapid method of sharing files. For example, without a LAN, files are shared by copying them to floppy disks. The disks are then carried from one computer to another. This rapidly becomes time-consuming when more than two or three computers are involved.

Expandability. A LAN is almost always easy to expand. As additional computers or printers become available, they can simply be added to the LAN. There are limits, however. Sometimes additional hardware and software must be purchased to allow a LAN to expand.

EDUCATIONAL APPLICATIONS

Computers have now become an integral component of the daily lives of many students and teachers. Teachers are now often responsible for managing and upgrading instructional software and tracking students' computer activities. A LAN makes it possible for all software to be centralized so that a single license for a specified number of users can be purchased for each piece of software. Most LAN software licenses specify a maximum number of concurrent users. This is usually smaller than the total number of workstations that are connected to the LAN because not all workstations will be using the same software at the same instant. Without a LAN, licensing issues are far more complex to manage as copies of a program become distributed throughout a school. The LAN is also able to assist with automatic inventory of all hardware attached to it, making it easy to keep track of the computer equipment in the school. When appropriate software is used, tracking student progress through instructional programs can be accomplished through the computer on the teacher's desk.

Although the initial investment in a school LAN may be high, the operation of a well-used, properly designed LAN consistently costs less over a period of time than the operation of a group of individual computers because of the centralization of software and management.

A simple example illustrates the relative efficiency of a LAN. Assume that 25 independent computers in a school have been equipped with a popular math tutorial. It is designed to keep track of student progress so that when a student returns to continue a lesson, the computer can pick up where the student left off a day earlier. Because the computers are not interconnected, each student is assigned to a specific computer that stores his or her records on its hard drive. A problem arises when two students assigned to the same computer want to use it at the same time. Even if an adjacent computer is available, neither student can switch to it because it does not have the appropriate records on it.

Now consider what happens when an improved version of the program arrives. Assume that even though the instructions for installing the new version are clear and direct, it still requires 30 minutes to install the new software. Unfortunately, this applies to *each* of the 25 student computers! This situation represents one of the most common problems with stand-alone computers: It takes more time to properly maintain the software. In this case, it would take an extra 12 hours just to install the new software on those computers.

With a LAN and a LAN version of the math tutorial, a different scenario unfolds. Because all student records are stored on the file server, a student can work at any available LAN computer. The LAN software keeps track of who is working and on what computer. It can also count the total number of students to make certain the total stays within the license requirements. When a new version of the software arrives, a teacher or media specialist spends half an hour loading the new software into the file server. After that, all the workstations can use the new software.

LAN BASICS

Most readers will not actually design, obtain, and install a LAN. Such activities are best handled by consultants or experts within the school system. However, all readers can develop sufficient knowledge about the general function of LANs to make informed decisions about their potential applications in educational settings.

A LAN is often described using technical buzzwords. For example, you might hear someone say that their LAN is an Ethernet star system running Novell Netware over 10BaseT lines. This technical terminology can be broken into four categories: the protocol, the topology, the operating system, and the interconnecting media. Our aim in the discussion of these categories is not to cover a vast amount of technical information but to provide a working knowledge that will help you communicate with the LAN experts who install a system in your school.

Network Protocols

The term *protocol* can have a variety of technical meanings in conversations about LANs. To keep things simple, we will discuss a *network protocol* as a set of standards that establishes how information travels through the LAN. For example, the Ethernet protocol uses an "etiquette" method of communication. Before a workstation sends anything through the LAN, it first listens to make sure that no other workstation is talking. If the LAN is clear, it then sends its data. Just as in conversations within a group, there are times when two workstations both listen but then start to "talk" at the same instant. These are called *collisions,* and the Ethernet protocol defines the method for resolving them.

Another popular protocol is the Token Ring protocol. A Token Ring network constantly passes a single electronic "permission to speak" token from one workstation to the next. If a workstation does not need to transmit information, it simply passes the token on. If it does need to transmit information, it holds the token until it is finished. As one might guess, these two approaches are different, and they cannot both function over the same set of cables. However, there are techniques to provide a "gateway" to LANs that use different protocols. Many aspects of a LAN, such as the computer network interface cards, the structure, and the type of wiring, become defined by the type of protocol chosen.

Network Topologies

The physical *topology* of a LAN refers to the overall shape formed by the way individual workstations are interconnected. The most common are straight lines of cable that are interchangeably called buses or trunk lines, rings that place each workstation on part of a big circle of cable, and stars that use central hubs to connect multiple workstations. Each topology has strengths and weaknesses, and it is common to find combinations of topologies in large LANs.

Operating System

Networks require their own operating systems. A popular operating system for microcomputer LANs is Netware by Novell, Inc. Other producers include Apple, IBM, and Microsoft. The network operating system (NOS) works with the disk operating systems (DOS) of the individual workstations to make all the LAN components work together. The NOS sends files from the file server to the appropriate workstation, controls use through passwords and levels of access, and makes certain that multiple users do not write to a single file at any one instant.

Interconnecting Media

In most cases, all the computers on a LAN are interconnected by some type of cable. (See fig. 7.2.) The type of cable you select can impact the speed of the network and other factors.

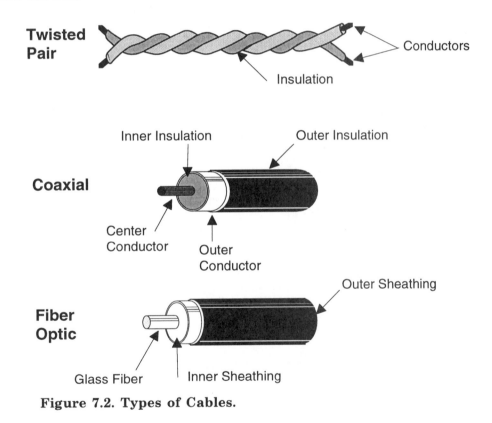

Figure 7.2. Types of Cables.

Twisted-Pair Cable

The least complex cabling system consists of simple, unshielded twisted pairs of wires (UTP). The quality of UTP may vary from telephone-grade wire to extremely high-speed cable. The cable has four pairs of wire inside the jacket, and each pair is twisted with a different number of twists per inch to help cancel out interference from adjacent pairs and other electrical devices. (See fig. 7.2.) The EIA/TIA (Electronic Industry Association/Telecommunication Industry Association) has established standards of UTP and rated five general categories of wire. (Please note that even though these standards provide a benchmark for upper levels of transmission rates, industry is continuously finding methods and adapting new technologies to take advantage of older wiring systems.)

Category 1:   Voice only (telephone wire)

Category 2:   Voice or data to 1Mbps (megabits per second)

Category 3:   Voice or data to 10Mbps

Category 4:   Voice or data to 20Mbps

Category 5:   Voice or data to 100Mbps

In general, you should buy the best cable you can afford (most schools purchase Category 3 or Category 5). Category 5 is highly recommended because it can support new, faster transmission rates. If you are designing a 10Mbps Ethernet network and considering the cost savings of purchasing Category 3 wire instead of Category 5, remember that the Category 5 cable will provide more "room to grow" as the transmission technologies increase.

A common transmission standard that is used with Category 3, 4, or 5 cables is called 10BaseT. This transmission standard defines a set of connectors and other interface devices that are manufactured by a variety of companies. 10BaseT can transmit data at up to 10Mbps on Ethernet systems. Token Ring systems can use this wire at 16Mbps over short distances. Most modern school and office telecommunication systems are installed with this standard in mind.

Unfortunately, twisted-pair cabling systems are susceptible to interference. External devices such as elevator motors and even vacuum cleaners can create enough electronic static to disrupt a LAN that operates through twisted-pair wires. Even ordinary telephone activity, such as dialing or a ring signal in an adjacent pair of wires, sometimes creates interference on lower-quality cables. LAN systems can usually identify and ignore this interference, but large amounts of interference may slow LAN operation.

Coaxial Cable

The next level of performance in LAN connections is provided through the use of coaxial cable. Although this type of cable is supplied in several thicknesses depending upon the distances involved, it all resembles television cable. Coaxial cable is almost immune to external interference, with the exception being direct lightning strikes.

Two common forms of coax cable are called Thinnet (10Base2) and Thicknet (10Base5). As the names imply, the main difference between these two types of cable is the thickness. The thicker cable is stiff and difficult to handle, but it allows workstation connections to be farther apart than the thin cable. Quite often a combination is used that incorporates thick cable between buildings or floors of buildings and thin cable to connect workstations within classrooms or offices.

Coaxial cables of both types are much less susceptible to external interference than twisted wire and also allow fast data transfer, from 16Mbps to more than 100Mbps. Coax cables are relatively expensive, however, and installation in an existing facility is labor intensive.

Fiber-Optic Cable

Another type of cable is being used in some LAN systems. Fiber-optic cable contains fine fibers of glass instead of metallic wires. Light, rather than electricity, is conducted through the cable. Fiber-optic cable offers many advantages over metallic cable. Extremely fast LANs of more than 100Mbps are possible and audio and video capabilities are integrated into the same cable. Also, fiber-optic cable is immune to all forms of electrical interference because it is nonmetallic.

Unfortunately, fiber optic cable is expensive and difficult to install and modify. That last point is important. With twisted-pair or coaxial cable, it is easy to add additional computers as the LAN grows. With fiber optics, however, specialized techniques and equipment are required to make outlets for additional computers. As a result, hybrid systems are often created wherein fiber-optic cables serve as *trunk lines* to link floors or buildings. Conventional metallic cables are then used in the classroom areas where frequent changes are likely to be made. (See fig. 7.3.)

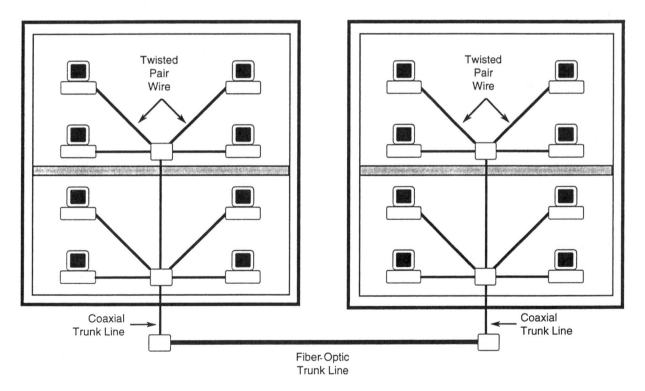

Figure 7.3. Hybrid LAN System.

Data-Transfer Rates

The previous paragraphs mention different LAN data-transfer rates for various cables. When a higher data-transfer rate is available in a LAN, more workstations can be in use at one time without noticeable delays. As a general guideline, small LANs with 20 or fewer workstations can function well with data-transfer rates in the area of 4Mbps. Larger LANs with around 100 workstations or LANs that use sophisticated multimedia workstations might require faster data-transfer rates. Rates up to 16Mbps are commonly available.

Some coaxial cable systems can transfer data at rates of 100Mbps, but that data "capacity" is just now becoming commercially available for twisted-pair wire. One standard, called 100 VG, uses four pairs of unshielded wire for each connection. This system uses two levels of priority, so time-sensitive data such as multimedia files get transferred first. At present, 100 VG has average rates of 96Mbps.

A second standard, 100BaseT, is derived from 10BaseT standards and can be integrated more easily into existing 10BaseT systems. It also can use up to four pairs of wires. Unfortunately, it is not quite as efficient in average transmission speed or distance as 100 VG. At this point, the associated high-speed equipment is expensive. See figure 7.4 for a summary of the data-transfer rates of the different cables.

	Wire Type	Speed	Max Length	Cost
10BaseT	Twisted Pair	10-16Mbps	100 Meters	Low
100BaseT	4 Twisted Pairs	~50Mbps	100 Meters	Medium
100 VG	4 Twisted Pairs	~96Mbps	200 Meters	Medium
10Base2	Thin Coax	10-100Mbps	185 Meters	Medium
10Base5	Thick Coax	10-100Mbps	500 Meters	High
Fiber	Glass Fiber	Up to 500Mbps	2000 Meters	Very High

Figure 7.4. Characteristics of LAN Cables.

Wiring Hubs

Wiring hubs are devices that bring the cables for a group of computers to one centralized location for connection to the LAN, resulting in a "star" LAN topology. A wiring hub simplifies cable connections and allows individual computers to be added or removed without interrupting the operations of the LAN. Some wiring hubs have signal-processing capabilities that help filter out interference before it gets into the main part of the LAN. Newer wiring hubs even have "intelligent" diagnostic capabilities that allow them to send warnings and information to the file server when a problem is detected in one of the computers connected to the hub. Wiring hubs must match the specific protocol and type of cable used in the system.

Network Interface Cards

A network interface card (NIC) creates the actual electronic connection between the LAN cable and the computer. With few exceptions, mentioned in the next paragraph, a NIC is added to every computer in the LAN. These cards define several features of a LAN, including the type of cable that goes to the computer, the protocol, and the transmission speed. A NIC can also contain a read-only memory (ROM) boot chip that allows the computer to immediately interact with a specific network operating system when the computer is turned on. For example, a NIC might be designed to work in a system that uses 10BaseT cable at 10Mbps using Ethernet. It might contain a "boot" chip that automatically connects it to the LAN when the computer is turned on.

Some computers such as the Macintosh contain internal network interfaces. This makes it easy to connect these computers to a LAN, provided the LAN matches the internal interface.

FILE SERVERS

The file server is the most important component of a typical LAN. It not only stores all the application programs but also serves as the traffic director to keep all the computers and printers working together. Because the capabilities of the file server directly determine the usefulness of the LAN, there should be no compromising on the features of the file server. This is one area in which a consultant can provide important advice during the planning phases for a LAN.

Processing Power

The file server is required to perform many operations quickly and, in some cases, concurrently. For example, at any one moment the file server might send a requested file to a workstation, route a letter from another workstation to a printer, and store an electronic-mail message for another individual. As a result, the file server should be a powerful computer. If the system is DOS-compatible, it should have at least an 486 central processor, running at no less than a 66-megahertz processing speed. A Macintosh file server should probably use a Power Mac central processor.

Mass Storage

Large amounts of storage are required for all the management and applications programs that will be used on the network. Consequently, the hard drive storage space must be much larger than that found on an ordinary stand-alone computer. It is common to find hard drive storage in thousands of megabytes (gigabytes). Most file servers also have space available for additional hard drives to be added. This allows the storage space on a file server to be increased as the network expands.

A file server stores and distributes the software that is used on a LAN, but it also stores the files that are created while teachers and students use word-processing programs, database managers, spreadsheet programs, and other productivity tools. Because so much important information can accumulate on the disk drives of a file server, it is essential to implement a dependable drive backup system. For years, various forms of tape have been used to make backup copies of the information on hard drives. Unfortunately, tape backup technologies have had trouble keeping up with the rapid growth in capacity of modern hard drives. It often takes an entire evening to make a tape backup of one large hard drive. As a result, backups are not made as often as they should be.

Recently, however, another technique was developed that makes use of redundant arrays of inexpensive disks (RAID). In such systems, two or more identical drives are grouped together. Whenever information is written to or erased from a drive, the same action happens to all the drives in the set. As a result, there is at least one *carbon copy* of every drive on the file server. If a drive should fail, a duplicate drive takes over until the broken drive is repaired. In these systems, the backup process is almost automatic, and it is rare that data is lost due to a failed hard drive.

PRINTER SERVERS AND PRINTERS

One of the economic savings of a LAN is in the reduction in the number of required printers. Stand-alone computers usually have a printer for each computer. This is not an efficient use of funding, as many printers are not used for long periods of time. A LAN allows one printer for a number of workstations.

When a printer on a LAN is accessible to any of the workstations, it is connected to a computer that acts as a printer server. Usually a printer server is a dedicated computer, meaning that it is not used as a workstation. (See fig. 7.5.) Because of the light computational load required of printer servers, they can be basic. Often old, entry-level, workstation computers are displaced by newer, more powerful computers. These old computers can find new lives as LAN printer servers.

The printer server runs special software that collects and stores files to be printed. As a printer finishes a job, the printer server sends the next appropriate file to that printer. When a printer server is running properly, students on the workstations are able to continue with their work after sending a file to the printer even if several other files

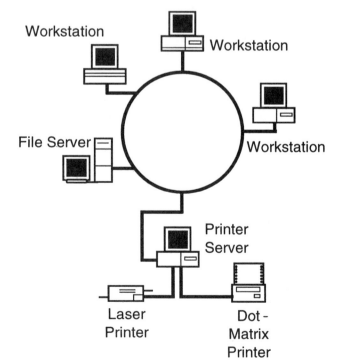

Figure 7.5. LAN with Dedicated Printer Server.

are in line to be printed first. Like the file server, the printer server must be kept running when the LAN is in use.

WORKSTATIONS

Workstations are the most visible components of a LAN. A typical workstation is a standard microcomputer that has had a network interface card added to it. Once this card is inserted into the computer, the LAN cable is simply plugged into it through the back of the computer.

Workstations usually have a floppy drive, but they do not need their own hard drives. Because the file server stores all program files on its drives, a hard drive on a workstation may be redundant. Data or text files that are created by individuals are saved on the hard drives of the file server, or they can be saved directly to a floppy disk at the workstation.

Diskless Workstations

Some of the workstations in a typical LAN design may not have either hard or floppy drives. These *diskless* workstations can be used to operate programs on the file server. Any data created are stored on the file server; there is no way for a student to enter or save information from a floppy disk. Such a design greatly reduces the chance that a computer virus will be introduced into the LAN. Also, it is impossible for a student to make illegal copies of software. Because of the secure nature of this type of workstation, many LAN operators choose to set up a few diskless stations in locations that are difficult to monitor properly. For example, they can be used for E-mail stations or information kiosks in an open area of the school.

Multipurpose Workstations

In contrast to the diskless workstation, some workstations on a LAN might have hard drives, tape backup devices, or multimedia peripherals such as digital sound boards and CD-ROM drives. In many cases, when an existing computer is added to a LAN, it is desirable to retain all the stand-alone characteristics of that computer. For example, a music teacher might connect his or her computer to a LAN only to monitor student activities in a music theory course that is on the LAN. The teacher might still intend to use his or her computer to compose music on a digital keyboard.

Usually, it is possible to set up a single computer to function part of the time as a LAN workstation and other times as a stand-alone computer. Care is required, however, to ensure that the LAN interface board and LAN workstation software do not interfere with existing applications. Such conflicts can be subtle. In the preceding example, the music teacher might find that everything appears to work fine after the LAN hookup has taken place. A bit later, however, the teacher may discover that the computer displays an "out of memory" message when the file for a long song is loaded into the composition program. The LAN workstation programs might have permanently taken up some of the computer memory, reducing the total amount of memory available for programs.

Grouped Versus
Distributed Workstations

LAN workstations can be placed almost anywhere. There are, however, sound reasons for grouping workstations when possible. Grouping workstations greatly reduces wiring costs. Also, when a number of workstations are placed in one room, it becomes practical for one individual to manage the activities within the room.

If workstations must be widely distributed, then the choice of cabling for LANs becomes important. Some LAN cable designs require amplifiers or *signal repeaters* on long connection lines. Other types of LAN cable designs simply will not work beyond a specified distance. As cable lengths increase, the chances of faulty or damaged cables also increase. In general, taking a LAN beyond a building, or even to many distant points within a building, requires an expert in the design and installation phases.

Hybrid LANs

It is possible to create a LAN that uses two incompatible types of workstations. For example, a LAN that has an MS-DOS file server and MS-DOS computers can also contain Apple Macintosh computers. The Macs will not be able to run any of the MS-DOS software, and the MS-DOS computers will not run any of the Mac software. However, they will be able to send E-mail messages and share data and text files with one another.

LAN COMPONENT
VARIATIONS

Local area networks have been designed to fit the needs of a variety of applications. Because of these variations, it is difficult to define a *typical* LAN. For example, the following three applications have one or more characteristics that contradict the common definition of a LAN.

Peer-to-Peer LANs

Not all LANs use a dedicated file server. For example, a LAN might consist of a series of workstations where all the hard drives and CD-ROM drives can be shared. Such a LAN is often called a peer-to-peer LAN because all workstations are equal and can access the programs and files on the other workstations. (See fig. 7.6.) Although this approach does not require an expensive, dedicated file server, there are some limitations to consider.

Most important, the LAN functions must be managed by the individual workstations. This means that performance on your workstation will be degraded when someone at another workstation is accessing the files on your hard drive or CD-ROM drive. This might be just slightly noticeable during a task like word processing, but it could be completely disruptive while processing digitized sound or video.

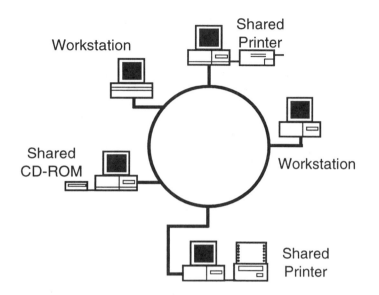

Figure 7.6. Peer-to-Peer LAN.

Second, it is impossible to access files from a computer that is not running. In a peer-to-peer system, all needed computers must be running. This might be simple to accomplish in a computer lab, but it can be difficult in a school office setting. For example, who has permission to unlock the principal's office to turn on that computer when he or she is absent?

A peer-to-peer LAN is intended for small applications, and it operates best when a maximum of 10 to 20 computers are involved. In addition, the users should have a reason to share files as opposed to simply needing to transfer files from one computer to another. For example, if several staff members need to access and modify a single student database, then a peer-to-peer LAN might be a good choice.

Another consideration is the expandability of a peer-to-peer LAN system. Some of these systems use proprietary interface cards and cabling; others use standard network interface cards and common network cabling. Although the peer-to-peer systems with standard equipment might be more expensive initially, they provide a cost-effective route for upgrading to additional workstations and a file server–based network as needs grow.

LANs Without Cables

There are locations such as large media centers or old buildings where it would be expensive to install LAN cables for a network. In such cases, wireless LAN technologies might be an appropriate solution. A wireless LAN uses radio waves or infrared light beams to replace the wiring between workstations and file servers.

Wireless LAN technologies are still in a stage of rapid growth, but several systems are available on the commercial market. In a typical system such as Proxim's RangeLAN2 wireless LAN, a PC Card adapter is connected to each workstation. A second component, an access point, connects to the existing wired LAN. Additional access points can be connected to a standard wire-based LAN to allow the portable computers to roam over large areas. Once regular LAN software is installed, the wireless LAN based upon the RangeLAN2 system behaves as if it were connected with wires. (See fig. 7.7.)

As with any technology, there are limits to wireless LANs. Most systems operate over short distances. The RangeLAN2 system, for example, requires a portable workstation to be within 500 feet of the nearest access point in most buildings. Wireless systems' data rates are not as good as wired LANs'. The RangeLAN2 system has a rated 1.6Mbps data-transfer rate, which is quite high by current wireless standards. Finally, wireless LANs are fairly expensive. Average prices for the equipment such as the RangeLAN2 access point are currently between $1,000 and $2,000 per unit, and several units might be needed to cover a large building. The adapter cards for the workstations are also expensive, with current prices ranging from $400 to $800 per workstation.

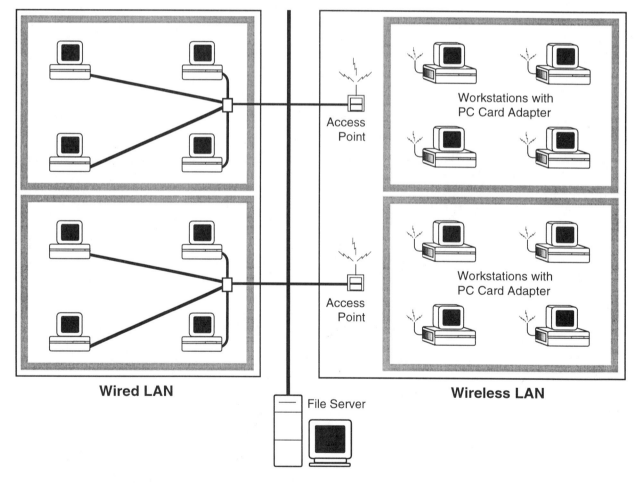

Figure 7.7. Configuration for LAN Plus Wireless LAN.

Wide Area Networks

There are situations in which workstations that need to be connected are simply too far apart for a LAN. In these cases, related technologies are used to create a wide area network, or WAN. A WAN might connect several schools in a district to one file server, or it might allow students and teachers to connect to the office LAN from home. In either case, telephone lines are used to tie the locations together.

When schools are interconnected, special high-speed leased lines that allow rapid data transfer are normally used. These lines allow such a high-speed transfer of data that the LAN appears to function as if all the computers were in one building. Unfortunately, these leased lines can cost thousands of dollars a month if they are in constant use. (See chapter 9 for more information on leased data lines.)

When a school LAN is used from a home computer, standard modems make the connections over normal dial-up telephone lines. Because common modems transfer data much more slowly than LAN connections, there are significant limitations to using the school LAN as a WAN from a home. For example, just the process of loading and starting a word-processing program stored on the school file server from home might take 10 or 15 minutes through a standard modem! The key to effective use is to install the large programs on the home computer, then use the WAN connection strictly to access small files such as memos or spreadsheet data.

LAN SOFTWARE

LAN software can be divided into two general categories: management software and applications software. LAN management software consists of the operating system and software that is used to supplement the operating system capabilities. Common features of LAN management software include enhanced diagnostics, workstation monitoring, and even automatic equipment inventory. Applications software includes programs that are to be used for instructional purposes. Computer-assisted instruction, word processing, database management systems, and other common applications are included in the applications category.

Management Software

Two types of management software are of most interest to the educator considering purchasing or using a LAN: network operating software and network monitoring software. Each has a specific function, and each affects the usefulness and configuration of the LAN.

Network Operating Software

As mentioned earlier in the chapter, the file server uses special network operating system (NOS) software to run the local area network. This software operates something like a regular disk operating system, but it must be able to keep track of many users at once. Complicated situations can arise when two or more workstations request the same programs or data files at the same time, and the network operating system must be refined enough to prevent mix-ups. For example, if one person is updating the telephone number of a student while another person is requesting the telephone number for that same student, the NOS must ensure that the second person gets the updated number.

One of the more popular network operating systems is Netware by Novell, Inc. Netware works with MS-DOS computers. In addition, one version works with Macintosh computers as workstations. The Netware file server software is highly adaptable and capable of operating on a variety of networks using Ethernet or Token Ring network interface cards. Because Netware has become one of the market leaders, many LAN application programs have been written to be compatible with it.

AppleTalk, the NOS by Apple Computer, is also popular in the schools. AppleTalk is integrated into Macintosh computers; however, it operates at a relatively slow 230.4 kilobits per second.

The market for network operating system software is becoming competitive; most major microcomputer manufacturers and a number of major software publishers offer products. It is important to confirm that a selected NOS product is compatible with the network interface cards and application software on the LAN.

Network Monitoring Software

It is convenient for a teacher to see at a glance who is doing what on the LAN. Sometimes network monitoring software is part of the NOS, but usually it is a separately purchased enhancement. Appropriate monitoring software goes beyond informing a teacher who is currently at the workstations on a LAN. Graphic illustrations of LAN capacity are common, and automatic alerts for questionable activities are often included. As an example, most systems will alert a teacher when multiple failed attempts to enter a student password have occurred. This type of activity might indicate that someone is attempting to gain unauthorized access to the LAN.

Frye Utilities for Networks is an example of modular network management software that includes components for server management, server-node troubleshooting and diagnostics, LAN documentation, hardware and software inventory, server monitoring, software distribution and file updating, and several other functions. This system allows the LAN operator to purchase and install only the components that are needed for a specific installation. (See fig. 7.8.)

LAN Applications Software

Most LAN applications software will be familiar to users. For example, word processors, spreadsheet programs, database managers, and many instructional programs are the same on a LAN as on a stand-alone computer. This is not to imply, however, that existing software can simply be copied onto the file server and run. There are two major considerations when evaluating the installation of existing software onto a LAN.

Software licensing. Most software comes with a license that specifies the conditions under which the software is to be used. Software should not be installed on a LAN if the software license does not clearly allow this. A software license that does permit LAN installation clearly specifies how many LAN users are authorized to use the software at the same time. The LAN management software should be set to restrict the application to that number of users. Note that violating software license specifications would make your organization vulnerable to legal action.

Software incompatibilities. Many single-user programs simply are not designed to work on a LAN. When such a program is installed on a LAN, unpredictable things may happen. In such situations it is common for the work of several students to become scrambled. For example, if two students are using a single-user word processor through a LAN, they might discover that their text is being intermixed in each other's files.

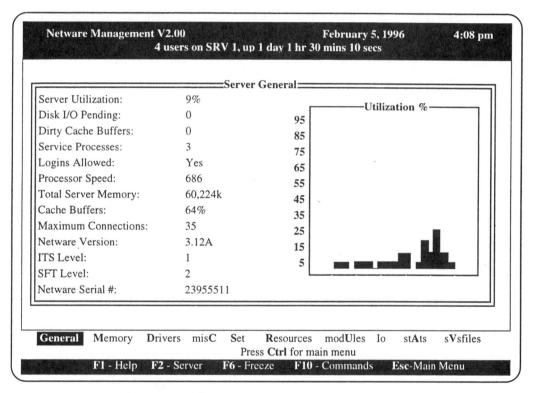

Figure 7.8. Monitoring Software for a LAN.

INTEGRATED LEARNING SYSTEMS

Several companies are making LANs and all the associated hardware and software more palatable by assembling packages called *integrated learning systems.* An ILS is a complete instructional package that includes

- Instructional applications software
- Instructional management software
- The LAN software
- The LAN hardware

The ILS concept is highly attractive to schools because it allows school personnel to concentrate on familiar issues of curricular content and instructional strategies rather than on the unfamiliar issues of LAN architecture, LAN operating systems, and software compatibility. A well-designed ILS arrives at the school with all the "mechanical" issues resolved.

Each ILS has unique strengths, and these strengths must be a major factor in any purchasing decision. CTB Macmillian/McGraw-Hill, for example, produces the *Macmillan/McGraw-Hill Open Integrated Learning System* for high school and community-college students. Wasatch Education Systems' *Projects for the Real World* provides real-world examples of reading, writing, and math to K-8 students.

Factors to consider when evaluating possible ILS products include

- *Age of students and their learning characteristics.* Is the software designed to address the needs of your students? Will it create an imbalance or form of discrimination by serving only a select group?

- *Frequency of revision of the instructional materials.* Are the instructional materials current? Is there a clear pattern of continuous revision, or are revisions few and far between?

- *Management options provided to teachers.* Can a teacher alter the curriculum to allow for individual learner differences?

- *Hardware platforms supported.* If a DOS platform, does the system support Microsoft Windows and multimedia presentations? If Macintosh, are all types of Macs fully supported?

- *Ability to integrate third-party, or add-on, programs.* Is it possible to add an instructional program or a productivity tool such as a word processor if it is not part of the original system?

- *Installation cost and maintenance cost.* Does the installation cost provide ownership of the hardware? Does the annual maintenance fee provide all software upgrades?

Research indicates that school "climate" is even more important than the essential training of teachers regarding the eventual successful implementation of an ILS. Cook (1994) has identified several factors of school climate that are critical:

- Goals that are clearly communicated by the principal

- Teacher participation in the decision to adopt the ILS

- Amount of interaction and collegiality among teachers regarding ILS use

- Encouragement of experimentation and risk taking

- The presence of a local "hero" who spearheads efforts to make the ILS a success

With good teacher training, a receptive school climate, and an appropriate integrated learning system, there is still no assurance of success. Two additional factors that appear to identify successful ILS applications are allowing learners to have adequate time on the system and careful integration into the curriculum. If the ILS is used only as a 30-minute break each week from the usual classroom activities, it is not likely to have much impact on learning.

The selection of an ILS is a major purchasing decision. Initial installation costs for the hardware and software can easily exceed $100,000 for 30 workstations. In addition, the supplier often charges an annual fee for hardware and software maintenance. The cost-effectiveness of ILSs is likely to improve over the next few years as the volume of sales increases and more competition enters the market.

LAN IMPLEMENTATION

Selecting a LAN for a school requires careful planning. Complete details are too extensive to cover in this text. The following discussion outlines two of the most important points to consider.

Physical Resources

In an existing building, a major part of the cost of a new LAN is the wiring required and the labor needed to install it. If your school already has a usable form of wiring, such as spare telephone connections or prewired coaxial cable, then a major component might already be in place.

If your school has invested heavily in specific software, it is important to determine the costs of changing that software to a version that is LAN compatible. Sometimes existing software is compatible with LANs; in other cases, the software simply will not work on a LAN. If existing software is not compatible with a proposed LAN, then the cost of appropriate new software must be considered. Be alert for hidden costs. For example, if old database software is to be scrapped in favor of new, LAN-compatible database software, there might be considerable costs associated with the labor of converting old database records to the new format.

Human Resources

It is most important to ensure that the LAN's strengths, which focus upon centralized control of resources, are compatible with the overall philosophy of management within the school system. If, for example, the administrative philosophy is to decentralize resources and control, it might be a waste of time to try to implement a LAN.

A LAN is a major funding investment and frequently requires clearly defined commitments in human support. For example, a school LAN might serve more than 1,000 students and many teachers. The basic activities of installing new software, deleting old software, and providing help would require several hours each day. It might even make sense to assign one person the primary responsibility of operating the LAN.

FOLLOW-UP

The installation and operation of a LAN requires careful planning. Because of the complex decisions that must be made during the planning and implementation of a LAN, it is advisable to have one or two capable employees receive some training in LAN design and operation.

Where You Can Learn More About LANs

Training can be formal, through a nearby university or community college, but care should be taken to confirm that an appropriate course is offered. Many college courses about LANs become involved in the computer science aspects of LANs and thus go into far more detail than is needed by individuals interested in the design and implementation of a LAN.

It is also possible to find appropriate training through commercial workshops. These workshops are usually offered on weekends in larger cities. Although such workshops can cost several hundred dollars per person, they are often targeted to address specific user needs. There is intense competition among the consulting companies that offer these workshops, so the quality of the workshops is usually high, and excellent resource materials are provided. Still, one should obtain client references before investing in this type of training.

Similar workshops are provided by hardware or software vendors. These workshops may be inexpensive or free, but they usually offer only a selected set of vendor-supported hardware or software. If an individual attends enough of these workshops from an assortment of vendors, it is possible to develop a good perspective on the market.

Some of the most productive training takes place through visits to area schools where LANs are already in use. Teachers are usually willing to discuss the successes and failures of their LAN implementations. After visiting several schools, you will be better able to identify the LAN application that meets the needs of your school.

How Your School Can Acquire a LAN

If the decision is to proceed with the procurement and installation of a LAN in your school, one of several procedures might be followed. District-level staff are often assigned to coordinate all significant technology development and purchases. Such districts frequently have specified standards to ensure equipment compatibility. If this is the case, you will work directly with these staff members to acquire your system.

Some school systems do not have a centralized technology development program, but they do have a central purchasing system. If this is the case in your school district, ensure that the purchasing staff has a complete set of your requirements and recommended hardware and software purchases. It is critical to stay in touch with the staff during equipment and software procurement to ensure that any changes are compatible with the original plan.

Finally, in some school systems you will be entirely on your own in coordinating the purchase of the equipment and software. If this is the case in your school, you will work directly with the appropriate vendors in obtaining the identified system. It is important to check with customers of the potential vendors to find out if they are satisfied with the level of support available from the vendor after the purchase.

ADVANTAGES AND DISADVANTAGES OF LANS

There are a number of reasons that a school might decide to connect a group of microcomputers to form a LAN. However, a LAN may not be the best arrangement for every situation. This section discusses the features and limitations of LANs.

Advantages of LANs

Connectivity. LANs offer a great deal of efficiency through connectivity. All workstations on a LAN can share the hardware and software resources of the LAN. Printers, programs, and information in databases can be shared by all.

Centralized management of learners. If the computers are used in an instructional lab setting, the LAN allows teachers a centralized approach to managing the learning process. A courseware management program allows a teacher to evaluate quickly the process of any learner on the LAN. Notes can be left for individual students, and teachers can even interact directly with students who are currently working on the LAN.

Control of software against pirating. Because all applications software programs are stored and managed through the file server, LAN management software controls access to the software. It is even possible to install diskless workstations that make it impossible to copy programs or to infect the system with computer viruses.

Ease of updating or adding software. Software is easy to update or change because only one copy of each program exists on the file server. If a revised version of a program arrives, only the file server copy must be updated. All workstations use that single copy of the software.

Disadvantages of LANs

File server failure. Perhaps the greatest weakness in any LAN is that a failure in the file server stops the whole system. It can be frustrating to have 20 or 30 computers that are all useless because the necessary software is on a broken file server. Fortunately, proper attention to LAN maintenance will prevent most serious problems.

Cable damage. Another potential area of weakness in most LANs is the interconnecting cable system. Problems with LAN cables can cause anything from minor interruptions to complete failures in LAN systems. Large, complex LANs might require complex diagnostic tools to help locate and correct cable problems.

Daily system management. One of the less obvious problems with LANs is that they demand consistent daily management. New students must be registered before they can use the LAN. Software must be updated or added on a regular basis. Minor problems with printers must be corrected before unmanageable backlogs of print requests accumulate. These maintenance requirements can become a burden to an otherwise busy individual.

High initial installation cost. A LAN can be expensive to install. This is particularly true when a LAN is installed in an older building in which the cabling requirements were not anticipated at the time the building was constructed. The apparent high price of a LAN can be misleading, though, because the actual cost of operating the same number of unconnected computers is usually even higher.

CONCLUSION

Local area networks are systems of computers, printers, and other peripherals that are linked together through a set of cables. Software is stored on one central computer, called a file server, and appropriate files are sent to the workstations as students need them. Printers can be shared by the workstations, making it possible to use dot-matrix printers for draft-quality printouts and a single laser printer for high-quality printouts.

LOCAL AREA
NETWORK GLOSSARY

AppleTalk. A proprietary LAN by Apple that has a data speed of 230.4 kilobits per second. AppleTalk interfaces are built into Macintosh computers.

Arcnet. An older network standard in use since 1977. Utilizes a token-passing protocol. Common transmission speed is 2.5 megabits per second.

ASCII (American Standard Code for Information Interchange). An established code that defines all characters, punctuation marks, and digits in binary form.

bandwidth. The range between the upper and lower limiting frequencies that a cable can transmit.

baseband. Digitally encoded information transmitted in such a way that the entire capacity, or bandwidth, of the cable is utilized.

bit (*binary digit*). A basic unit of computer information expressed numerically as a 0 or a 1.

bit-transfer rate. The number of bits transmitted per unit of time. Frequently stated in millions of bits, or megabits, per second for LANs.

bridge. A LAN computer that links two similar networks.

byte. A grouping of eight bits. A byte provides sufficient information to define one ASCII character.

cable. One or more conductors contained within a protective shell.

coaxial cable. A cable made up of one central conductor surrounded by a shielding conductor.

collision. A simultaneous transmission of data by two or more LAN workstations.

Ethernet. A baseband LAN communications standard developed by Xerox. Data transmission speed is typically 10 megabits per second.

fiber-optic cable. A cable that contains a fine strand of glasslike material. Light, not electricity, is conducted through the cable.

file server. The computer in a LAN that stores and distributes the files for the workstations.

gateway. A computer in a LAN that links two dissimilar LANs. It is capable of translating data between the two LANs.

gigabyte. One billion bytes. Equal to 1,000 megabytes.

hub. *See* wiring hub.

ILS (integrated learning system). Commercial computer-based educational systems that are delivered complete with hardware, software, management systems, and faculty training.

ISDN (Integrated Services Digital Network). A new technology for telephone systems that is totally digital. Computer data can be intermixed with voice communications.

LAN (local area network). An interlinked microcomputer system, the dimensions of which are usually less than 2 miles. Transmission rates are usually above 1 megabit per second.

LocalTalk. A network standard used by Apple Macintosh computers. Uses shielded or unshielded twisted-pair wire at a relatively slow data-transfer rate of 230.4 kilobits per second.

megabit. One million bits.

NIC (network interface card). The interface card that is added to a computer to make it a LAN workstation. It determines the LAN standard for the network cable. Common standards are Arcnet, Ethernet, and Token Ring.

100BaseT. An extension of the 10BaseT standards that defines much faster LAN data transmission. Requires network interface cards and hubs that are compatible with the 100BaseT standard, but most new hardware can run at lower 10BaseT speeds until the entire network is upgraded.

100 VG. A new standard for LANs that operate on unshielded twisted-pair (UTP) cable. Similar to but incompatible with 100BaseT. Allows faster transmission speeds and greater cable lengths than 100BaseT.

packet. A grouping of binary digits, often a portion of a larger file. Treated within a LAN as an entity.

packet switching. A transmission technique commonly used in LANs. Packets are transmitted in an intermixed manner, with each one going to its predetermined destination. This allows all workstations on a LAN equal access to files.

printer server. A computer on a LAN that runs software to control one or more shared printers.

RAID (redundant array of inexpensive disks). Two or more disk drives are used as mirror images of each other. This provides an effective method of automatically backing up data.

10Base5. A standard that defines a thick coaxial cable system, sometimes called Thicknet. This cable is often used in parts of LANs that cover large distances, such as from one building to another.

10BaseT. A standard that defines a twisted-pair cable system. This is an inexpensive cable system that is often used in LANs and office telephone systems.

10Base2. A standard that defines a thin coaxial cable system, sometimes called Thinnet. This cable is often used in LANs.

Thicknet. Thick coaxial cable used to connect parts of a LAN that are separated by long distances.

Thinnet. Thin coaxial cable used to connect parts of a LAN separated by medium distances, such as between floors of buildings.

token. A special message or flag used in some LANs. The token is passed from workstation to workstation, and the workstation that has the token can transmit. This prevents data collisions.

Token Ring. A network standard that uses token-passing techniques to prevent data collisions. Transmission rates are 4 or 16 megabits per second, depending upon interface cards and type of cable.

unshielded twisted-pair cable (UTP). Two wires twisted together. This type of cable is used for telephone communications and many LANs. Categories 2 through 5 are in use, with the higher numbers allowing faster LAN data transmission rates.

WAN (wide area network). A network of computers that is spread out over large distances. Usually high-speed telephone lines are used to interconnect the computers.

wireless LAN. A LAN that uses infrared light beams or radio waves to interconnect the computers. This allows portability and ease of placement of workstations.

wiring hub. The central connecting point for a number of computers on a LAN. Wiring hubs simplify LAN connections and allow computers to be added or removed without interrupting the LAN itself.

workstation. Individual microcomputer on a LAN that is used by students and teachers to run programs.

LOCAL AREA NETWORK RESOURCES

Local Area Network Manufacturers

Apple Computer, Inc.
1 Infinite Loop
Cupertino, CA 95014
800-776-2333

AST Research, Inc.
16215 Alton Parkway
Irvine, CA 92713
714-727-4141

Control Data Corporation
Computer Products Group in Marketing
4201 N. Lexington
Saint Paul, MN 55126
612-482-2100

Corvus Systems, Inc.
160 Great Oaks Boulevard
San Jose, CA 95119
415-674-1102

Data General
4400 Computer Drive
Westboro, MA 01580
508-366-8911

Gateway Industries
2941 Alton Avenue
Irvine, CA 92714
714-553-1555
800-367-6555 (outside California)

IBM Corporation
Old Orchard Road
Armonk, NY 10504-1783
914-765-1900

McDonnell Douglas Computer Systems Company
1801 E. Saint Andrews Place
Santa Ana, CA 92707
714-566-4000

Motorola
50 E. Commerce Drive
Schaumburg, IL 60173
800-934-4721

Novell, Inc.
Communications Department
122 E. 1700 South
Provo, UT 84606
800-453-1267

Proteon, Inc.
9 Technology Drive
Westborough, MA 01581
508-898-2800

Proxim, Inc
295 N. Bernando Avenue
Mountain View, CA 94043
800-229-1630

3-Com Corporation
5400 Bayfront Plaza
Santa Clara, CA 95052-8145
408-764-5000

Ungermann-Bass, Inc.
3900 Freedom Circle
Santa Clara, CA 95054
408-496-0111

Integrated Learning Systems

Computer Curriculum Corporation
1287 Lawrence Station Road
Sunnyvale, CA 94089
800-227-8324

Computer Networking Specialists
2211 Rimlend Drive
Bellingham, WA 98226
800-372-3277

CTB Macmillan/McGraw-Hill
20 Ryan Ranch Road
Monterey, CA 93940
800-538-9547

Jostens Learning Corporation
7878 N. 16th Street
Phoenix, AZ 85020
800-422-4339

New Century Education
220 Old New Brunswick Road
Piscataway, NJ 08854
800-833-6232

Wasatch Education Systems
5250 S. 300 West, Suite 350
Salt Lake City, UT 84107
800-877-2848

WICAT Systems
1875 S. State Street
Orem, UT 84058
800-759-4228

Other Resources

Black Box Catalog
Black Box Corporation
P.O. Box 12800
Pittsburgh, PA 15241
800-552-6816

Carbon Copy
Microcom Inside Sales
500 River Ridge Drive
Norwood, MA 02062
800-822-8224

Frye Utilities for Networks
Frye Computer Systems, Inc.
31 St. James Avenue
Boston, MA 02116
800-234-3793

Local Area Networking Sourcebook
Phillips Publishing, Inc.
1201 Seven Lakes Road
Potomac, MD 20854
800-777-5006

Netware and Netware Care
Novell, Inc.
122 E. 1700 South
Provo, UT 84606
800-453-1267

Sitelock
Brightwork Development
766 Shrewdury
Tintine Falls, NJ 07724
800-552-9876

REFERENCE LIST

Cook, C. (1994). Factors affecting ILS implementation. *Media & Methods* 30(3): 66–67.

RECOMMENDED READING

Boyle, P. (1996). Wireless LANs: Free to roam. *PC Magazine* 15(4): 175–204.

———. (1995). Wireless LANs: No strings attached. *PC Magazine* 14(1): 215–37.

Brush, T. (1995). The effectiveness of cooperative learning groups for low- and high-achieving students using an integrated learning system (Dissertation). Indiana University, 136 pp. Note: Dissertation Abstracts International, volume 56–07, section A, page 2595.

Carlitz, R. D. (1995). Standards for school networking. *T.H.E. Journal* 22(9): 71–74.

Derfler, F. J. (1994). Peer pressure: Peer to peer networks. *PC Magazine* 13(8): 237–74.

Dyrli, O. E., and D. E. Kinnaman. (1995). Connecting classrooms: School is more than a place! *Technology and Learning* 15(8): 82–88.

Farmer, L. (1995). Networking: Moving beyond sneaker net. *Technology Connection* 2(5): 37–39.

Garris, J. (1995). Shifting into high gear: Fast Ethernet adapters. *PC Magazine* 14(22): 201–32.

Hativa, N., and H. Becker, eds. (1994). Computer-based integrated learning systems: Research and theory. *International Journal of Educational Research* [Theme issue] 21(1): 1–119.

Hazari, S. I. (1995). Multi-protocol LAN design and implementation: A case study. *T.H.E. Journal* 22(9): 80–85.

Hess, P. (1996). Tips and tricks for K-12 educational LANs. *T.H.E. Journal* 23(9): 84–87.

Laub, C. (1995). Computer-integrated learning system and elementary student achievement in mathematics: An evaluation study (Dissertation). Temple University, 121 pp. Note: Dissertation Abstracts International, volume 56-06, section A, page 2110.

Maddux, C. D., and J. W. Willis. (1993). Integrated learning systems: What decision-makers need to know. *Ed-Tech Review* (Spring/Summer): 3–11.

Mastel, V. L. (1996). Building a school district's wide area network. *T.H.E. Journal* 23(9): 69–75.

McCandless, G. (1996). Networked multimedia: Not quite ready for prime time. *Syllabus* 9(5): 33–36.

McFarlane, A. (1994). Enter, the teaching machine. (Integrated learning systems in response to students' educational needs). *Times Educational Supplement* (Sept. 23, 1994): n4082, pA24.

Ray-Overstreet, A., and C. DeVane. (1995). Schoolwide response to integrated learning systems. *Media & Methods* 32(3): 54–55.

Satchell, S., and H. Clifford. (1995). Make your notebook a network node: PCMCIA LAN adapters. *PC Magazine* 14(2): 232–38.

Schuster, J. (1995). 5 things you should know about districtwide networking. *Electronic Learning* 14(5): 32–44.

Stetten, G. D., and S. D. Guthrie. (1995). Wireless infrared networking in the Duke paperless classroom. *T.H.E. Journal* 23(3): 87–90.

Tristram, C. (1995). Bottleneck busters [Methods of sending digitized video over LANs]. *New Media* 5(4): 53–56.

Weiss, A. M. (1995). What's in the walls: Copper, fiber or, coaxial wiring? *MultiMedia Schools* 2(4): 35–39.

Weiss, J. (1996). Networks serve up CD-ROMs. *New Media*: 6(2): 39–42.

Wiberg, K. (1995). Integrated learning systems: What does the research say? *Computing Teacher* 22(5): 7–10.

LOCAL AREA NETWORKS

An Overview Of

Dr. Ann E. Barron
University of South Florida

Dr. Gary W. Orwig
University of Central Florida

This brochure is an excerpt from:

New Technologies for Education

A Beginner's Guide

Third Edition

To obtain the complete book, contact:

Libraries Unlimited
P.O. Box 6633
Englewood, CO 80155-6633
800-237-6124

Advantages

• *Centralized Management.* The greatest advantage of a LAN is the centralized management of the software in the school.

• *Software Licensing.* A LAN can restrict the number of users to the number allowed by each software license.

• *Software Management.* Software can be installed or upgraded from a single location.

• *Student Management.* A LAN also makes it easy for teachers to monitor the progress of students who are working through computer programs.

• *Electronic Mail.* Teachers can write E-mail comments for individual students to read the next time they use their workstations.

Disadvantages

• *Expensive to Install.* The cost of installing a LAN in an existing building can become prohibitive if extensive wiring is required.

• *File Server May Fail.* The dependable operation of the file server is critical. Because the file server runs the LAN and stores the software, its failure causes the whole system to stop.

• *Requires Administrative Time.* LAN maintenance requires significant time for a system operator.

LAN Basics

A local area network or LAN consists of a group of interconnected microcomputers. Because the computers can share the same software, the licensing of the software is easy to manage. The LAN is also able to assist with automatic inventory of all hardware attached to it, making it easy to keep track of the computer equipment in the school. When appropriate software is used, tracking students through instructional programs can be accomplished with a computer on the teacher's desk.

In a typical LAN, one computer is designated as the "file server." This computer runs the software that makes the whole system work, and it contains a large hard disk drive that stores the programs used on the LAN.

All of the other computers connected to the LAN are called "workstations." A student working on one of these computers can use the programs on the hard drive of the file server as easily as though the files were stored on a drive in the workstation itself. A teacher can use a workstation to evaluate the work of the students and to communicate with them.

A LAN requires regular attention to keep it running smoothly. One person, called a system operator or "sysop," is usually assigned the responsibility of installing new software, updating older software, and keeping track of the students and teachers using the LAN.

Configuration

A typical LAN consists of a file server, workstations, a printer server, printers, and connecting cables.

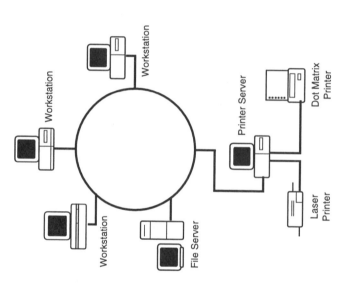

Workstation

Workstation

Workstation

File Server

Printer Server

Laser Printer

Dot Matrix Printer

A LAN makes it possible for a group of computers to share one or more printers. In most cases a separate computer, called a "printer server," is connected to the LAN in a convenient location. The printer server is often connected to a fast dot matrix printer and a high quality laser printer. For rough drafts of text, the dot matrix printer is used, and for quality printouts, the laser printer is used.

Peer-to-Peer LANs

A peer-to-peer LAN looks like an ordinary LAN, except it does not use a file server. Instead, files on the hard drives of all of the workstations connected to the LAN are shared by other workstations. This is an inexpensive solution if only a few computers need to share information and printers.

Wireless LANs

Computers on most LANs are connected with cables, but there are times when cables are very difficult to install, such as when linking two stories of an old school building or buildings on a school campus. It is possible to use wireless transmitters and receivers to take the place of some of the cables in a LAN. Some systems use beams of infrared light that require a direct line of sight between transmitters and receivers. Other systems use radio waves that can go through walls and floors. With proper equipment, distances of several hundred feet can be covered with a wireless LAN.

Workstations with PC Card Adapter

File Server

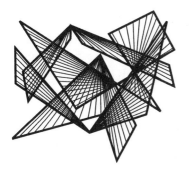

8

Telecommunications

A Scenario

The basic World Wide Web home page for Washington Middle School had been easy to make. The school district had several templates to choose from, and Mr. Steffy's sixth-grade class looked over all of them before choosing one. They downloaded the chosen template, then set about selecting pictures of their classroom, school, and community to take the places of the temporary ones that were already in the template.

The project came to a standstill, however, when students and teachers in other classes heard about it. Some of them had ideas for a home page too, and they were wondering if each class should work alone or if there should be some kind of master plan. Mrs. Atkinson, the principal, asked Mr. Steffy to stop further work on the project and to chair a committee of teachers and students to develop a master plan for a Web page for the whole school.

The committee turned out to be a good one. Everyone was enthusiastic, and a number of creative ideas were discussed. The group decided that there would be a central home page with branch pages for each class or group that wanted to develop one. Because Mr. Steffy was the only faculty member who had created a class page, they appointed him the Webmaster for the school. It was his job to help the other teachers and students implement their ideas. In return, they sent a recommendation to Mrs. Atkinson that some of Mr. Steffy's other assignments be scaled back, and she agreed.

The committee defined the content of the school home page, and while doing so they agreed on the specific school logo, fonts, and backgrounds that would carry over to the individual class pages. Much of what Mr. Steffy's class had already created fit into the school home page, so his class got a special thank-you credit at the bottom of the page.

However, the final plan did not really fit the original template anymore, so Mr. Steffy had to develop some of the home page on his own. He had learned a little bit of the *Hypertext Markup Language* (HTML) that World Wide Web pages use, but the language was difficult. After a couple of E-mail messages to some friends he had met in an Internet class, he found out about a new shareware program that made it easier to create Web pages. He quickly located this program on the Internet, downloaded it, and installed it.

This new program was a *what you see is what you get* (WYSIWYG) tool in that you positioned text and pictures on the screen the way you wanted them to look on the Web page, then the program created the HTML for you. It was not perfect, but it made Mr. Steffy's job much easier. He soon had all the pictures and text placed in the new home-page form for his school. He also had links to his class page and all the pages that other teachers planned to help their classes build.

Next Mr. Steffy uploaded all the HTML files and associated image files to the Web server at the district level, and then he logged into the Internet with his Web browser. When he went to the new school home page, almost everything worked just the way they had planned it. He called the committee together to examine his work, and they were excited. They found just a few little "bugs" that needed minor repair, and once Mr. Steffy had made the necessary changes in the file, he uploaded the corrected file to the Web server, and, just like that, the bugs were gone!

Soon students were showing their parents how to get to their home page from America Online, CompuServe, and other online services. The school home page and class pages were quickly the talk of the community. Within the first two weeks, the pages started to generate E-mail messages from around the world. In fact, a teacher in Australia wrote with the address for his school's home page. He was interested in setting up some shared class projects that could benefit students at both schools.

Telecommunications techniques are not just technologies that might become useful in the near future. They are here now and are used by millions of people every day. Telecommunications can provide teachers and students with an abundance of up-to-date information, increase their multicultural awareness, and help them develop friendships throughout the world. This chapter examines educational applications of telecommunications and explains the hardware and software that make it all possible. This chapter

- Surveys basic educational applications of telecommunications
- Explores the Internet
- Explores the World Wide Web within the Internet
- Explains the operation of modems and fax-modems
- Provides resources for further information

INTRODUCTION

In education, *telecommunications* generally refers to using personal computers to send and receive information over a distance. Recently, our ability to access information and to communicate with others on a global scale through telecommunications has increased tremendously. It is now possible for students on different continents to debate political issues, exchange stories, and send sounds, images, and data to one another on a daily basis.

There are a growing number of telecommunications services available to students and educators, including the Internet, statewide educational networks, commercial integrated services, and local bulletin board systems. Most telecommunications resources provide three basic services: electronic mail, file transfers, and remote access. Although modern point-and-click hypermedia interfaces shield computer users from the complex Unix or DOS commands that were previously needed to use these basic services, the three services still exist in almost all telecommunications systems, including the World Wide Web.

Electronic mail (E-mail). E-mail messages are created by a person on a computer workstation, transmitted to other computers, and read by one or more persons on their computer workstations. E-mail is possible when a group of people have their desktop computers linked together through a local area network, a commercial telecommunications system, the Internet, or a local bulletin-board system. E-mail messages can be addressed to an individual, a group, or the members of an entire organization.

In many situations, electronic mail is more efficient than traditional paper communications because it can be distributed instantly. An electronic memo about a problem might go through two or three rounds of discussion, and a solution might be found before an original paper memo can be duplicated and delivered to its destinations.

The use of E-mail also reduces overall mail and telephone costs. Although the amount of savings depends upon the system, many E-mail programs make use of computer networks that are already in place, and the added expenses of E-mail are minimal. Even international communications can be economical.

File transfers. Computer files often need to be moved from one computer to a distant computer. They could be copied to diskette and sent via parcel post, but there are more efficient electronic methods of moving a file from one location to another. The exact procedures for electronic file transfers vary, but in most cases a person can view a directory of files available on a remote system, select those that are needed, and issue a command to have the files transmitted to the local workstation. The entire process is generally complete in a matter of minutes.

Remote access. Many telecommunications systems offer the benefit of connecting your computer directly into another computer system at a remote location. With remote access, you can log on to a distant system, search the directories, read the files, leave messages, run the programs, or download files as if you were sitting right in front of that particular computer.

THE INTERNET

The growth of the Internet is perhaps the single greatest contribution to the communications explosion. The Internet is a worldwide telecommunications network that connects thousands of other, smaller networks. It began in 1969 as a U.S. Department of Defense project that was called the Advanced Research Projects Agency Network (ARPANET). In 1986, the National Science Foundation formed NSFNET, which replaced ARPANET, and built the foundation of the U.S. portion of the Internet with high-speed, long-distance data lines. The Internet has now gone commercial, and almost any individual or company can subscribe to a service that connects to it.

Because the original purpose of the Internet was for efficient military communications, it was designed to get the message through even in the worst of conditions. Messages—E-mail, data files, images, and so on—are broken into small packets that contain the address for the destination and a sequence number that allows reassembly of the complete file when it gets to the destination. Once a file goes into the "net," each packet is on its own. The Internet is designed to seek out the most efficient path at any instant, and packets can scatter all over the Internet as they seek a clear path to their destination. Once at the destination, they reassemble into the correct order of the original file. The protocol, or language, that is used on the Internet to send and receive packets of information is called TCP/IP (Transmission Control Protocol/Internet Protocol).

Internet E-Mail

To send E-mail through the Internet you must meet some basic requirements. First, you must be able to access a host computer at an *Internet Service Provider* or ISP. The ISP might be a university or school, a commercial service, or an integrated online service such as America Online, CompuServe, or Prodigy.

Second, you need an account that provides an Internet user address. Such an address might be something like *barron@typhoon.coedu.usf.edu*. This address would be spoken as "barron at typhoon dot coedu dot usf dot edu." The address is made up of two components. To the left of the @ sign is the identification or name of the user on the system where he or she has an account. To the right of the @ sign is the Internet designation of the user's system, called the host name or the domain name. The host name follows a predefined structure. The last right-hand component (*edu* in this case) represents a type, or domain, of organization or country. Some common domains are *edu* for education, *com* for commercial, *mil* for military, and *uk* for United Kingdom. (See fig. 8.1.) The remainder of the host name identifies a specific computer. For example, *typhoon.coedu.usf* identifies the computer called typhoon in the College of Education *(coedu)* of the University of South Florida *(usf)*. If you access the Internet through a commercial vendor, you might have an address like *smith@aol.com,* where *smith* is the identification of the user on the commercial America Online system.

The last component you need to access Internet E-mail is a software program. A popular, easy-to-use program in school and university settings is called PINE and is by the University of Washington. PINE runs on the host computer and provides menus that allow users to make simple choices for reading messages, composing and sending messages, and creating address lists. (See fig. 8.2.)

ID	Major Domains
EDU	Education
COM	Commercial Organization
MIL	Military
GOV	Government Sites
NET	Special Network Resources
ORG	Other Organizations
UK	United Kingdom
CA	Canada

Figure 8.1. Types of Organizations and Their Internet Identifiers.

PINE 3.93	MAIN MENU	Folder: INBOX 8 Messages

?	HELP	-	Get help using Pine
C	COMPOSE MESSAGE	-	Compose and send/post a message
I	FOLDER INDEX	-	View messages in current folder
L	FOLDER LIST	-	Select a folder OR news group to view
A	ADDRESS BOOK	-	Update address book
S	SETUP	-	Configure or update Pine
Q	QUIT	-	Exit the Pine program

Copyright 1989 - 1996. PINE is a trademark of the University of Washington.

[Folder "INBOX" opened with 8 messages]

? Help
O Other CMDS   L [ListFldrs]   P PrevCmd   R RelNotes
       N NextCmd   K KBlock

Figure 8.2. PINE E-Mail Menu.

With these components—a host computer, an Internet user address, and a software interface—it is a simple matter to use a computer at school or home to compose, send, and receive E-mail on a global scale.

There are variations of E-mail that allow group communications on the Internet. A *listserv* is simply a group address list that automatically distributes information. Any message that is sent to the listserv is sent to all names on the list. Some listservs are private; most have automated procedures that allow anyone to *subscribe* or *unsubscribe*. Care should be taken in joining listservs because they may generate dozens of messages a day. Getting out of an unwanted listserv can be frustrating if the specific unsubscribe procedure is lost.

Another form of group communications on the Internet is called USENET. USENET is an electronic bulletin-board system where people can read messages that other people have written, or they can "post" messages for others to read. There are more than 10,000 special-interest groups on USENET, referred to as *newsgroups*.

Internet File Transfers

The Internet also allows individuals to transfer files from a computer at one location to a computer at another location. Anything that can be digitized into a computer format can be transferred on the Internet, including text, databases, spreadsheets, public-domain programs, images, music, and digital video. The process of transferring a file on the Internet is called FTP, which stands for *file transfer protocol*. A typical transfer might proceed as follows:

Let's say that you teach music and would like to introduce MIDI music to your students. You have the MIDI hardware required to play the MIDI music, but you do not have any MIDI music files appropriate for your class. In an E-mail conversation with a fellow music teacher, you learn that there is a free collection of music on the Internet that would be just right for your students. After you obtain the Internet address of the MIDI music from your friend, the rest is simple. You simply log on to your Internet account, type the appropriate commands, and within minutes you can download the music files of your choice and play them on your computer.

There are an incredible number of images (weather satellite pictures, NASA launches, museum pieces), sound files (music, sound effects, MIDI files), and public-domain software programs available for FTP transfer on the Internet. To help locate the files you need, searching tools are available on the Internet. Whenever you download files from the Internet, be sure to read any copyright restrictions that may accompany the files.

Internet Remote Access

E-mail provides a route for person-to-person communication, and file transfers provide a way of moving files from one place to another. However, much of the information in the world exists in various forms of databases that operate only on the computer where they are stored. Examples might be electronic library catalogs, online periodical bibliographies, and electronic encyclopedias. A major benefit of the Internet is the ability to connect your computer directly to another computer system at a remote location. The remote-access feature of the Internet provides fast, easy entry into huge storehouses of information.

The Internet method of accessing these databases is through a program called *telnet*. When a command such as *telnet spacelink.msfc.nasa.gov* is issued from a computer connected to the Internet, that computer connects to the NASA computer in Alabama. The NASA computer is open to the public: Just log on as *guest*. After you have logged on, you can use the NASA computer to search the directories, download images and programs, and conduct research in the files. There are thousands of telnet sites around the world that allow access to anyone on the Internet. In addition, if you are traveling and you have access to the Internet, you can use the telnet program to check your E-mail messages back home.

One disadvantage of using the telnet command to reach another computer is that you must know the name of the site you are telnetting to: for example, *spacelink.msfc.nasa.gov*. To make navigation a little easier, many Internet computers use a resource called *Gopher* that was created at the University of Minnesota to present menus of selections. When an item on a Gopher menu is selected by a user, the program branches to another Internet location or "goes for" the information related to the item. Gophers permit automatic, invisible links between computers connected to the Internet. Figure 8.3 is a sample Gopher menu. Note that if you choose item 4, you will access another Gopher menu of libraries all over the world. If you then select a specific library from the menu of libraries, you will automatically be connected to that location. (A / at the end of the line indicates that the selection branches to another Gopher menu.)

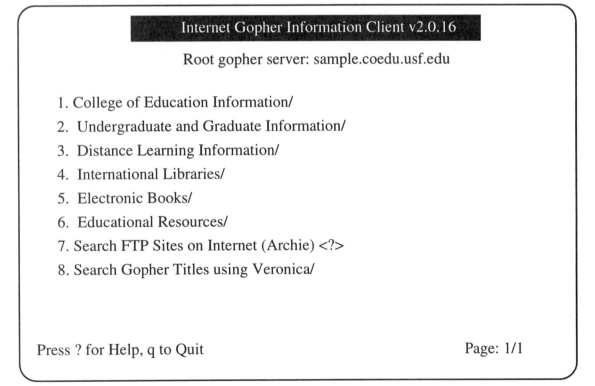

Figure 8.3. Sample Gopher Menu.

World Wide Web

The first wave of public access to the Internet was through programs such as telnet and Gopher that were alphanumeric (text and number), line-oriented programs that at best provided menus as a user interface. Recently, most Internet users have switched to a graphical user interface (GUI) to the Internet that is called the World Wide Web.

The concept of the World Wide Web—often shortened to Web—was created in Switzerland in 1991 to allow *hyperlinks* within documents. In other words, while you are reading one document, there may be words or buttons that you can choose or click on to take you to another document or file. Recent software programs called Web browsers are designed to access the Web and use common mouse point-and-click interfaces. For example, *Netscape Navigator* is a browser for the Web that allows the user to forget about cryptic commands because the program automatically activates whatever commands are needed. When multimedia Web sites are accessed, sounds, pictures, or motion images can result from a mouse click. See figure 8.4 for an example of a Web screen.

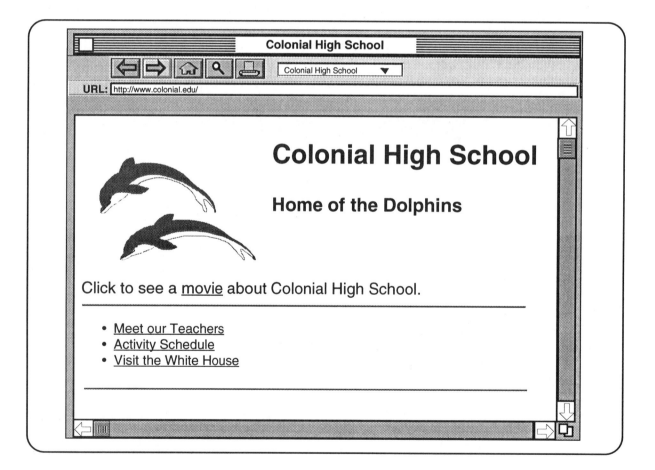

Figure 8.4. Sample Web Page.

Web Pages

A Web browser, such as Netscape Navigator, is a software program that creates screens or *pages* of information from files that it accesses throughout the Web. If a particular file creates a Web page that is a focal point or main menu for an individual, group, or organization, it is called a *home page*. For example, a person might say that the home page for the University of Central Florida is at *http://www.ucf.edu/*.

The *http://www.ucf.edu/* is a Web address that is called a *Uniform Resource Locator* or URL. Every Internet location that stores and provides access to Web pages must have a unique URL. For a person using a Web browser, the URL is the most direct route to access a particular Web page.

URLs for Web sites begin with http (HyperText Transfer Protocol) followed by a colon, two slashes, and the address for the Web page or site. At the end of the address, another slash may appear, followed by a path and file name. For example, *http://fcit.coedu.usf.edu/holocaust/index.html* will take you to the first page of the Teacher's Guide to the Holocaust at the University of South Florida. (Note that the addresses may be listed as a series of numbers rather than letters.)

In addition to Web documents, URLs can be used to reach Gopher menus, telnet sites, and FTP directories. For example, *gopher://fcit.coedu.usf.edu* will access a Gopher site with lesson plans for technology; *telnet://spacelink.msfc.nasa.gov* will reach NASA's telnet site; and *ftp://typhoon.coedu.usf.edu* will reach the FTP site at USF.

If you do not know the URL for a specific location, search tools are available on the Internet to help find a Web site. These search tools, including Yahoo, Lycos, Infoseek, and others, will provide a list of sites that match the search criteria that you enter. (See the Resource section at the end of this chapter for a list of some of the educational sites on the Web.)

INTERNET EDUCATIONAL APPLICATIONS

The Internet provides endless research and communication opportunities for education. Some of the instructional activities involve a simple exchange or transfer of information; others involve high-level problem solving and synthesis. This section presents a variety of educational applications for integrating the Internet into your curriculum.

Research

The Internet provides a wealth of information for research, including access to international libraries; government databases; and collections of text, graphics, sounds, digital video, and computer files. Information on virtually every topic is available on the Internet and is usually more up-to-date and extensive than the information in the libraries or textbooks. Research on the Internet can be divided into three broad categories or levels: basic, advanced, and original. Although these categories are not exclusive, they can be used to help classify Internet projects based on the number of sites visited, the sources of the research, and the complexity of the research questions (Barron and Ivers 1996).

Basic Research

Basic research involves finding and comparing facts from a single or several preselected sources and reporting the information. In most cases, students' initial uses of the Internet involve basic research. For example, they may access the Library of Congress or the CIA World Factbook to write a research report. A good site to begin is My Virtual Reference Desk at http://www.refdesk.com/.

When conducting Internet research, students should be encouraged not only to practice their research skills and locate the desired information but to analyze the results of their searches, compare the facts, and report them appropriately. They should also begin to question the data and reject poor, incomplete, inaccurate, and inconsequential facts.

Advanced Research

Advanced research includes a wider variety of sources, including several sites on the Internet as well as print or CD-ROM sources. Another difference is that the sources in advanced research are not preselected. In other words, the students must determine which source or sources to investigate.

Advanced research consists of a six-step cycle:

1. *Questioning.* Before going online, students structure their research questions.

2. *Planning.* Students develop a search strategy and a list of sites to investigate.

3. *Gathering.* Students go online to collect information.

4. *Sorting.* After signing off the Internet, students analyze and categorize their data.

5. *Synthesizing.* Students integrate the information and draw conclusions.

6. *Evaluating.* Students assess the results; if necessary, the cycle begins again with a refined research question.

Original Research

The Internet is an excellent place to conduct original research through surveys and collaborative experiments. For example, students may conduct surveys through E-mail messages as they collect and compare food prices or other items from around the world. After the information is compiled, it can be graphed, analyzed, and reported. Cooperative experiments can also be performed. For example, students from different geographical locations may collaborate to plant the same kind of seeds on the same day. They follow the same directions for care of the plants as they grow, measure the plants, and send data to other participants. The data are then used for graphing, analyses, and drawing conclusions.

Communication

One of the major advantages of the Internet is the potential for worldwide communication. This type of communication is often described as time shifted, meaning a student may send a message and receive an answer two minutes or two days later. In comparison to the postal system, however, the time delays can be short. Another advantage of using the Internet to communicate is that the cost is minimal; in many cases, there is little or no charge to educators for sending messages whether they go across the street or around the world.

Pen-Pal Activities

Perhaps the most common form of telecommunications projects is electronic pen pals, or key pals. Similar to traditional pen pals, electronic pen pals exchange personal thoughts, stories, ideas, questions, and experiences through E-mail messages. They can learn from others in a risk-free environment both within and beyond their communities, practice written communication skills, become aware of other cultures, and make new friends. If you are looking for classrooms and students to communicate with, try the Intercultural E-mail Classroom Connections site at http://www.stolaf. edu/network/iecc/.

Peer-to-Peer Tutoring

Another form of electronic communications is peer-to-peer tutoring or mentoring. These exchanges provide a formal use of E-mail that specifically pairs students with other students or with adults who can provide one-on-one assistance and guidance on a routine basis. In some cases, online tutoring takes place totally through E-mail messages. In other cases, the "chat" feature of the Internet or other telecommunications systems may be used for real-time communications. Electronic chatting enables two or more people to type on a "collective" computer screen. They can see what they are typing as well as the input from others—all at the same time on the same screen.

Electronic Appearances and Impersonations

Electronic networks can often bring students into direct contact with distinguished authors, national figures, or other notable people. In other cases, someone may impersonate a famous author, character, or person to provide a unique perspective. For example, Virginia's educational network (VA-PEN) has a forum entitled the Electronic Village. In this "village," students can send messages to Willy Wonka and other fictional characters. Teachers or graduate students answer the questions from Willy's perspective. Other examples include portrayals of fictional characters such as the Great Pumpkin or of historical characters such as George Washington.

Simulations

Students can participate in electronic simulations by taking on the role of another person or country in a particular situation or event. For example, different classrooms from around the world might take the perspective of a particular country in a fictional or real international conflict. Moderators of the simulation post the news or events, and the classrooms must react to the "news" as well as to the reactions of the students in the other classrooms.

Electronic Publishing

Formal and informal publishing are other means of communication through the Internet. Round-robin stories are an example of informal publishing. In this approach, a participating class starts a story with one paragraph. The story starter is sent to a predetermined class (class 1 sends its story to class 2 and so on). Students work in small groups to add a new paragraph to the story. The story variations then rotate to the next class, and that class adds to the story variation before they forward it. This cycle continues until the story reaches the original class in the round.

Formal publishing can take place when a student or a class posts a story or other document in an electronic journal or on a bulletin board. In most cases, electronic documents are prepared offline in a word processor such as *Microsoft Word* or *WordPerfect* and then saved as straight text files. After the document has been proofread and spell checked, it can then be uploaded to the electronic journal or bulletin board. Many schools have used this method to share information about their school and other topics on the Internet. For example, Patch High School in Germany produced a World Wide Web document devoted to D day. Students at Patch wrote research reports and accumulated graphics, text, video, and sounds about D day. Visit their site at http://192.253.114.31 to witness the work of the students.

Web Publishing

Many schools, classes, teachers, and even students have published their own home pages on the World Wide Web. A school home page can serve as an information center for the community. The school calendar, building layouts, special events, course materials, and even the school song can be part of the page. Teachers often form students into groups to plan and collect materials for various parts of a school home page. There are many HTML tutorials online to help get students started, such as http://www.coedu.usf.edu/inst_tech/publications/html. In addition, students can use HTML editors, such as PageMill (Adobe) or Netscape Gold, to simplify the programming aspect of the production.

The process of creating home pages and other Web pages that link to home pages is called *Web publishing*. There are two fundamental stages to Web publishing. First, the page files and all associated images, sounds, and so forth must be created and tested. Second, the files must all be transferred to a host computer called a Web server at an Internet Service Provider.

All Web pages are derived from data files that store the information that makes up the pages. As with most data files, Web page files adhere to a specific format or language. For Web pages, the language is called *HyperText Markup Language* or HTML. HTML uses *tags* to define how information is formatted on a screen.

⟨H2⟩Home of the Dolphins⟨/H2⟩

In this example, ⟨H2⟩ and ⟨/H2⟩ are tags that represent the beginning and ending of a line of text. In this case, ⟨H2⟩ is a command to start a second level headline—a single line of text. Headlines have six levels available, with 1 being the largest and 6 being the smallest. The ⟨/H2⟩ is the instruction to cancel the headline style and return to the normal font. If the ⟨/H2⟩ were not used, all following text would continue to be displayed in the headline font. See figure 8.5 to view the HTML file that creates the Web page in figure 8.4.

```
<HTML>
<HEAD>
<TITLE>Colonial High School</TITLE></HEAD>
<BODY>
<IMG SRC ="dolphin.gif">
<H1> Colonial High School</H1>
<H2>Home of the Dolphins</H2>
<P>
Click to see a <A HREF="CHS.mov">movie</A> about Colonial High
School.
<P>
<HR>
<UL>
<LI><A HREF="http://www.col.edu/teachers/">Meet our Teachers</A>
<LI><A HREF="http://www.col.edu/sports/">Activity Schedule</A>
<LI><A HREF="http://www.whitehouse.gov/">Visit the White
House</A>
</UL>
</BODY>
</HTML>
```

Figure 8.5. HTML Tags Used to Create the Sample Web Page in Figure 8.4.

There are about 50 HTML tags in common use, but companies such as Netscape have developed their own enhanced or extended tags. Although all Web browsers can correctly interpret the basic tags, enhanced tags are sometimes unique to specific browsers.

Creating a Web page by using the HTML language appears to be intimidating, but even elementary school students have done it. In many cases, individuals learn a basic dozen HTML tags and then gradually expand their "vocabulary" as they become more experienced. In other cases, individuals rely on HTML *editors* to help them out. HTML editors vary in form and function, but they insulate the author from most of the HTML tags. The editors allow the author to concentrate more on the content and form of the page and less on the mechanics of HTML. PageMill by Adobe and Netscape Gold are two popular programs that can easily create Web pages.

Another method used to create a Web page is to use an HTML converter. For example, Microsoft Internet Assistant will convert Microsoft Word documents into HTML files. Also, HyperStudio by Roger Wagner Publishers offers additional software (to HyperStudio) that allows it to display pages on the Web (see http://www.hyperstudio.com/).

Once a Web page and its associated materials have been created and tested, it must be transferred to a location, or host, on the World Wide Web so that it can be accessed by all. The host is usually an Internet Service Provider (ISP) that manages a computer, or *Web server,* that stores the Web pages.

INTERNET CONNECTIONS

There are two basic methods to connect to the Internet: indirect access and direct access. The type of connection affects the speed of transmission and the level of activity that is possible. As one might expect, a graphic multimedia interface such as Netscape requires a more advanced connection than simply sending E-mail messages.

Indirect Access

With indirect access to the Internet, your desktop computer, the client, is simply communicating through a modem and a regular telephone line to another computer, or host, that has an Internet address. The host computer can be located at an ISP that might be an integrated online service such as America Online—a company that provides access only to the Internet—or it can be a computer at a district office, statewide educational center, or university. Once authorized to use the host computer, the user is given an identification name and a password that allows access. The basic activities of E-mail, file transfer, and remote access on the Internet are all possible when using a host computer for indirect access to the Internet (depending on the services provided by the host computer). With indirect access, the actual programs that access the Internet usually run on the host computer. The client's computer simply displays the results of the activities of these programs. Hypermedia interfaces such as Netscape, however, require a more powerful *direct* connection.

Direct Access

A direct connection to the Internet provides your desktop computer with its own Internet address. Direct connections provide fast transmission rates and allow all possible activities on the Internet, including the use of graphic interfaces such as Netscape that access the World Wide Web. School computers can be provided with direct connections to the Internet through a local area network that has a *leased data line* connection (see chapter 9) to an Internet service provider. Unfortunately, direct connections are more challenging and often more expensive to establish than indirect connections. Leased data lines and the necessary hardware to connect into them are still fairly expensive.

Direct connections can also be established through standard telephone lines and fast modems. Two techniques are possible: serial line Internet protocol (SLIP) and point-to-point protocol (PPP). To establish a SLIP or a PPP connection, you must contract with an ISP and obtain special software. SLIP and PPP connections are not as fast as direct leased line connections, but they provide affordable access to the World Wide Web.

Internet Service Providers

To connect to the Internet, you must "belong" to some organization that can provide Internet access. In some cases, the organization may be a university or educational system that provides free access to students and faculty. If you do not have free access, you will have to subscribe to a commercial Internet Service Provider (ISP).

Several commercial companies, generically called *integrated online services,* provide a variety of electronic services to their customers. America Online, CompuServe, and Prodigy are among the best known of these companies that offer services ranging from topical bulletin boards and E-mail to electronic encyclopedias and online airline reservations.

When services of this type first started, they charged fees directly related to the amount of use. Like long-distance telephone charges, these fees were usually higher during the peak activity of the day and lower during evening and weekend hours. Until recently, off-peak rates of $12 to $15 an hour were common. Competition has had an impact, and now monthly fees are common among integrated service vendors, with rates as low as $10 a month for unlimited online time during evenings and weekends. A word of caution: Most of these systems charge an additional fee for Internet access. If you are a seasoned surfer and spend large amounts of time on the Internet, this type of service can easily become too expensive.

Another option is to subscribe to an ISP that operates through the telephone company, cable company, or as a small business. These providers usually charge about $20 per month for unlimited access—including the Internet. Most of the providers will supply all the software you need and a local or toll-free telephone number for your modem.

MODEMS

Modems have been mentioned several times in this chapter. Because they are critical components in telecommunications, it is appropriate to explore them in greater detail.

Overview

A modem might seem like a complicated device, but it is designed to perform two simple processes. Most standard telephone lines transmit only analog audio tones, such as those in human voices. A computer manipulates digital information in a binary code of 0s and 1s. The modem translates, or *modulates,* the 0s and 1s of an outgoing message into a fluctuating tone that goes through the telephone line. At the same time, the modem listens for a different tone that comes from the distant computer's modem. As this tone comes through the telephone line, the local modem translates, or *demodulates,* it back into the 0s and 1s of the binary language of the local computer. Thus, the modem—*mo*dulator-*dem*odulator—allows the two computers to behave as though they are connected directly even though they might be thousands of miles apart.

If everything goes right, the stream of 0s and 1s going out of one computer is translated into a rapidly fluctuating tone. This tone is transmitted through the telephone line, and at the other end the distant modem translates the tone back into the identical pattern of 0s and 1s that earlier departed the original computer. (See fig. 8.6.)

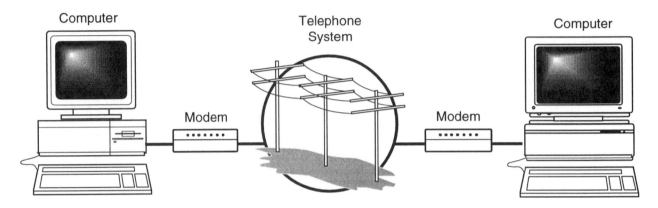

Figure 8.6. Typical Modem Computer Application.

Modems have settings that must be matched so that two modems can communicate. Some of these settings are automatically determined by the modems when the telephone call connects; other settings must be established manually. Required settings are usually published along with the telephone numbers of most telecommunications services.

Modem Speed

Manufacturers have been able to increase dramatically the transfer rate or speed of modems. Although this has been partly because of improvements in telephone lines, the largest improvements have come through discoveries concerning how to send and receive more information over the telephone lines and how to correct common telephone-line interference.

Baud—named after Emil Baudot, who invented a telegraph teleprinter code in 1874—is a term often used to define the speed of modems. A modern measurement, *bits per second,* or *bps,* has replaced baud as a measurement of speed for modems. A *bit* is a binary digit having a value of 0 or 1. The more bits a modem can process per second, the faster it can send or receive data.

Bits define each character and the spaces between characters; it takes about 10 bits to transmit or receive a single character of information. A 2,400bps modem can transmit or receive about 240 characters per second. This sentence, which is 107 characters long (counting spaces), would require about 0.4 seconds to transmit.

Until recently, a modem that operated at 2,400bps was considered fast because the first popular modems that were used with computers operated at only 300bps. Now, however, 28,800bps (28.8Kbps) dominate the market, and even faster speeds are now possible by using *digital modems* on new telephone lines that are part of the Integrated

Service Digital Network, or ISDN system. Faster speeds mean less time connected to a telephone, and shorter telephone connection times result in lower charges for long-distance calls and lower connection fees for many services that charge by the hour.

Handshaking Protocols

As two computer modems exchange information, a series of rapidly changing tones goes through the telephone lines. The modems convert these tones into binary 0s and 1s, but software in the computers must work with the modems to reassemble this stream of information into the original data. The computers at each end must look for the same structure within the binary data to translate them properly.

Certain bits represent the start and end of each character (start and stop bits) and whether it has been transmitted without error (parity bit). In addition, both computers must agree on the number of bits in each character (data bits). Finally, a signaling technique that allows each computer to know when the other is ready to receive information is used to prevent the loss of information. This signaling process is most accurately called *handshaking,* but now all these parameters are commonly grouped into handshaking discussions. For one computer to communicate with another through a modem, the handshaking settings must be properly set. (See fig. 8.7.)

Transmitted information is defined by seven or eight data bits. With seven data bits 128 characters can be defined, including uppercase and lowercase letters, punctuation marks, and some simple graphics symbols. Seven data bits are common for modems attached to mainframe computers.

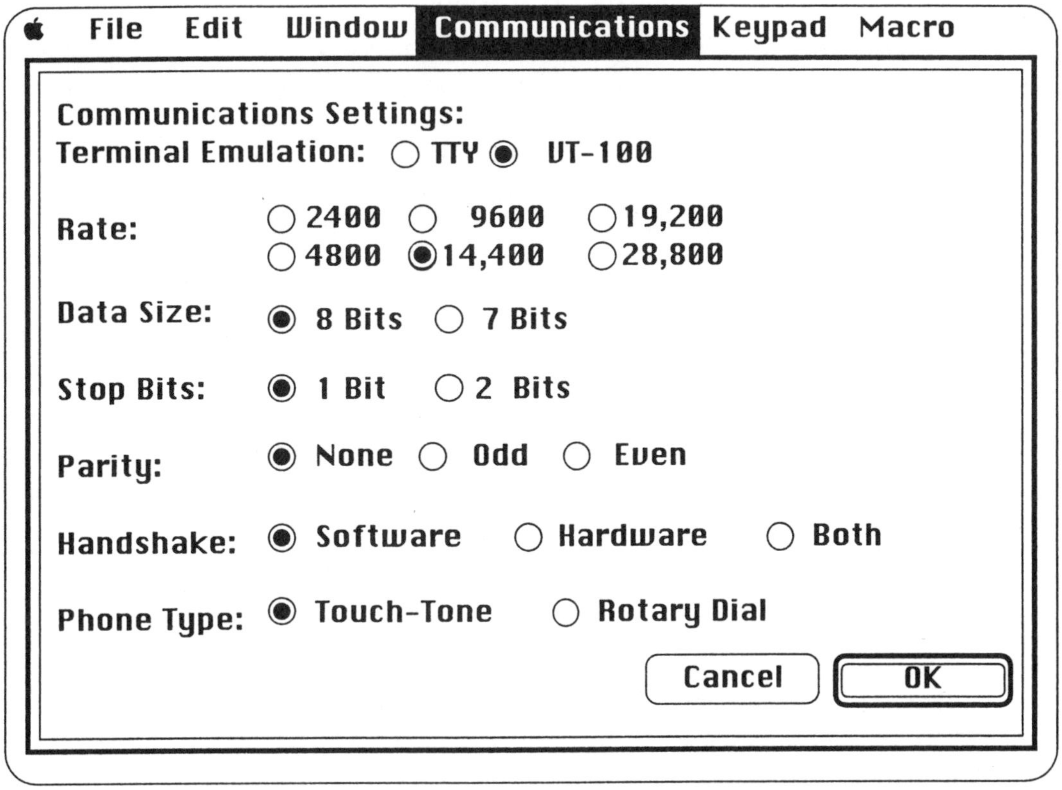

File Edit Window **Communications** Keypad Macro
Communications Settings:
Terminal Emulation: ○ TTY ● UT-100
Rate: ○ 2400 ○ 9600 ○ 19,200   ○ 4800 ● 14,400 ○ 28,800
Data Size: ● 8 Bits ○ 7 Bits
Stop Bits: ● 1 Bit ○ 2 Bits
Parity: ● None ○ Odd ○ Even
Handshake: ● Software ○ Hardware ○ Both
Phone Type: ● Touch-Tone ○ Rotary Dial
[Cancel] [OK]

Figure 8.7. Communications Software Settings Menu.

Eight data bits allow for the definition of 256 characters, including uppercase and lowercase letters, foreign-language characters, punctuation marks, and some graphics symbols. Eight-bit data transmission matches the eight-bit-per-byte memory format of many computers, making it much easier to transmit whole computer programs or other files. When microcomputers communicate with one another through modems, eight data bits are commonly used.

One handshake signal is a form of error checking that is called *parity*. The most common settings for it are *even, odd,* or *none*. Parity checking is a low level of error control, and it is not used much anymore. As a result, most modem communications between microcomputers use *none* as the setting for parity. Mainframe computer modems, however, sometimes use *even*.

Start and stop bits are the handshaking bits used to separate one character from another. Current modem transmission techniques always use one start bit, but several values can be used for the stop bits. The single stop bit is by far the most common.

In summary, the most common settings are either seven or eight data bits per character. Seven-bit requirements show up frequently when communications involve a mainframe computer, and eight bits are common when two microcomputers are connected to each other. Parity is usually *none* or *even;* the stop-bit setting is almost always *one*.

Finally, the original concept of handshaking must be addressed. If one computer sends information through a modem before the computer at the other end is ready to receive it, the information will be lost. For modem communications to be effective, the computer at each end must be able to tell the other: "Wait a second. I'm not quite ready." These signals can be handled directly through the hardware of each modem, or they can be generated as specific character codes by the computers' software. Software techniques seem to be used most commonly at present. Only rarely is it necessary to make changes in handshaking techniques. When necessary, the modem manual and the telecommunications software documentation should be consulted.

All this seems complicated, but it does not have to be. Most modems with appropriate computer software automatically match up the bps rates and some of the handshaking protocols. It usually pays to know the settings for data bits, parity, and stop bits for the computer services that you are going to call, however. These settings are usually supplied with the telephone number of the service.

Internal and External Modems

Modems can be installed inside the computer, or they can sit next to the computer in their own box. Both types of modems have some advantages. The advantages of one type of modem generally turn out to be the disadvantages of the other type.

Advantages of Internal Modems

Internal modems are less expensive because they do not have their own power supply or container. They are better used with portable or laptop computers. Because internal modems become part of the computer, they are always ready for use and cannot be left behind. Internal modems connect directly to the computer, so there is no need for a cable between the modem and the computer. (See fig. 8.8.)

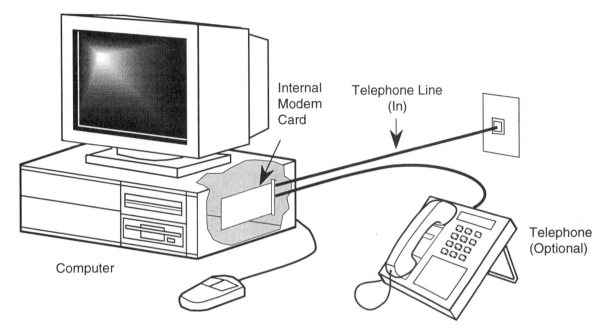

Figure 8.8. Internal Modem and Connections.

Advantages of External Modems

External modems can be moved from one computer to another with ease. They make use of a communications port that is standard on virtually all computers. (See fig. 8.9 on page 216.)

Modem Software

Modems allow computers to communicate through standard telephone lines, but the computers still have a lot of work to do. Computer programs that operate modems are called telecommunications software. These programs perform a number of activities. For example, they format the arriving text for your computer screen by inserting carriage returns and line feeds as needed. They may also contain a dialing directory so that you can select the appropriate number from a list. Once selected, the telephone number is dialed and the modem settings associated with that telephone number are used to prepare the modem for action.

More sophisticated functions are also common in telecommunications software. For example, people often want to keep the information that comes through a modem. Appropriate software can turn on a printer or save text to a file on a disk.

Modem software also makes it possible to transfer complete files from one computer to another over telephone lines. Although the speed of the process depends upon the speed of the modems that are in use, the effect is about the same as copying a file from one disk drive to another.

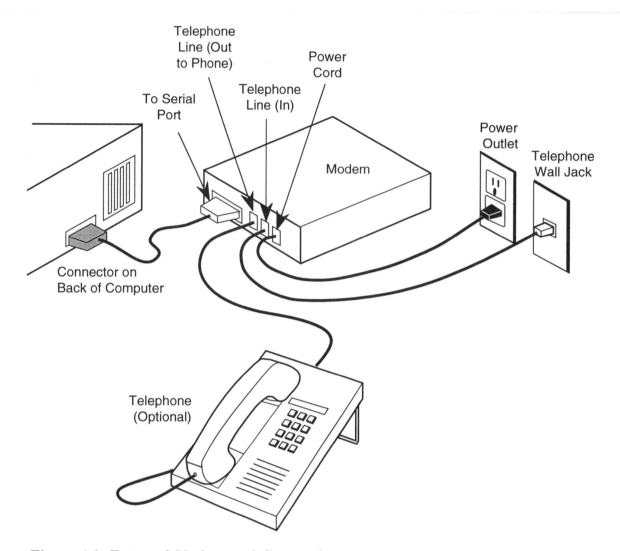

Figure 8.9. External Modem and Connections.

If you are using a modem to connect to the Internet, the software program you use will depend on the type of Internet connection you are establishing. Indirect connections will require telecommunications software such as *Windows Terminal, ProComm, ZTerm,* or *White Knight.* These programs determine the terminal emulation, set the parameters, dial the phone number, and send and receive the files.

If you are connecting via a point-to-point connection, then you will need different software that contains the PPP protocols. This software, including ConfigPPP and WinSock, is available free of charge on the Internet, or it may be supplied by your Internet Service Provider.

Direct and PPP connections are becoming so popular that part of the software that is needed—the TCP/IP software—is now included in the system software of Macintosh and Windows-compatible computers. Check with your service provider to determine the exact software programs you need and the settings that will be required.

Advice for Setting Up and Using a Modem

It takes some advanced preparation to get a modem to work on the first try. To begin with, be sure that you can connect the modem to the computer that you plan to use. For example, some computers are not designed to hold an internal modem. Also, internal modems tend to be more sensitive to fast computers.

External modems also have some potential problems. First, you must confirm that you have an available communications serial port on your computer. Quite often a mouse is connected to such a port, and sometimes printers use serial ports. If you are already using all your available serial ports, you should ask a local dealer about possible alternatives. It is possible that the serial port on an older computer is too slow for a fast modem. Internal modems come with their own state-of-the-art serial ports, so they may work better with an older computer.

Finally, connection problems can show up where you least expect them—in the telephone line. You can use a modem on almost any standard single-number telephone, but a separate line for just the modem is best. When a modem shares a line with regular telephones and someone picks up an extension while the modem is in use, that person will be greeted with a loud blast of computer tones, and your modem will be disconnected.

If you have a multinumber telephone, you will need specialized telephone equipment to separate a single number for the computer modem. Telephone companies or telephone product stores can help determine precisely what is needed for your system.

More complex telephone systems can create even greater problems. Some modern private telephone exchanges found in universities, businesses, or even large schools are completely incompatible with modems. If you plan to use your modem at school or another place of work, make certain that the telephone lines to your office or classroom are compatible with computer modems. In general, if you have a wide variety of internal office features such as voice mail, call waiting, call parking, group conferencing, and so forth, your telephone system might be too modern for standard modems.

ISDN "Modems"

As telephone companies modernize their switching equipment, they are expanding the Integrated Services Digital Network (ISDN) system. An ISDN connection is a dial-up connection much like the standard telephone system, but all similarities end there. ISDN is all digital, and a single ISDN line can permit data transmission at speeds up to 128,000 (128Kbps) bits per second. It is possible to split the available bandwidth into two parts so that one half—64,000bps—is used for data transmissions while the other half is used for a standard voice telephone call.

ISDN telephone lines use interface devices with computers that are sometimes called ISDN modems, but this term is misleading. A modem is designed to convert digital data into outgoing analog audio tones—modulation—for standard telephone lines. Incoming audio tones from a distant modem are converted back into digital data, known as demodulation.

Since an ISDN line transmits digital data, there is no need for the modulation-demodulation of a standard modem. Instead, computer information goes from start to finish in true digital form.

As mentioned earlier, ISDN lines require a device to connect them to a computer. This device is called an ISDN terminal adapter, and it is what is usually incorrectly called an ISDN modem. To confuse the issue, some terminal adapters also have standard modems built into them. This is because it will be a long time before all telecommunication services provide ISDN lines. Until that happens, a computer needs a standard modem to connect to services that still use only modems. Combining the terminal adapter with the modem means that only one serial port is needed instead of two, and configuration conflicts will also be less likely. The built-in modem on the terminal adapter takes over any time the computer dials a service that answers with a standard modem tone. More detailed information on ISDN lines is included in chapter 9 in the discussion of high-speed data lines.

Other High-Speed Data Connections

The telephone line is no longer the only way that data can get to and from a home or school. Several cable television companies are introducing services that allow very high speed connections to the Internet through the same cable that provides cable television service. While standards are still evolving in this area, data transmission speeds can theoretically be as high as 36Mbps. Most of the initial systems are targeting to provide data to a home at around 10Mbps and to receive data at lower rates ranging from 200Kbps to 2Mbps. The transmission rate is designed to go faster in one direction than the other because research indicates that most home Internet users receive far more data than they send.

A second approach also capitalizes on the fact that most home Internet users receive more information than they send. The same digital satellite technology that makes small dish antennas possible can also be used to send computer data to specific receivers. Using satellite Internet access, home users can currently receive (or download) information at speeds up to 428Kbps. This is strictly a one-way communication; standard telephone connections and modems are used to send data from the home back to the Internet Service Provider.

Both of these technologies are new and evolving. Standards are not fully set in either case, and it is possible that interface or "modem" equipment that is in use might not meet the standards that evolve in the next few years. However, for individuals who now have a critical need for high speed downloading of Internet data at home, the speed advantages of either of these two technologies might be worth the risk of being on the "crest of the technology wave."

Fax Modems

Facsimile machines, or *fax* machines as they are frequently called, have become almost as common as modems. Fax machines are used to send copies of paper documents from one location to another. (See fig. 8.10.) The machines function in much the same way as modems in that they generate tones that are sent over standard telephone lines.

Recent advances in modem technologies now make it possible to use the modem to send and receive fax messages. Such a modem allows one computer to connect to another to share data, but this type of modem can also connect to a distant fax machine. When it operates as a fax machine, it can receive a picture or image of whatever the fax machine at the other end is sending. With proper software, this image can be printed, stored, or immediately displayed on the computer screen. The image might contain text, numbers, line drawings, or photographs. However, even if the image is entirely text, the text cannot be fed directly into a word processor for further editing.

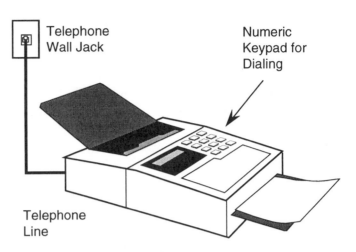

Figure 8.10. Fax Machine.

Fax modems can also be used to send information from a computer to a distant fax machine. The information must be either an image or a text file that is stored in the computer. After the appropriate software converts the file to a format that is compatible with fax machines, the distant fax machine is dialed and the file is transmitted. At the other end, the image of the page comes out of the receiving fax in the usual manner.

ADVICE FOR GETTING STARTED IN TELECOMMUNICATIONS

The incredible number of options that are available in this technological field may intimidate the novice. Perhaps the best advice is to start out with one useful application, then gradually determine what additional options are available in your setting. Once you begin, you will almost certainly find other people who share your interests. The following are some additional tips.

1. *Take an informal course* through a local computer store, computer club, university, or community college. It is much easier to learn the basics of telecommunications with somebody helping you through the confusing parts.

2. *Join one of the inexpensive subscription services,* such as Prodigy. A few months on such a system will make you a telecommunications veteran. As you explore such a system, you will learn how it might be used in your classroom. In addition, you will learn about other programs that are directed specifically toward teachers and classrooms. If you find that a particular subscription service does not meet your needs, terminate your membership and try another one.

3. *Start small.* Your first telecommunications project does not have to involve a school in Russia. Instead, begin with someone who is in your school or a nearby school so that you can help each other through the initial procedures.

4. *Look for projects with specific goals.* The most successful telecommunications projects are those with specific goals, structure, and time lines.

5. *Ask questions.* Find someone who might have already solved the problem that has you stumped. If you can use telecommunications to ask the questions, all the better. You will be amazed by the willingness of other people to help you get going in this field.

CONCLUSION

The variety of applications for telecommunications is almost unlimited. It is now possible to use libraries after they are closed. Banking can be accomplished on national holidays. A message can be sent to a traveling scholar even if you do not have the faintest idea where that person is at the moment. Groups of people separated by local, state, or even national boundaries can work together to solve common problems.

TELECOMMUNICATIONS GLOSSARY

Archie. An Internet program that allows an individual to search for specific files on the Internet.

ARPANET (Advanced Research Projects Agency Network). The government research network that served as the basis for the Internet.

ASCII (American Standard Code for Information Interchange). A standard that establishes the structure of binary 0s and 1s that define the letters of the alphabet, digits, and common punctuation marks.

baud rate. A term sometimes used to define the speed of serial data transmissions, such as those found with modems. The term is derived from Emil Baudot, a nineteenth-century inventor. The term is being replaced by *bits per second* (bps).

BBS (bulletin-board system). An electronic bulletin-board system (EBBS, sometimes shortened to just BBS). A computer-based equivalent of the traditional bulletin board. Most BBSs also offer an option for private E-mail.

bit (*binary digit***).** The smallest unit of information in a digital computer. It is usually represented with values of 0 or 1.

bits per second. A common method of measuring the speed of a modem. Modems range in speed from 1,200 bits per second (bps) to more than 28,800bps. Modem bps rates must match before they can communicate with each other.

capture. Most telecommunications software allows you to save, or *capture*, data to a disk. This makes it possible to review or use the results of a telecommunications session at a later time.

chat. An option on some telecommunications systems that makes it possible for a user to communicate directly with the system operator or other users. The chatting is not vocal, however; the information typed into each system keyboard is displayed on the other computer monitor(s).

communications software. *See* telecommunications software.

conferences. Bulletin boards on a telecommunication system that are labeled for specific topics. A number of conferences might be available on a typical BBS, and users may select those in which they are interested.

connect time. The amount of time a computer is connected to a telecommunications service, such as a BBS or an online database. Charges are often based on connect time.

data bits. The number of bits used to define one character of information during telecommunications. Most systems use eight data bits to define each character. Telecommunications software has a menu selection to set data bits.

dedicated telephone line. A normal telephone line that is used for nothing but telecommunications. This reduces the likelihood that someone will pick up an extension or otherwise interrupt while the modem is online.

download. To receive a file through a telecommunications system. Normally the system does not allow any other activity while the file is being transferred. Contrasts with *capture,* where just the text of the session is saved to a disk.

electronic mail (E-mail). Mail or communications sent and received through electronic, nonpaper methods. Usually a mainframe, a LAN, or a BBS is the vehicle.

FTP (file transfer protocol). The set of rules that allows files to be moved from one Internet site to another.

Gopher. An Internet program that allows an individual to access text and files that are listed in menus in Internet Gopherspace. Gophers automate the process of connecting to resources.

GUI (graphical user interface). Software that allows an individual to make selections by simply pointing and clicking with a mouse. A GUI often incorporates images as active parts of menus.

handshake. Modem settings that must be matched before two computers can communicate through the modems.

host computer. The computer one calls when initiating telecommunications. It might be a mainframe, a LAN, a BBS, or just another personal computer.

HTML (HyperText Markup Language). Coding language used to create hypertext documents to be posted on the Web. HTML code consists of embedded tags that specify how a block of text should appear or that specify how the word is linked to another file on the Internet.

HTTP (HyperText Transfer Protocol). The protocol for moving hypertext files across the World Wide Web.

Integrated Services Digital Network (ISDN). An enhancement to telephone switching systems that allows telephone lines to transmit voice and data in digital form.

Internet. A group of networks connecting governmental institutions, military branches, educational institutions, and commercial companies.

Internet address. A series of letters or numbers that identifies a unique node on the Internet.

Internet Service Provider (ISP). Organizations that provide connections to the Internet. They may be universities or private companies.

logoff. A simple, typed command telling the host computer that the user is finished. Usually it is a choice from an on-screen menu, but sometimes the user actually types *logoff* or *logout*.

logon. The procedure followed to start a telecommunications session. Often it requires the user to enter a name and a correct password.

modem (*modulator-dem*odulator). Modems are used to link computers through telephone lines. *Modulation* is the process of changing computer data into tones that can be sent through a telephone line, and *demodulation* is the process of changing the tones back into computer data.

NSFNET (National Science Foundation Network). The high-speed "network of networks" that serves as the present Internet backbone in the United States.

online. Having a computer connected via modem and telephone lines to another computer.

parity. A specific structure added to the data bits that are going into a modem to check for errors when the data bits arrive at the destination. Parity is usually defined as even, odd, or none. None means that no parity error checking is conducted.

PPP (point-to-point protocol). A data communications technique that allows a direct Internet connection to be established over a standard telephone line. Superior to and replacing SLIP connections.

protocol. In telecommunications, refers to the complete structure of the information that is going from one modem to the other. Data speed in bits per second, parity, the number of start bits, the number of data bits, and the number of stop bits all constitute the protocol. The same settings must be used in both computer modems.

SIG (special-interest group). In bulletin-board systems, about the same as a conference. Some BBSs are set up so that selecting one SIG automatically selects all appropriate conferences on that BBS.

SLIP (serial line Internet protocol). A data transmission method that allows a direct Internet link to take place through a standard telephone line. Similar to a PPP connection.

start bits. (This is a term that you do not normally need to worry about.) Every character of information that goes through a modem is preceded by one or more start bits. All common modem protocols use one start bit.

stop bits. Every character of information that goes through a modem ends with one or more stop bits. Most common telecommunications systems use one stop bit. Communications software has a menu selection to set the number of stop bits.

system operator. The person in charge of maintaining a BBS. The "sysop" monitors the system, answers questions, and checks files that are uploaded.

TCP/IP (Transmission Control Protocol/Internet Protocol). The rules, or protocols, for data transfers on the Internet.

telecommunications software. Program used to allow the computer to communicate through a modem. Most software of this type dials the requested number and sets the modem for the system that is being called.

telnet. The Internet process of providing remote access to computers. Telnet enables a person to run a computer program from a remote location.

terminal emulation. Most mainframe computers are designed to communicate with specific workstations called *terminals*. For a microcomputer to communicate with a mainframe, the microcomputer telecommunications software must be able to perform like, or *emulate*, an appropriate terminal. Most telecommunications software can emulate a variety of common computer terminals.

Uniform Resource Locator (URL). The address structure for the World Wide Web. A unique URL identifies each Web site, allowing others to locate it.

upload. The process of sending a complete file to the host computer.

Veronica. An Internet program that makes it possible to conduct keyword searches for information in Internet Gopherspace.

Web browser. A computer program designed to make it easy for an individual to utilize the World Wide Web portion of the Internet. A Web browser almost always uses a graphical user interface (GUI).

World Wide Web. Hypermedia-based Internet information system. Graphical user interfaces allow users to click a mouse on desired menu items, resulting in text, sound, pictures, or even motion video from all over the world.

TELECOMMUNICATIONS RESOURCES

Telecommunications Services

America Online
8619 Westwood Center Drive
Vienna, VA 22182
800-827-6364

Applelink
P.O. Box 10600
Herndon, VA 22070
408-974-3309

AT&T Learning Network
5501 LBJ Freeway
Dallas, TX 75244
800-367-7225

Big Sky Telegraph
Western Montana College of the
University of Montana
710 S. Atlantic
Dillon, MT 59725-3598
406-683-7870

Classroom Prodigy
Prodigy Services
445 Hamilton Avenue, H8B
White Plains, NY 10601
800-PRODIGY

CompuServe
P.O. Box 20212
Columbus, OH 43220
800-848-8199

Delphi
1030 Massachusetts Avenue
Cambridge, MA 02138
800-544-4005

EcoNet, PeaceNet
Presidio Building 1012, First Floor,
Torney Avenue
P.O. Box 29904
San Francisco, CA 94129-0904
415-561-6100

FidoNet
1151 S.W. Vermont Street
Portland, OR 97219
503-280-5280
jmurray@psg.com

GEnie
GE Information Services
401 N. Washington Street
Rockville, MD 20850
800-638-9636

Global School Net Foundation
P.O. Box 243
Bonita, CA 91902
619-475-4852

GTE Education Services
5525 MacArthur Boulevard
Irving, TX 75038
800-927-3000

International Education and Resource Network (I*EARN)
345 Kear Street
Yorktown Heights, NY 10598
914-962-5864
ed1@copenfund.igc.apc.org

Internet Society
12020 Sunrise Valley Drive, Suite 210
Reston, VA 22091-3429
703-648-9888

Knight-Ridder Information
2440 El Camino Real
Mountain View, CA 94040
800-334-2564

Learning Link
Learning Link National Consortium
356 W. 58th Street
New York, NY 10019
212-560-6613

Microsoft Network
Microsoft Corporation
1 Microsoft Way
Redmond, WA 98052-6399
800-426-9400

National Geographic Kids Network
National Geographic Society
Educational Services
P.O. Box 98019
Washington, DC 20090
800-368-2728

Prodigy
P.O. Box 8129
Gray, TN 37615-0667
800-776-3449

Scholastic Network
Scholastic, Inc.
P.O. Box 7502
Jefferson City, MO 65102
800-246-2986

TERC's Global Lab and LabNet (TERC)
2067 Massachusetts Avenue
Cambridge, MA 02140
617-547-0430

Communications Software

BBN Systems and Technologies
10 Moulton Street
Cambridge, MA 02138

Cello (Internet graphical interface)
Use Internet FTP to log on to:
fatty.law.cornell.edu
type *anonymous* at the login prompt
Enter your E-mail address as
    the password
Currently Cello files are located in
    /pub/LII.Cello

Crosstalk
Attachmate Corporation
3617 131st Avenue SE
Bellevue, WA 98006
800-348-3221

HyperAccess/5
Hilgraeve, Inc.
111 Conant Avenue, Suite A
Monroe, MI 48161
800-826-2760

Internet in a Box
SPRY, Inc.
316 Occidental Avenue South, Suite 200
Seattle, WA 98104
206-957-8998

MicroPhone II
Software Ventures, Inc.
2907 Claremont Avenue
Berkeley, CA 94705
703-709-5500

Microsoft Works
Microsoft Corporation
1 Microsoft Way
Redmond, WA 98052-6399
800-426-9400

Mosaic (Internet Web browser)
Note: The trademark for Mosaic is
held by the board of trustees of
the University of Illinois
ftp://ftp.ncsa.uiuc.edu
Explore the subdirectories for Windows
and Macintosh versions

Netscape (Internet Web browser)
Netscape Communications Corporation
501 E. Middlefield
Mountain View, CA 94043
800-638-7483

PCBoard (BBS software)
Clark Development Company
P.O. Box 571365
Murray, UT 84157
800-356-1686

Point-to-Point
Beagle Brothers
1555 N. Technology
Orem, UT 84057
800-321-4566

Procomm Plus
Datastorm Technologies, Inc.
3212 Lemone Industrial Boulevard
Columbia, MO 65201
800-315-3282

RBBS-PC (BBS software)
Capital PC User Group Software
Library
P.O. Box 1785
West Bethesda, MD 20827-1785
301-762-6775

TBBS (BBS software)
eSoft, Inc.
15200 E. Girard Avenue, Suite 3000
Aurora, CO 80014
303-699-6565

White Knight
FreeSoft Company
105 McKinley Road
Beaver Falls, PA 15010
412-846-2700

Tools for Creating Web Pages

HyperStudio
Roger Wagner Publishers
1050 Pioneer Way
El Cajon, CA 92020
800-421-6525

Internet Assistant
Microsoft Corporation
1 Microsoft Way
Redmond, WA 98052-6399
800-426-9400

Netscape
Netscape Communications Corporation
501 E. Middlefield
Mountain View, CA 94043
800-638-7483

PageMill
Adobe Systems Incorporated
1585 Charleston Road
P.O. Box 7900
Mountain View, CA 94039
415-961-4400

Educational Resources
on the World Wide Web

Academy One Server	http://www.nptn.org/cyber.serv/AOneP/
AskERIC	http://ericir.syr.edu
Classroom Connect	http://www.classroom.net/
EdWeb	http://k12.cnidr.org:90/
Exploratorium	http://www.exploratorium.edu/
Global Schoolnet Foundation	http://www.gsn.org/
GlobalLearn	http://www.globalearn.org
Human Languages Page	http://www.hardlink.com/~chambers/HLP/
Intercultural E-mail Classroom Connections	http://www.stolaf.edu/network/iecc
Library of Congress	http://www.loc.gov
Louvre Museum	http://www.paris.org/Musees/Louvre
My Virtual Reference Desk	http://www.refdesk.com/
NASA Internet in the Classroom	http://quest.arc.nasa.gov/
Newton's Apple	http://ericir.syr.edu/Projects/Newton/
Oregon Trail	http://www.isu.edu/~trinmich/Oregontrail.html
Shakespeare Web	http://www.shakespeare.com
Smithsonian Institute	http://www.si.edu/
Teacher's Guide to School Networks	http://fcit.coedu.usf.edu/network
Teacher's Guide to the Holocaust	http://fcit.coedu.usf.edu/holocaust
Technology Lesson Plans	http://fcit.coedu.usf.edu/tnt/
U.S. Holocaust Museum	http://www.ushmm.org/
Web66	http://web66.coled.umn.edu/
White House	http://www.whitehouse.gov/

REFERENCE LIST

Barron, A. E., and K. S. Ivers. (1996). *The Internet and instruction: Ideas and activities.* Englewood, CO: Libraries Unlimited.

RECOMMENDED READING

All about E-mail. (1996). *Microsoft Magazine* 3(2): 14–26.

Ayre, R. (1995). New paths to the Net [Review of integrated online and Internet services providers]. *PC Magazine* 14(17): 109–49.

Ayre, R., and T. Mace. (1996). Internet access: Just browsing [Review of Web browsers]. *PC Magazine* 15(5): 100–147.

Ayre, R., and K. Reichard. (1995). The web untangled. *PC Magazine* 14(3): 173ff.

Barron, A. E. (1995). *Getting started with telecommunications.* Tampa, FL: Florida Center for Instructional Technology.

Barron, A. E., D. Hoffman, K. Ivers, and L. Sherry. (1995). *Telecommunications: Ideas, activities, and resources.* Tampa, FL: Florida Center for Instructional Technology.

Barron, A. E., and G. W. Orwig. (1995). Digital video and the Internet: A powerful combination. *Journal of Instruction Delivery Systems* 9(3): 10–13.

Barron, A. E., and D. Tai. (1995). The World Wide Web as an instructional delivery tool. *Florida Technology in Education Quarterly* 7(3): 111–18.

Black, L., K. Klingenstein, and N. Songer. (1995). Observations from the Boulder Valley Internet project. *T.H.E. Journal* 22(10): 75–80.

Blankenhorn, D. (1995). ISDN modems push ahead. *Interactive Age* 2(21): 21–22.

Bull, A. (1995). Making waves on the Web: How to create better looking graphics for the Internet. *Photo Electronic Imaging* 38(7): 34–35.

Bush, R. (1993). FidoNet: Technology, tools, and history. *Communications of the ACM* 36(8): 31ff.

Caputo, A. (1994). Seven secrets of searching: How and when to choose online. *MultiMedia Schools* 1(1): 29–33.

Carmona, J. (1995). Educators make faster connections with latest modems and software. *T.H.E. Journal* 22(7): 12–17.

Clyman, J., and L. Seltzer. (1996). The browser battle between Microsoft and Netscape. *PC Magazine* 15(10): 40–41.

Cohen, F. L. (1995). How to plan for Internet access. *MultiMedia Schools* 2(5): 39–43.

Duncan, L. (1995). How to create your first Web page, part 1. *Photo-Electronic Imaging* 38(10): 33–43.

———. (1995). How to create your first Web page, part 2. *Photo-Electronic Imaging* 38(11): 34–36.

———. (1995). How to create your first Web page, part 3. *Photo-Electronic Imaging* 38(12): 10–11.

———. (1996). How to create your first Web page, part 4. *Photo-Electronic Imaging* 39(2): 40–43.

Dutcher, W. (1993). How to retrofit a LAN to access the Internet. *PC Week* 10(45): 1.

Dyrli, O. E., and D. E. Kinnaman. (1996). Energizing the classroom curriculum through telecommunications. *Technology and Learning* 16(4): 65–70.

———. (1996). Teaching effectively with telecommunications. *Technology and Learning* 16(5): 57–62.

Grunin, L.. (1995). Publish without paper! *PC Magazine* 14(3): 110ff.

Hargadon, T. (1995). The state of the info highway. *New Media* 5(10): 44–53.

Johnson, D. (1995). Captured by the Web: K-12 schools and the World Wide Web. *MultiMedia Schools* 2(2): 24–30.

Marcus, S. (1996). Truth and consequences. *Electronic Learning* 15(6): 42–43.

Mendelson, E. (1995). Publish to the Web: No experience required [Review of HTML editors]. *PC Magazine* 14(17): 203–25.

Norr, H. (1995). It sounds darn nice: ISDN. *MacUser* 11(11): 100–104.

Owen, F. G. (1996). Use of the Internet in Florida learning support systems. *T.H.E. Journal* 23(9): 64–68.

Ozer, J. (1996). Sound blasts the Web [Evaluation of continuous delivery audio software]. *PC Magazine* 15(6): 103–28.

———. (1996). Web TV tunes in [Evaluation of Web-based video software]. *PC Magazine* 15(6): 129–45.

Rosenthal, S. (1995). Writing tools for Web pages. *New Media* 5(10): 65–68.

Ross, P. (1995). Relevant telecomputing activities. *Computing Teacher* 22(5): 28–30.

Roth, C. (1996). ISDN modems come to town. *New Media* 6(4): 35–38.

Stout, M., and J. Thompson. (1995). Instructional design issues and the World Wide Web. *Educators' Tech Exchange* 3(1): 24–35.

Talab, R. (1994). Copyright, legal, and ethical issues in the Internet environment. *TechTrends* 39(2): 11–14.

TELECOMMUNICATIONS

An Overview Of

Dr. Ann E. Barron
University of South Florida

Dr. Gary W. Orwig
University of Central Florida

This brochure is an excerpt from:

New Technologies for Education

A Beginner's Guide

Third Edition

To obtain the complete book, contact:

Libraries Unlimited
P.O. Box 6633
Englewood, CO 80155-6633
800-237-6124

The Internet

The Internet is a worldwide group of interconnected computers. It allows a student or teacher to communicate through E-mail, to transfer files, or to access computers at remote locations. It is an excellent resource for global and cultural education because it involves numerous computers from many nations.

There are a wealth of instructional applications for the Internet. For example, students may engage in:

- Pen-pal activities
- Peer-to-peer tutoring
- Simulations
- Electronic publishing
- Basic research
- Original research

The World Wide Web

The World Wide Web, or Web, is the most rapidly evolving portion of the Internet. It consists of documents on the Internet that contain hyperlinks to other documents or files. Recent software programs designed to access the Web (generically called Web browsers) use common mouse "point and click" interfaces. Currently, Microsoft Internet Explorer and Netscape Navigator are the most popular browers.

When multimedia Web sites are accessed, sounds, pictures, or motion images can result from a mouse click.

MS-DOS Configuration

A modem can be external (outside the computer) or internal. An external modem is connected to an MS-DOS computer through a communication port (often called a COM port). Most MS-DOS computers have one or two COM ports, but sometimes it is necessary to purchase an add-in card if the computer does not have the needed port.

An internal modem is a computer card installed inside the computer. Internal modems are very useful for portable computers.

Macintosh Configuration

All Macintosh computers have a built-in modem port (the one with the telephone icon). A cable is needed to connect the modem to this port. The telephone line connects directly into the back of the modem.

Telephone
Wall Jack

Computer

Telephone
Line

Modem

Modems

Modems are required for many of the applications of telecommunications. A modem (MOdulator-DEModulator) allows two computers to communicate as though they were connected directly together, even though they might be thousands of miles apart.

Modems connect computers to standard telephone lines. Most standard telephone lines transmit only audio tones, such as those found in human voices. A computer, though, manipulates digital information in a binary code of 0s and 1s.

The modem translates (or modulates) the 0s and 1s of an outgoing message into a fluctuating tone that will go through the telephone line. At the same time, the modem listens for a different tone that comes from the distant computer's modem. As this tone comes through the telephone line, the local modem demodulates it back into the 0s and 1s that the local computer can understand. In this way, the two computers can communicate with each other.

Computer programs that can operate modems are called telecommunication software. These programs can perform a number of activities. For example, they format the arriving text for your computer screen by inserting carriage returns and line feeds as needed. They also contain a dialing function so that you can input the telephone number of the receiving computer.

Overview

Telecommunications allow individuals to connect their computers to other computers around the world. One person can communicate with another simply by typing a message on a computer keyboard, and information previously available only at libraries is now just a keypress or two away. Even pictures and sounds can be selected and downloaded from collections around the globe.

Applications

E-mail
E-mail stands for "electronic mail." E-mail messages are created by a person on a computer and then electronically sent to one or more people. As long as everyone involved has an E-mail address, the mail can be sent almost anywhere in the world.

File Transfers
With telecommunications software, you can transfer files from one location to another. Text files, computer programs, pictures, and sounds can be uploaded to a remote location or downloaded from another location.

Remote Access
Telecommunications software allows a person at one location to run programs on a computer at another location. For example, a university library might have its catalog online.

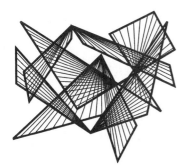

9

Teleconferencing and Distance Learning

A Scenario

Marcelo is so excited that he can hardly sit still, but he has to. He is sitting at a multimedia workstation at his school. If he moves much he goes off the screen of the small video camera that is pointing at him.

Marcelo is an international exchange student who is in the eighth grade in an Orlando, Florida, school. His home is in Brazil near Rio de Janeiro. He has been in Orlando for six months and has survived the worst of his homesickness, but he still misses his family and friends a lot.

One of Marcelo's diversions has been to learn as much about technology as he possibly can. His school back home does access the Internet, but the connections are not as advanced as the Internet access at his Orlando school.

Marcelo has used the Internet to send E-mail to friends in Brazil, but it usually takes a week or so to get an answer back. This isn't because it takes a long time for the messages to go back and forth but because there are only a couple of workstations at his school in Brazil, and students get just a few minutes a week to work on them.

Marcelo has been impressed with the multimedia aspects of the Internet. After he learned some of the basic searching and downloading techniques that are used on the World Wide Web, he assembled a multimedia presentation about his hometown. It included photographs, maps, sounds, and the current weather report.

A couple of months ago, the Orlando school added a simple little camera, costing less than $100, to one of the workstations in the media center. Some software called CUSeeMe was downloaded from the Internet, and suddenly it was possible to see and talk to other people around the world. The images were black and white and tended to be "jerky," but they were images of real people. Marcelo quickly discovered that there were two ways to use the software. He could join *reflectors* that served as meeting rooms for small groups, or he could go *point-to-point* to see and talk with individuals. He learned that the point-to-point process worked better when long distances and slow transmission rates were likely.

Marcelo used CUSeeMe to bring Brazil to his Orlando classroom. He found a Brazilian university that had a beginning teacher program, and he scheduled a conference between several college students who were studying to be teachers and the students in his Orlando classroom. The Brazilian students were anxious to try out their English abilities but often had to revert to their native Portuguese. Marcelo translated quickly and efficiently for his fellow students in Orlando. The Orlando students were amazed that most of the Brazilian students could speak two or three languages. There was a lot of discussion and a number of spin-off projects about international isolationism in the United States.

But none of that explains why Marcelo is sitting in front of the workstation and the excitement he feels. Unknown to him, several parents in Orlando had been in contact with his school in Brazil. They discovered that just one key item was needed to allow two-way video conferences with Marcelo's home school. It took only a week to raise the $100 needed for a simple camera, and now that camera had arrived at his school in Brazil. Marcelo was about to click on the *connect* button to establish a point-to-point connection that would let him see his friends for the first time in six months.

The connection went smoothly, but what followed was far less than organized. As soon as the image started to build in the corner of his screen, Marcelo recognized his best friend Carlos from Brazil. The same thing obviously happened at the other end, because suddenly the screen became jerky as Carlos and other friends started jumping around and pointing. The speech was also a problem because the connection was fairly slow. Speech was delayed by a couple seconds, was slightly broken up, and could only go one way at a time.

At first the awkward communications were frustrating for everyone, but gradually Marcelo taught his friends to sit still, to talk slowly, and to pause for a couple of seconds after talking. Soon the conversation was going pretty smoothly. Then came the biggest surprise of all. Marcelo's picture from Brazil suddenly went blurry as it does when someone moves quickly or when the scene changes. As the picture reformed, he realized that he was looking at his mother! His school in Brazil had invited his family to the event! It was obvious that his family had been paying close attention during the first part of the teleconference, because as his mother and father sat in front of the camera they were so stiff that they barely moved. They did talk though, and they seemed even happier to see him than he was to see them. His brother and sister even seemed happy to talk with him. That was a first!

After about 20 minutes it was time to sign off. As happy as everyone was to see and talk to each other, the Internet videoconference technology was a real strain. It took a lot of concentration to sit still, and it was even harder to talk slowly with appropriate pauses. Marcelo's family reminded him to be sure to thank his classmates' parents for sending the camera, and Marcelo's friends in Brazil had already set up another time a few days later to meet again. They were really excited about meeting with Marcelo's American classmates and had already suggested a couple of topics to discuss.

Teleconferencing is the process of communicating with one or more people who are at distant locations. Unlike E-mail, teleconferencing usually takes place in real time and provides interactive conversations. Many educators think that educational applications of teleconferencing are in the distant future. Although it is true that techniques such as high-quality two-way video teleconferencing are still too expensive for many schools, a number of other approaches for distance learning are currently in use in school systems. This chapter includes the following:

- An introduction to the three most common teleconferencing technologies
- Educational applications for teleconferencing
- Audio teleconferencing
- Audiographic teleconferencing
- Videoconferencing
- Digital data lines
- Resources for further information

INTRODUCTION

Teleconferencing techniques are essential components of several forms of distance education. When compared with other educational delivery strategies, teleconferencing has historically been complex, difficult to administer, and expensive. However, recent advances in technology are creating more practical teleconferencing options for school systems. Three distinct categories of teleconferencing technologies are considered in this chapter.

Audio teleconferencing. This technology uses standard telephones for audio conferences. Minimal equipment is required, but the lack of visual interaction can limit learner engagement. Audio teleconferencing requires substantial advanced planning and preparation of adjunct materials to keep the educational process productive.

Audiographic teleconferencing. This technology adds the element of two-way image transmission to audio teleconferencing. With computer and facsimile technologies, this variation allows figures, charts, and still pictures to be exchanged during the conference. The interactive exchange of images along with the audio enhances the free expression of ideas during the educational process without inordinate expenses.

Videoconferencing. This technology combines full-motion video with audio. It is useful for situations that require the use of motion to enhance the course content. Most forms of videoconferencing still require careful cost justification in educational settings, but recently developed digital techniques promise a variety of cost-effective applications.

EDUCATIONAL APPLICATIONS

There are several applications for teleconferencing in educational settings. Although some applications, such as using guest speakers through audio teleconferencing, require minimal expenditures, other applications, such as the contract delivery of courses, require major curricular decisions and significant financial commitments.

The Classroom Guest Speaker

Teleconferencing allows the instructor to bring into the classroom a guest who would normally be unable to visit. Long distances, difficult travel conditions, or busy schedules make it impractical for many individuals to visit school classrooms as guest speakers. A telephone line into the classroom and a good speakerphone often solve these problems. Prominent persons are usually more willing to take 15 minutes to talk with a class by telephone than to spend a couple of hours traveling to and from the school.

Homebound Students

One of the original educational applications of teleconferencing was to provide a classroom connection for students who were homebound because of illness or injury. The same basic equipment that brings guest speakers into the classroom can be used to bring the classroom to a student. Typically, this approach is used briefly during the day for special discussions or other activities that directly involve the distant student.

Distance Tutoring

Some school systems have implemented audio-teleconferencing systems to provide students access to tutors during the early evening hours. Depending on the system, the tutors can work at their own homes or at a central location, such as the school. Active community programs often encourage students and parents to become involved in the tutoring program.

Distributed Classes

A number of school districts in less-populated areas are using teleconferencing to share teachers among several schools. In this way, the few students who need a course in each school can add up to a single class large enough to justify the cost of a teacher. The teacher stays at one school, but classrooms in several other schools can be linked through telephone, audiographic means, or video to the teacher's classroom. Proctors or teacher's aides supervise the students in the remote classrooms, distribute learning materials, and administer tests.

Contract Courses

Sometimes, teacher shortages or low enrollments make it impossible for a school system to offer certain classes. A number of companies now provide selected courses to schools that cannot teach those courses in the traditional manner. Foreign-language and advanced math topics are among the most common courses available through commercial services. These courses are normally delivered through satellite television channels with audio teleconferencing for student interaction.

AUDIO TELECONFERENCING

Standard telephone technologies have been in use since the 1940s to provide educational opportunities to people who are separated by distance. Audio teleconferencing is noted for its simplicity, its adaptability to a variety of situations, and its relatively low cost. Although some of the equipment, such as speakerphones and directional microphones, has become more highly refined over the years, the primary component of audio teleconferencing remains the inexpensive and common dial-up telephone line.

To prepare for an audio-teleconferencing technique such as interviewing a distant guest speaker, the teacher needs only a telephone line and a speakerphone. (See fig. 9.1.) If the classroom is large or if frequent student interaction is expected, a system with an amplified speaker and additional microphones for the students will be useful. The addition of sound-absorbing materials, such as an acoustic ceiling or draperies, greatly reduces the "talking in a barrel" distortion that often degrades a speakerphone conversation.

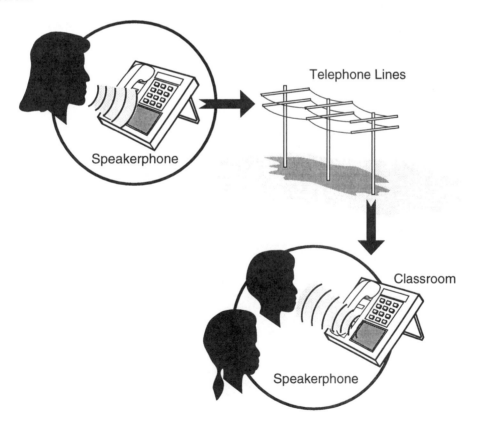

Figure 9.1. Basic Audio-Teleconferencing System.

Speakerphones

Speakerphones have been improved in the past several years, but they still have some limitations. Common speakerphones are called *simplex* message devices. This means they do not allow simultaneous two-way conversations. In other words, the people at both ends of the connection cannot talk at the same time. In some ways, this process is like that of water flowing through a pipe. The water can go in either direction, but it can go in only one direction at any one moment.

This flow is in contrast to the standard telephone handset, which is called a *duplex* message device. A standard handset is more like a water system with two pipes—one for water going in each direction. In a standard telephone handset, the earpiece and the microphone are sufficiently separated to prevent faint sounds coming through the earpiece from feeding back into the microphone.

When a person's voice is coming through a speakerphone, however, the standard speakerphone must turn off its microphone. If it is not turned off, the incoming sound will be picked up by the microphone and almost instantly routed directly back to the person originating the message. At the least, this creates a strong echo of the speaker's voice. More likely, it causes a feedback squeal similar to that generated when a microphone is too close to a loudspeaker in a public-address system.

When the distant person pauses, or when someone in a classroom talks loudly, the standard speakerphone switches off its speaker and activates its microphone. At this point, the voice of the distant person is cut off, and the flow reverses so that the distant person can hear what is being said in the classroom. Modern speakerphones are capable of making these simplex changes in direction so quickly that it is usually only a minor distraction. As both guest speakers and students become familiar with the limitations, they learn to establish a pattern of brief pauses during interactive discussions to prevent interruptions.

Long-distance telephone communications may be further complicated by the slight delays created when the telephone call is routed through satellites. Signals may be routed to one or two distant satellites to travel halfway around the globe. When this happens, delays from a quarter second to a half second occur as the signals travel these long distances. These delays, combined with the simplex communications of speakerphones, can cause awkward false starts in conversations. If satellite links are involved in an audio teleconference, longer pauses must be built into the conversation.

New, full duplex speakerphones are rapidly dropping in price. What cost $2,000 just a few years ago now costs $400 to $500. The ConferenceLink CS1000 by USRobotics, for example, currently sells for around $400. It offers full duplex technology, three microphones, a speaker, and automatic gain control that adjusts as people speak from different locations in the room. When a modern full duplex speakerphone is used in a small classroom, conversations can flow just as easily as they can through regular telephone handsets.

Telephone Bridges

Many telephone lines have simple conference-calling features that make it easy to connect three locations. The person at a telephone line with conference-calling features simply dials the other two locations, and with the press of a button, all three are interconnected. If speakerphones are used at all three locations, the volumes might have to be adjusted so that they are evenly balanced. If either of the other people involved in the call also has conference-calling features, then it is possible to tie in, or *daisychain,* additional locations, but this process often results in audio levels that are too low for comfortable use.

When more than three locations must be connected in a teleconferencing process, the best solution is the use of a technology called the telephone *bridge.* The bridge is an electronic system that links multiple telephone lines and automatically balances all audio levels. The bridge can be provided through the telephone company or competing long-distance services, or it can be owned and operated by the school system. Unless a bridge is used several times a day, it is usually more economical to rent one.

A telephone bridge does not involve any classroom equipment other than the standard telephone line. The actual bridge system is located at the telephone company or, in the case of a privately owned system, at the school switchboard. Most school systems do not own bridges because of the number of outside telephone lines required. For example, to connect a bridge of 25 students with each in a different location, 25 telephone lines would be required. (See fig. 9.2.) Most school systems are not able to justify the number of telephone lines required for a bridge. In any case, prior arrangements must be made to reserve the bridge for the date and the length of time the conference is expected to last.

A bridge can be either call in or call out. With a call-in bridge, participants in the telephone conference are given the bridge telephone number ahead of time. The participants then call the number at the beginning of the conference. The bridge system automatically connects the calls to the conference. A call-out bridge arrangement requires a person, usually an operator, to dial the telephone numbers of all the locations that will participate in the conference. As each number is reached, it becomes connected to the conference.

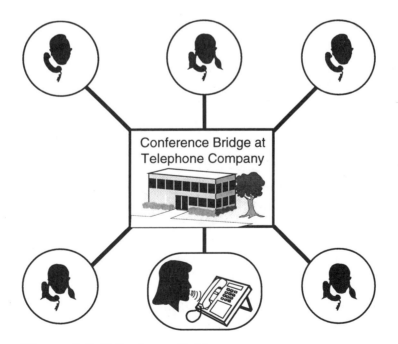

Figure 9.2. Telephone Bridge.

Each of these techniques has some strengths and some weaknesses. The call-in technique allows individuals to call from any location, but the conference must be planned far enough in advance to distribute the telephone number for the bridge. In addition, the individual participants will be charged for any long-distance fees that might apply. However, a participant can enter the conference late or reenter the conference if accidentally disconnected. The bridge telephone number can be set to remain open during the entire meeting.

The call-out process does not require advance distribution of a telephone number for the bridge. In fact, most telephone companies and long-distance services offer on-demand call-out bridge systems that can be operated entirely through a Touch-Tone telephone. In these systems, the conference leader calls a number for the bridge management system and then uses an automated process to enter the telephone numbers to be connected together for the conference. With a call-out system, all charges for the conference, including any long-distance fees that might apply, are billed to the conference leader's telephone number. One major disadvantage of a call-out system is that it is difficult for a participant to enter the conference late or be reconnected if accidentally disconnected during the conference.

Internet Audio Conferencing

The Internet and the World Wide Web in particular have been used for some time to transfer digitized sound files. In the last couple of years, there has been a gradual expansion of this capability into the digitization and transfer of real-time conversations. An early stage has been called almost-real-time audio because two separate stages were involved in the transmission of a conversation. First, a person digitized and compressed a sentence or two. As soon as the *push to talk* key (usually a mouse click) was released, the sentence was transmitted. Although conversations could take place, there were long pauses between sentences during the data transmissions.

More recent software (given the generic name of Internet *telephony* software) has the ability to digitize and compress sound on the fly, meaning that it is transmitted almost the instant it is spoken. An example is Speak Freely version 6.1 by John Walker. Speak Freely is freeware that is available on the World Wide Web at http://www.four-milab.ch/speakfree/windows/. (See the Resource section at the end of this chapter for additional Internet telephone resources.)

There are some limits, however, that are determined by the specific sound-digitizing boards in the computers. Perhaps the most significant limitation is simplex versus duplex communication. Many earlier soundboards were not designed to produce sound from the distant source at the same time they were digitizing sound from the microphone. As a result, people must use a *push to talk* button, and sound can go only one direction at a time. New soundboards for PCs and built-in circuitry on new Macs have been designed to handle full-duplex communication. When appropriate software is used with these boards, two-way communications can take place.

Internet telephony software is in a period of rapid growth. There are indications that a standard may evolve soon, but currently there is little likelihood that competing products will be compatible. It is most likely that a popular software product will eventually dominate the market, and others will follow it. For example, the latest version of the Netscape Navigator Web browser incorporates the CoolTalk program.

Because Netscape Navigator is popular and works on Macs, PCs, and Unix machines, the CoolTalk program will receive wide coverage.

Other factors also enter into the eventual success of Internet telephony software. (See fig. 9.3.) In particular, talking over the Internet allows individuals and businesses to bypass standard telephone charges and taxes. Because long-distance communication over the Internet is currently far less expensive than standard long-distance communication, there will almost certainly be a noticeable economic impact in the near future on long-distance carriers and the taxes they pay to governmental agencies. With that decline in taxes, there may be increased efforts to recover more taxes out of Internet usage.

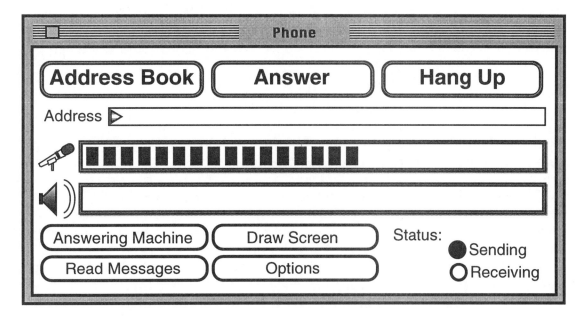

Figure 9.3. A Typical Internet Telephony Screen.

Words of Advice

Audio teleconferencing is the most economical method available for interactive distance education. The strength of the technology is attributed to the extensive telephone network within the United States and many other countries. The greatest weakness of the method is its inability to use visual information. All visual materials must be planned and distributed prior to the distance-education event. Practical experience has also shown that audio-only communication is stressful to many learners. An audio-teleconference lesson should contain short segments of audio interaction—not more than 15 minutes—intermixed with other activities.

Having a speaker visit by telephone often takes more planning than having the speaker visit in person. The speaker should be contacted days in advance to attend to the following details:

Topic and objectives. Confirm that the speaker is knowledgeable about the topic and understands the objectives of the lesson.

Length of presentation. Be specific about the amount of time that can be allocated. Many adults have forgotten that in most schools it simply is not possible to take an extra 10 minutes to finish a discussion. If the end-of-class bell is going to ring at 1:45, make certain that the speaker realizes it and plans accordingly.

Style of presentation. Understand in advance the style of presentation that will take place. If the speaker wants to speak first and answer questions at the end, prepare your students for this particular style.

Supplementary materials. Ask the speaker to anticipate any handouts or other visual materials that might be of value during the presentation. Distribute these materials ahead of time so that they will be ready for the class.

AUDIOGRAPHIC TELECONFERENCING

Audiographic teleconferencing includes the exchange of still images along with telephone communications. Depending on the equipment used, the images can be black and white or color; however, they will always be static images rather than motion pictures. A variety of equipment choices is available to create or capture the image at the site where it originates and to display the image at the distant location.

The addition of graphics to an audio conference allows the exchange of spontaneously drawn sketches or illustrations. For example, it is much easier to show an image of a complex formula than it is to describe it. In the same vein, it is better to discuss an organizational chart when everyone in the conversation can see it. Graphics devices can also eliminate the need to distribute materials before the conference. Instead, each graphic is transmitted to all sites at the time it is displayed by the conference leader.

Facsimile Machines

The most basic equipment needed for an audiographic teleconference is a pair of facsimile, or fax, machines added to the speakerphones that are used in a standard audio teleconference. The fax machines allow paper sketches to be sent back and forth during the conference. To avoid interruptions in the audio, a second telephone line should be dedicated to the fax machines.

Fax machines, like many other audiographic devices, are designed to work only in pairs. In other words, if five sites are involved in the teleconference, then a fax machine at one site can send an image to only one of the remaining sites at a time. Newer fax machines allow the creation of mailing lists, however, so that additional sites can be sent the same image in quick succession. The use of faxes at multiple sites mandates that each site has one line for the telephone and a separate line for the fax; otherwise, the interruptions in the conversation would become too distracting as images were sent to and from the multiple locations.

Computers

Audiographic teleconferencing is one of the most rapidly evolving areas of distance education. Although fax machines can be used to supply basic graphics requirements, computers and related peripherals have become the primary vehicles of audiographic teleconferencing.

A computer used for audiographic teleconferencing uses a color display system connected to a large classroom monitor or a projection system. (See fig. 9.4.) The computer also contains a video-capture card that is connected to one or more external video cameras. (See chapter 5 for more information about video-capture cards.) One of these cameras may be mounted on a copy stand and provide controls for zooming in and out and focusing on whatever documents might be placed on the stand. A mouse or graphics tablet is used to allow the creation of freehand drawings and to position a pointer on a captured video image.

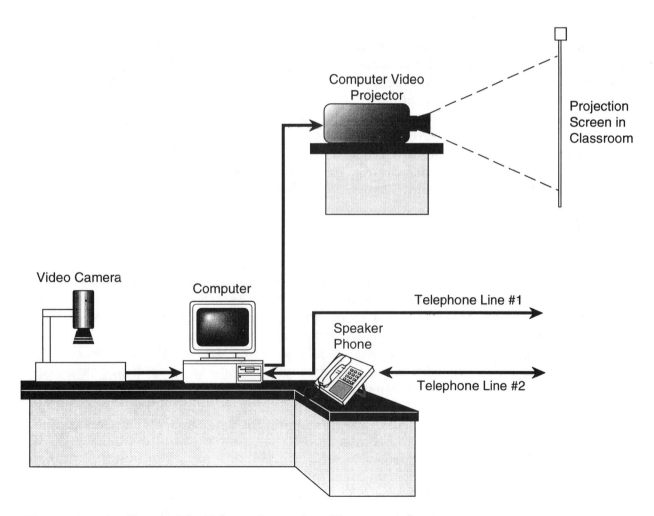

Figure 9.4. Audiographic Teleconferencing Classroom System.

Finally, the computer must contain a high-speed modem or fax modem that connects the system to the telephone line. The images used during the teleconference are sent or received through the modem. Fax modems are most useful when visuals have been prepared in advance using appropriate computer-based software, such as a graphics program. (See chapter 8 for more information on modems and fax modems.)

Although these hardware components have been available for several years, convenient software that integrates the hardware into a complete audiographic system is just starting to become available. Many computer-based audiographic systems use custom-developed software or collections of commercial programs that are still not fully integrated. As software improves, it will be much easier for a teacher to select or prepare appropriate illustrations as an audiographic conference is taking place. At present, teachers must be well trained in the use of the systems and must prepare most materials before the class.

Audiographic Teleconferencing on the Internet

Just as the Internet has become a factor in audio teleconferencing, it is also entering the audiographic domain. Several Internet products that have audio capabilities also have graphic-display areas that are often called *white boards*. A white board allows an image or text to be *clipped* from an application and *pasted* onto it. Once this has taken place, the workstations at both ends of the conversation display the image. Simple drawing tools then allow people at either end to draw arrows, circles, or other simple symbols to highlight portions of the image. Two popular Internet programs that incorporate audio and white boards are Netscape Navigator's CoolTalk and White Pine's Enhanced CUSeeMe. CUSeeMe has an added feature—motion video.

Words of Advice

Audiographic teleconferencing is a compromise between inexpensive but visually limited audio-only techniques and the more costly and complex motion-video techniques. If the intended lessons can benefit from the interactive use of still visuals and only two sites are involved, then audiographic techniques are the medium of choice. Because audiographic teleconferencing is currently going through such a dynamic stage of development, it is impossible to recommend specific hardware and software. However, common sense should be used when trying to match systems to applications. Some of the following factors should be considered.

Number of simultaneous sites. Most audiographic systems connect two sites. If equipment is advertised to connect more than two sites, ask for demonstrations to see just how easy it is to exchange images among the sites.

Resolution of images. The greater the detail or resolution of the transmitted image, the longer it takes to transmit it. Most systems allow a choice of several resolutions. There is not much reason to send images in greater detail than can be displayed at the other end. For example, if a projection system can display only 640 by 480 pixel-level (VGA) graphics, there is no reason to send 800 by 600 pixel-level (SVGA) images. The higher-level pictures will take longer to send, but they will not look much different on the limited projection system.

Color of images. The more colors in a transmitted image, the longer it takes to transmit the image. If only 16-color images can be displayed on the systems, there is little reason to transmit 256-color images: The latter will not look much different but will take two times longer to transmit.

Type of telephone lines required. Most audiographic systems require one or two standard dial-up telephone lines. A few systems require special digital telephone lines, which will be discussed later in the chapter. Because of the differences in cost, ensure that any additional benefits offered by digital line systems are essential before committing to the expense.

Software compatibility with other packages. Audiographic software is still limited in commercial availability. Many audiographic systems are sold as complete packages with custom-written software that cannot be modified. It is preferable to have a system that allows simple modifications in the set up program so that it can adapt to new or different peripherals. The software should also be compatible with images and text that are created through commercial word-processing and graphics programs.

VIDEOCONFERENCING

Full-motion video teleconferencing, or videoconferencing, offers the closest option to actually being there. The most common form of videoconferencing is one-way video with two-way audio; two-way video and audio techniques are becoming popular for applications such as desktop videoconferencing through microcomputers.

In a typical videoconferencing application, the television image is distributed from the teleconference leader's classroom through cable, microwave, or satellite to distant sites. Two-way video uses additional channels to return images from distant sites back to the teleconference leader's classroom. Audio is usually managed through a standard telephone bridge, although two-way systems often transmit the audio and video signals together.

Videoconferencing is the method of choice for many forms of business, military, and industrial training. Though it can be expensive, it is far less costly than transporting people from all over the country to one location for training. New technologies are reducing the costs of some types of videoconferencing to the point where many school systems are now contracting for teledelivery of courses when they do not have teachers available for the courses. By using some of the newest digital techniques, schools can set up desktop videoconferencing systems that function on a worldwide scale through the Internet.

Satellite Videoconferencing

Satellite videoconferencing is one of the older, more established techniques. Two distinct sets of equipment are needed for satellite systems: *uplink,* which creates and transmits the signal to the satellite, and *downlink,* which is necessary to receive and display the signal. (See fig. 9.5.)

Satellite videoconferences usually require a studio classroom for the teacher. This classroom must be properly wired for the lighting, microphones, and cameras needed to produce an acceptable lesson. The studio is usually connected to a control room, where one or more technicians control the television cameras and microphones. The resulting television signal is then connected to an uplink transmitter—a large satellite dish that beams the signal to the satellite. Uplink transmitters are expensive and are often shared with other schools or businesses.

The receiving sites of satellite videoconferences must have satellite downlinks. The most critical part of a downlink is the receiving dish antenna and its associated electronics. These dishes, common even in backyards, select and amplify the desired satellite signals. The signal is then fed into the distant classrooms, where it is displayed on standard television monitors or projection systems.

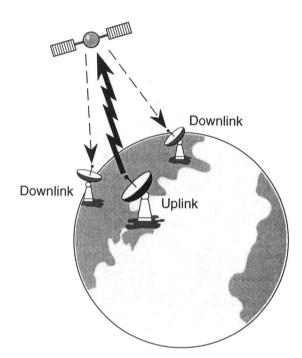

Figure 9.5. Videoconferencing via Satellite.

With regular satellite transmissions, the outgoing audio is combined with the picture much as it is in commercial broadcasts. To provide audio interaction with the instructor or other students, the distant classrooms must also have an audio-teleconferencing system—usually a telephone bridge.

Satellite videoconferencing is expensive. It would not be cost effective for most school systems to use uplinks to originate distance-education classes unless the school systems were in a position to market the classes over wide geographic areas. It is reasonable, however, for a school to use a downlink to receive purchased courses that are delivered through satellite channels.

Microwave Television Conferencing

Satellites are a popular method for enabling video communications over long distances. Microwave transmissions provide a cost-effective method for educational applications of video teleconferencing in more localized areas. Most microwave systems are designed to transmit video signals to areas that are not more than 20 miles apart. The most popular systems use microwave frequencies that have been designated by the Federal Communications Commission (FCC) as Instructional Television Fixed Service

(ITFS) stations. When compared with satellite or commercial broadcast television, ITFS stations operate at a low power that makes the transmission equipment relatively inexpensive. Reception equipment is also relatively inexpensive as long as the receiving sites are located within 20 miles of the transmitter and there are no hills or tall buildings to block the signal.

ITFS has become popular with community colleges and universities as a method of distributing courses throughout communities. By using pairs of ITFS channels, two-way video teleconferencing can be set up between a main-campus classroom and a branch-campus classroom.

One drawback of microwave ITFS communication, however, involves the limited number of channels available in any one area. Many metropolitan areas already have all available channels in use, so no further expansion of ITFS teleconferencing is possible in these areas.

Cable Television

Almost all cable television systems allow schools to transmit television courses over their systems. In some areas, school systems use this technique to offer informal or formal education courses to the community at large. This is most effective in areas where a high percentage of the community subscribes to the cable television system.

A second use for cable television is to link the schools in a community with common course offerings or contract courses. For example, if two area high schools do not each have enough students to justify an advanced math course, they might team up to teach a single course delivered through cable television. In one school the teacher would conduct a regular class; in the other the students would be connected through a standard cable television channel.

Course distribution through cable television systems is cost effective. In some cases, only the basic studio classroom equipment is needed if the cable company can provide a direct link to the cable system. In other cases, a microwave link or other connection is required to send the television signal from the classroom to the *front end* or origination point for the cable television signals.

Cable companies will soon be able to use the technology of digitizing video to offer hundreds of channels to each home and school. Whereas many of these channels will be used for commercial entertainment purposes, it is almost certain that a larger number of channels will become available for education.

Because audio and video can now be digitized into data, cable television companies and telephone companies are negotiating with government agencies to broaden their services. Telephone companies seek to provide video services traditionally offered by cable companies, and cable companies seek to provide communications services typically provided by telephone companies. If communications systems do become less regulated, then the distinctions between cable television and telephone systems will blur.

Desktop
Videoconferencing

Desktop videoconferencing is a technique that uses a computer along with a camera and microphone at one site to transmit video and audio to a computer at another site. Several companies using MS-DOS, Macintosh, or UNIX computers have demonstrated such systems, which can place a small, live image of another person at another location onto the computer screen. To transmit and display the video, all the computers involved must have a videoconferencing board installed. (See fig. 9.6.) These boards often have the ability to *c*ompress and *de*compress the digitized video, and thus are called codec boards (see chapter 5 for more information on digital video).

There are a couple of limitations to desktop videoconferencing at the moment. First, the images are usually transmitted at 15 images per second—half the normal video speed. This causes the video to appear somewhat jerky if any rapid motion takes place in the scene.

A second restriction is related to the connection between the computers. Most systems have been demonstrated either through LANs or through ISDN lines. Because the fast, new digital lines are still expensive in many areas, desktop videoconferencing systems might be limited to localized applications for several years. Still, products such as the PictureTel ISDN Videoconferencing System have produced amazing results at a fraction of the cost of videoconferencing just a few years ago.

Desktop videoconferencing is still in its infancy, but it will almost certainly become a major force in educational applications of videoconferencing. The present focus is on business communications, conferences, and document sharing, but the predicted low cost of this technology will make it appealing to schools.

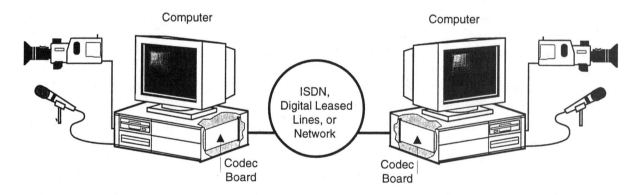

Figure 9.6. Desktop Videoconferencing.

Internet
Videoconferencing

Software is now evolving that allows limited videoconferencing over the Internet. At this moment, the best known product is Cornell University's shareware product called CUSeeMe. A commercial version, Enhanced CUSeeMe, is marketed by White Pine Software. CUSeeMe works on Macs, PCs, and UNIX machines. To transmit video, a video camera and digitizing card are required on the workstation. A microphone, speakers (or headset), and an audio card are required for audio.

CUSeeMe produces a small 160-by-120-pixel window of "motion" video. Depending upon the speed of the connection, the motion can range from 1 to about 15 frames per second. The size of the image window can be increased to 320 by 240 pixels, but the resolution is not increased. The pixels are simply made bigger. The shareware version produces a black-and-white image, while the commercial version can produce either black-and-white or color images.

In addition to the motion image, CUSeeMe transmits sound. Depending upon the type of soundboards in use in the workstations, either *push to talk* simplex sound or *bidirectional* duplex sound are possible. Sound quality also varies with the speed of the connection. With a high-speed connection such as an ISDN line or a direct LAN connection, sound is at least as good as a telephone conference. When slower modems and long distances are involved, an extremely long delay—up to 30 seconds—can sometimes be involved in the audio.

The enhanced version of CUSeeMe also has a white-board capability. In theory, it is possible to clip an image from an application, place it on the white board, then watch your conversation partner as you both mark or further illustrate the image on the white board. For this to go smoothly, however, a high-speed ISDN or direct LAN connection is essential.

Finally, CUSeeMe offers one other useful feature. In addition to one-to-one connections, it is possible to use a CUSeeMe reflector to establish multiple connections. A reflector functions like a telephone bridge in that it is an Internet server computer that is running special CUSeeMe software. When a group of people "dial in" by specifying the reflector's Internet address, they can all see and talk to each other. Multiple little windows open on each workstation, each with an image of one of the other participants. (See fig. 9.7 on page 248.) It is possible to speak to the entire group or privately to individuals. However, for a CUSeeMe reflector to be functional, it must have extremely fast connections. Usually a direct LAN connection or a high-speed data line is required.

Although all the technology sounds exciting, it is still early in the development process. The images that are produced by such products as CUSeeMe are extremely low in quality and have limited instructional uses at this point. With luck, it is possible to identify an individual if he or she fills the entire window, but even then there is no synchronization between lips and sound. Internet videoconferencing is an emerging technology that needs to be tracked carefully.

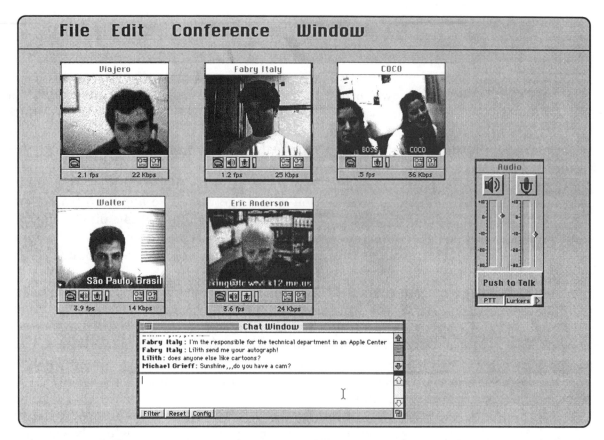

Figure 9.7. CUSeeMe Reflector. Printed with Permission from White Pine Software, Inc.

DIGITAL DATA LINES

Telephone companies and other vendors provide a variety of communications services beyond the basic dial-up voice lines. Several new techniques digitize and compress television signals and video so that they can be sent through digital telephone data lines. These are not the same telephone lines used in regular telephone conversations or modem connections. Instead, digital data lines are designed to allow the transmission of digitized information more efficiently than standard audio telephone lines. Digital data lines are important for videographic and video teleconferencing as well as for interconnecting LANs into wide area networks.

In general, the most commonly used services fall into two categories: digital dial-up (called circuit switched) and dedicated leased lines. Digital data lines can transmit data at rates that start at 56Kbps and go up to 45 million bits per second (Mbps). The higher transmission rates allow digitized video and audio to be transmitted from place to place in direct competition with satellite video transmission.

Circuit-Switched Systems

Circuit-switched digital systems are the most like standard telephone lines. Usually, a set monthly fee provides access to the system, and additional fees accumulate as the system is used. In most cases, a dial-up process connects the sites. There are two common digital circuit-switched systems. The oldest is the 56Kbps line, which is used exclusively for computer data transfer. These systems cost about $50 a month plus 8¢ to 30¢ per minute for use. Switched 56Kbps lines are used mainly by businesses and schools to interconnect small LANs into a wide area network (WAN).

A new standard called Integrated Services Digital Network (ISDN) is rapidly replacing all older circuit-switched systems. ISDN systems are designed to handle voice and data in a variety of combinations. A typical ISDN line is called a Basic Rate Interface, or BRI. Each BRI has the capacity for two *bearer* or B channels and one *delta* or D channel. Each B channel can transmit a standard voice telephone conversation or each can transfer data at 64Kbps. The two B channels can be combined for a transmission rate of 128Kbps. The D channel is usually used for internal purposes.

ISDN has great potential because it can use the copper telephone wire system currently in place. To implement ISDN on a large scale, telephone companies need to upgrade switching equipment, and homes and schools need to upgrade their telephones and computer interfaces. This transition will happen gradually as older equipment reaches the end of its useful life. ISDN has the potential of bringing true digital transmission to every home and school in the nation.

At present, ISDN availability and costs vary dramatically. In some areas, ISDN lines are available for nearly the same cost as standard voice lines, but in other areas they are either expensive or unavailable. In the southeastern United States, a basic ISDN bill for a home in a metropolitan area would currently be about $75 per month. Part of the reason for the high cost is that some governmental agencies insist that an ISDN line must cost at least the equal of two standard lines because two "conversations" can take place at one time. Many taxes are based upon basic rates for individual telephone lines, and some politicians fear losing a growing source of income. Costs are expected to drop, however, as availability and demand increase over the next several years.

Dedicated Leased Lines

If a school requires 24-hour-a-day access to computers in branch centers or videoconferencing, then leased data lines might be the most sensible route. Although almost all telephone services are technically leased from a telephone company, a *leased* data line refers to one that provides a constant, private connection between two points. There is no need to dial a number to connect to the distant point because the line continuously links the two points.

A common voice line can be leased as a dedicated line, but there is no technical and little economic advantage to doing this. Instead, most higher performance digital data lines are usually leased. The two most common types of leased lines are referred to as T1 and T3. The capabilities of these lines are incredible.

T1 leased digital lines. A standard T1 line allows digital information to be transmitted at 1.544Mbps. This transmission speed is almost 54 times faster than a 28,800-bit-per-second modem. The standard T1 line can transmit digitized video conferences, although video-compression techniques are still needed. T1 lines are also commonly used to link large local LANs into a wide area network or the Internet. Large amounts of data can flow through such a linkage, so the entire system functions smoothly.

Performance has its price, however. Distance is a primary factor in the cost of a leased T1 line, and a transcontinental T1 line could cost $20,000 per month. This might seem astounding to the average person, but consider the cost of keeping open 54 long-distance lines for 24 hours a day for one month. A quick calculation indicates that the cost could approach $500,000 per month.

T3 leased digital lines. If T1 lines do not provide enough data power, there is an even faster alternative: the T3 line. This leased line can transmit data at 44.736Mbps. This is roughly equivalent to 29 simultaneous T1 lines. T3 lines are expensive, though. For example, one telephone company charges a basic monthly fee of about $4,000 plus approximately $220 per mile for the distance between the two points. A T3 connection between two buildings 10 miles apart would cost about $6,200 per month, while a connection between two buildings 1,000 miles apart might cost $224,000 per month. Although there are increasing numbers of T3 lines in use, the primary customers have needs for tremendous data transmission. For example, the government uses T3 lines for its interconnections of the supercomputers that make up government defense and research backbones.

On-demand leased digital lines. Few schools can afford or justify 100 percent use of T1 or T3 lines; however, some school systems could make short-term use of one of these lines for a teleconference or a large data transfer. A hybrid of circuit-switched and dedicated lines has evolved. Vendors have quickly caught on to the transient data needs of schools and have started renting out their dedicated leased T1 and T3 lines. The vendors also rent the equipment needed at each end to make the necessary connections, and they supply technical support during the time the line is in use. After a school system signs a contract with one of the vendors, access to the T1 or T3 line is controlled by a circuit-switched process that is much like an ISDN line.

It is reasonable for a school system to use a leased-line vendor if such a line is needed only an hour or two each week. For example, a television course can be much less expensive and more secure when transmitted over a leased digital line than when transmitted by a satellite. See figure 9.8 for a comparison of telephone data lines.

Although there will be significant variations in the results, all forms of digital data lines can be used to send a video teleconference from one location to another. In general, the slower lines, such as ISDN, will be able to provide audio with a small, step-motion image. The fastest lines, such as a T3 line, will provide a video teleconference of a quality equal to that of a satellite transmission.

	SPEED	COST per MONTH	PRIMARY USE
56 Kbps Line	56Kbps	$50/month + usage	Data
ISDN	128Kbps	$50/month + usage	Voice/Data
T1	1,544Kbps	$3,000/month*	Data/Video
T3	44,736Kbps	$12,000/month*	Data/Video

Highly dependent upon distances involved -- can be much higher for long distances

Figure 9.8. Comparison of Telephone Data Lines.

Words of Advice

Video teleconferencing offers the highest level of information exchange of the three forms of teleconferencing. However, some forms of video teleconferencing are still expensive and probably impractical for most schools. The most affordable and accessible video techniques include the use of community-access cable television to provide formal and informal education to the community, contract satellite courses to fill in for courses that are not available in the school, and ITFS television to connect two or more sites in a community. Desktop videoconferencing is rapidly developing, and as schools connect to the Internet and wide area networks, videoconferencing will indeed arrive at the desktop. All these educational applications of video teleconferencing require careful planning, however. In particular, the following details should be considered.

Curricular justification. Video teleconferencing involves significant commitments of financial and personnel resources. Before commitments are finalized, careful evaluations should be conducted to ensure that the curriculum will benefit from the changes.

Physical facilities. Regular classrooms can be adapted to receive video teleconferencing, but a special facility will probably have to be constructed if video courses are to originate from the site. The special requirements for the cameras, lighting, and sound systems exceed what can be accomplished through minor renovations of traditional classrooms. An expert should be consulted prior to developing a studio classroom that originates video classes.

Faculty training. Most faculty are not naturals when it comes to getting in front of cameras and teaching effectively. It takes training and practice to know which camera is active, how much to gesture, and how to prepare visual materials. If faculty are expected to teach video classes, they should be supported with the proper training.

Alternate planning. No matter how carefully the video teleconference is planned, things can go wrong. A cable might be accidentally cut at a construction site, or a sudden storm might twist your satellite dish out of position. These possibilities emphasize the importance of having an alternate plan to cover the situation. In most cases, the standard audio telephone bridge is sufficient to provide a two-way audio backup.

CONCLUSION

Teleconferencing technologies have developed to the point where a number of techniques are now practical for school systems. When properly integrated into the curriculum, these techniques can provide enhanced learning experiences to many students. A summary of teleconferencing techniques is provided in figure 9.9.

Teleconferencing Technique

	Audio	Audiographic	Video Satellite	Video Desktop
Features	2-way audio	2-way audio 2-way still images	2-way audio 1-way motion images*	2-way audio 2-way video
Course Content	Highly verbal	Verbal/visual	Visual	Verbal/visual
Teacher Training	Slight	Moderate	Extensive	Moderate
Advance Planning	Slight	Moderate	Extensive	Slight
Class Location	Two or more sites	Two sites	Two or more sites	Two or more sites
Student Interaction	Verbal	Verbal or still image	Verbal or video*	Verbal or video*
Relative Costs	Low	Moderate	High	Moderate

* Some video systems offer two-way video communications

Figure 9.9. Summary of Teleconferencing Features.

TELECONFERENCING GLOSSARY

audio teleconferencing. Voice-only communications linking two or more sites. In most cases, standard telephone lines and speakerphones are employed.

audiographic teleconferencing. Voice communications supplemented with the transmission of still images. Pictures, graphs, or sketches can be transmitted during the conference. Standard facsimile, or fax, machines are used, or computer-driven systems can be used.

bridge. A device, often leased through a telephone company, that links three or more telephone lines together for audio teleconferencing. *See* call-in bridge and call-out bridge.

call-in bridge. A telephone bridge where the conference is established by having all the distant sites call in to the bridge telephone number. Long-distance charges are billed to the distant locations.

call-out bridge. A telephone bridge where one location calls all distant sites to connect each site to the teleconference. Any long-distance charges are billed to the one originating location.

codec (*compression-decompression*). An electronic device that converts standard television signals into compressed digital signals for transmission. The same device can convert incoming compressed digital signals back into viewable television signals. A codec allows motion images to be transmitted through special telephone lines.

compression. Digital signal processing techniques that are used to reduce the amount of information in a video signal. This allows the video signal to be sent through telephone data lines.

daisychain. A connection from one device to another to create a chain of devices. For example, it is possible to use several conference-call telephones to link more than three people to one conversation.

desktop videoconference. Multimedia microcomputers are used to display live video images that are transmitted over LANs or digital data lines.

digital data line. A telephone line that is designed to transmit computer data rather than human voices. *See* 56Kbps data line, ISDN, T1 line, and T3 line.

downlink. A location that receives a video teleconference from a satellite.

duplex. A process that allows information to flow in both directions at once as in a standard telephone conversation. Contrasts with simplex.

facsimile machine (fax). An electronic device that transmits text or graphics material over telephone lines to other locations.

56Kbps data line. A special telephone line that is designed to transmit computer data at 56Kbps. It will probably be replaced by ISDN lines over the next few years.

freeze frame. *See* still frame.

graphics tablet. A computer device that converts hand-drawn images into digital information that can be displayed on computer screens.

ISDN (Integrated Services Digital Network). A modern telephone system that allows rapid digital transmission of sound, data, and images. These systems are becoming more common in private exchanges, such as in schools or businesses. Eventually, many public telephone systems will be upgraded.

ITFS (Instructional Television Fixed Service). A set of microwave frequencies that have been designated for use by educational facilities. Allows television transmissions over ranges of about 20 miles.

microwave. A high-frequency transmission that can be used for television signals or computer data. Microwave transmissions are said to be *line of sight,* which means that they cannot pass through tall buildings or mountains.

simplex. A communication process that allows information to flow in only one direction at a time. Common speakerphones are simplex devices because only one person can speak at a time. Contrasts with duplex.

still frame. A single frame of video. Most video-capture cards capture only a single video frame, representing a ⅓₀th-of-a-second snapshot. This is sometimes called a *freeze frame* if it is captured from a moving image.

T1 line. A special type of telephone line that transmits digital information at a high rate. These lines are much more expensive than regular telephone lines.

T3 line. A telephone line that is capable of transmitting digital information at rates even higher than those of a T1 line.

teleconferencing. Electronic techniques that are used to allow three or more people at two or more locations to communicate.

uplink. The site for a video conference from which a signal is sent to a satellite.

videoconferencing. Transmitting motion video and audio to two or more locations for the purpose of interactive conferencing.

white board. A graphic display that can be shared by two or more users on a network.

TELECONFERENCING
RESOURCES

For an overview of resources, see the Desktop Videoconferencing Product Survey at http://www2.ncsu.edu/eos/service/ece/project/succeed_info/dtvc_survey/survey.html.

Annenberg/CPB (Corporation for Public Broadcasting)
P.O. Box 2345
South Burlington, VT 05407
800-532-7637

Apple Computer, Inc.
1 Infinite Loop
Cupertino, CA 95014
800-776-2333

AT&T Global Business Video Services
51 Peachtree Center Avenue
Atlanta, GA 30303
800-828-9679

Community College Satellite Network (CCSN)
1 Dupont Circle NW, Suite 410
Washington, DC 20036
202-728-0200

Compression Labs, Inc.
350 E. Plumeria Drive
San Jose, CA 95134-1911
408-435-3000

Connectix Corporation
2655 Campus Drive
San Mateo, CA 94403
800-950-5880

Cornell University
Copyrighted Freeware version of
CUSeeMe
Contact via the World Wide Web only
http://cu-seeme.cornell.edu/

Crosswise Corporation
1545 ½ Pacific Avenue
Santa Cruz, CA 95060
408-459-9060

CUSeeMe
Cornell University
Ithaca, NY 14851
607-255-7566

Education Satellite Network
Star Schools Clearinghouse
2100 I70 Drive S.W.
Columbia, MO 65203
800-243-3376

Educational Management Group
P.O. Box 610
Scottsdale, AZ 85252
800-842-6791

ETC
700 14th Street NW, Suite 500
Washington, DC 20005
202-393-3666

GPT Video Systems, Inc.
737 Canal Street, 35A
Stamford, CT 06902
800-442-4788

Great Plains National
P.O. Box 80669
Lincoln, NE 68501-0669
800-228-4630

The Guide
PBS Adult Learning Service
1320 Braddock Place
Alexandria, VA 22314-1698
800-257-2578

Hitachi America, Ltd.
Telecommunications Division
2990 Gateway Drive
Norcross, GA 30071
404-446-8820

IBM Corporation
P.O. Box 2150
Atlanta, GA 30302-2150
800-342-6672

Intel Corporation
2200 Mission College Boulevard
P.O. Box 58119
Santa Clara, CA 95052
800-538-3373

Intelecom
150 E. Colorado Boulevard
Pasadena, CA 91105
714-828-5770

International Teleconferencing Association
703-506-3280
http://www.itca.org

Kentucky Educational Television Star Channels (KET)
600 Cooper Drive
Lexington, KY 40502
606-233-3000

Learnstar Corporation
5966 La Place Court
Carlsbad, CA 92008
800-292-1505
http://www.ntn.com/learn/

Miami-Dade Community College
Product Development and Distribution
11011 S.W. 104th Street
Miami, FL 33176
305-347-2158

National Distance Learning Center (NDLC)
Owensboro Community College
4800 New Hartford Road
Owensboro, KY 42303-9990
502-686-4556

NEC America, Inc.
Data and Video Communications Division
1525 Walnut Hill Lane
Irving, TX 75038
214-518-4598

Northern Telecom
P.O. Box 13010
RTP, NC 27709
919-992-5000

Panasonic Communications & Systems Company
2 Panasonic Way
Secaucus, NJ 07094
201-348-7000

PBS-ALS
PBS K-12 Learning Services
1320 Braddock Place
Alexandria, VA 22314-1698
703-739-5402

PictureTel Corporation
222 Rosewood Drive
Danvers, MA 01923
800-716-6000

Pierce-Phelps, Inc.
2000 N. 59th Street
Philadelphia, PA 19131
215-879-7171

ShareVision Technology, Inc.
2951 Zanker Road
San Jose, CA 95134
408-428-0330

Sony Corporation of America
Conference and Satellite Systems
3 Paragon Drive
Montvale, NJ 07645
201-930-7194

South Carolina Educational Television
P.O. Drawer L
Box 11000
Columbia, SC 29211
800-277-0829

Star Schools Program
910 N. Ash
Spokane, WA 99201
509-323-2722

United States Distance Learning Association
510-606-5160
http://www.usdla.org

USRobotics
7770 N. Frontage Road
Skokie, IL 60077
800-342-5877
http://www.usr.com

Videolabs
10925 Bren Road East
Minneapolis, MN 55343
612-988-0055

White Pine Software, Inc.
Commercial Enhanced Version of
CUSeeMe
40 Simon Street
Nashua, NH 03060
800-241-7463
http://www.wpine.com/ng.htm

INTERNET
TELEPHONE RESOURCES

CoolTalk
Netscape Communications
Corporation
717-730-9501
http://www.netscape.com

DigiPhone
Third Planet Publishing
214-713-2630
http://www.planeteers.com

FreeTel
FreeTel Communications
http://www.freetel.com

Internet Phone
VocalTec, Inc.
201-768-9400
http://www.vocaltec.com

Net Phone
Electric Magic
214-713-2630
http://www.emagic.com

Speak Freely
John Walker
http://www.fourmilab.ch/speakfree/
windows/

TeleVox
Voxware, Inc.
609-514-4100
http://www.voxware.com

WebPhone
NetSpeak Corporation
407-998-8700
http://www.netspeak.com

WebTalk
Quarterdeck Corporation
310-309-3700
http://webtalk.qdeck.com

RECOMMENDED READING

Abouzeid, M., and V. Scott. (1995). The TEMPO model: Outreach program for educators. *T.H.E. Journal* 23(5): 61–63.

Angell, D. (1996). The ins and outs of ISDN. *Internet World* 7(3): 78–82.

Battaglino, L. (1996). Videoconferencing alliance to develop international special education programs and practices. *T.H.E. Journal* 23(6): 72–73.

Desmond, M. (1996). Ma Bell goes digital. *Multimedia World* 3(2): 16–17.

Freed, L. (1996). Fast connections [Review of ISDN adapters]. *PC Magazine* 15(11): 143–83.

Fyock, J., and D. Sutphin. (1995). Adult supervision in the distance learning classroom: Is it necessary? *T.H.E. Journal* 23(4): 89–91.

Galbreath, J. (1995). Compressed digital videoconferencing: An overview. *Educational Technology* 35(1): 31–38.

Gasper, R., and T. Thompson. (1995). Current trends in distance education. *Journal of Interactive Instruction Development* 8(2): 21–27.

Gellerman, E. (1994). Teleconferencing systems facilitate collaboration and distance learning. *T.H.E Journal* 22(3): 16ff.

Jafari, A. (1996). Video to the desktop and classrooms: The IUPUI IMDS project. *T.H.E. Journal* 23(7): 77–81.

Jerram, P. (1995). Videoconferencing gets in synch. *NewMedia* 5(7): 48–55.

Jordahl, G. (1995). Bringing schools closer with "distance" learning. *Technology and Learning* 15(4): 16–19.

Mather, M. A. (1996). Cutting-edge connectivity: ISDN and beyond. *Technology and Learning* 16(8): 28–33.

Petersen, S. (1995). Easy video conferencing. *PC Graphics and Video* 4(1): 26–32.

Pihlman, M. (1995). Desktop videoconferencing challenge [Videoconferencing system evaluations]. *NewMedia* 5(11): 55–66.

Rees, F., and B. Safford. (1995). Iowa's approach to distance learning. *T.H.E. Journal* 22(11): 63–66.

Tucker, R. W. (1995). Distance learning programs: Models and alternatives. *Syllabus* 9(3): 42–46.

Tuttle, H. G. (1996). Learning: The star of videoconferencing. *MultiMedia Schools* 3(4): 37–41.

Venditto, G. (1996). Internet phones: The future is calling. *Internet World* 7(6): 40–52.

Walsh, J., and B. Reese. (1995). Distance learning's growing reach. *T.H.E. Journal* 22(11): 58–62.

Whitaker, G. (1995). First-hand observations on tele-course teaching. *T.H.E. Journal* 23(1): 65–68.

TELECONFERENCING

Dr. Ann E. Barron
University of South Florida

Dr. Gary W. Orwig
University of Central Florida

An Overview Of

This brochure is an excerpt from:

New Technologies for Education

A Beginner's Guide

Third Edition

To obtain the complete book, contact:

Libraries Unlimited
P.O. Box 6633
Englewood, CO 80155-6633
800-237-6124

Educational Applications

Classroom Guest Speaker

Perhaps one of the most practical applications of teleconferencing is to bring into the classroom a guest who would not normally be able to visit.

Homebound Students

Another application of teleconferencing is to provide a classroom connection to students who are homebound because of illness or injury.

Distance Tutoring

Some school systems have set up audio teleconferencing systems to provide students access to tutors during the early evening hours.

Distributed Classrooms

A number of school districts in less populated areas use teleconferencing to share a teacher among several schools. This makes it possible to offer classes that a school could not otherwise afford to teach.

Contract Courses

A number of companies now provide selected courses to schools that cannot teach those courses in the traditional manner.

Audio Teleconferencing

Audio teleconferencing is the most mature and the least expensive of the teleconferencing techniques. A telephone line and speakerphones are the only components needed.

When more than three locations must be connected for a teleconference, the best solution is to use a telephone bridge. The bridge (usually located at a telephone company) links multiple telephone lines and balances the audio levels.

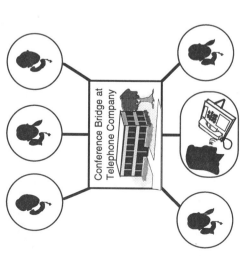

Conference Bridge at Telephone Company

An audio teleconference allows students to talk with experts who are unable to travel to the school. This technique is also an inexpensive method for communicating with homebound students.

Audiographic Teleconferencing

Computer technologies make possible this teleconferencing technique that adds the interactive transmission of charts, graphs, and still pictures to regular audio teleconferencing. An audiographics site contains the following components:

- A standard speakerphone for the audio portion of the conference

- A desktop computer to manage the images for a teleconference

- A device to capture images, such as a scanner or copy stand

- A modem to allow the computer to send and receive the images

- A large computer monitor or projection system to display the images for the class

Most audiographic teleconferencing systems use two telephone lines for each site. This allows the audio to continue without interruption while graphics are transmitted back and forth through the second phone line.

Some systems work with a single telephone line, but most of these systems require a pause in the conversation while an image is being transmitted.

Satellite Videoconferencing

Videoconferencing combines video with audio. Videoconferencing via satellites uses an uplink station to send the video signal to the satellite, where it is broadcast back toward the earth. Numerous downlink sites can then receive the signal. Standard telephone lines are used to allow the remote participants to ask questions.

Desktop Videoconferencing

Microcomputers can be used for two-way videoconferences if each workstation is equipped with a camera, microphone, speakers, and internal computer boards to process the video and sound. Desktop videoconferencing is most commonly used through local area networks, but it can also be used over wide area systems such as the Internet. Special high speed data lines such as ISDN, T1, and T3 must be used to connect the computers.

TYPE	SPEED
ISDN	128Kbps
T1	1,544Kbps
T3	44,736Kbps

10

The Computer as an Assistive Technology

A Scenario

The finishing touches were just going into place on Anita's research paper. She had worked hard to gather the basic resources and had collected some excellent textual materials, current E-mail from several experts on the topic, illustrations of some of the devices that were used, and even some World Wide Web links to current pages on the topic.

Anita was working on a paper about how computer-assistive technologies are used by people with disabilities who want to take control of their academic lives. Her paper included an introduction to the topic, a case study of the trials and successes of one student, and examples of how standard microcomputers are adapted to meet the needs of individuals with disabilities.

She used the online library catalog from home to identify the books she wanted to locate at the library. In a similar manner, she used an online bibliographic tool to locate journal articles that might help her. A search of the World Wide Web quickly produced several sites that had all kinds of useful information. She was also able to use the Web sites to contact several experts who helped clarify a couple of complicated issues.

Anita is a highly motivated, independent, and technology-accepting teenager of the late 1990s, not unlike many of the other teenagers in her class. She has also had cerebral palsy since birth and has limited control of her feet and hands.

Although Anita still needs help in some everyday activities, such as getting books off the top shelf in the library stacks or in getting a bound journal volume onto a copy machine, she is now experiencing more intellectual freedom than she had ever dreamed of just a few years ago. It would take her days to type a paper on an electric typewriter a few years ago, and inserting illustrations was out of the question. Now, with a specialized keyboard in front of her, a mouse in her toes—she has better luck with them for fine motor movements—and word-prediction software linked to her word processor, she can type more than 20 words a minute. Anita is intelligent, in control, and confident.

When microcomputers first emerged as practical tools to enhance everyday life, many people with disabilities feared that the small computers would be yet another resource to which they had limited access. However, instead of becoming tools of exclusion, microcomputers have become tools of inclusion for many people. When fitted with appropriate input devices, output devices, and software, a standard microcomputer can quickly become an indispensable part of everyday life for people with disabilities.

In this chapter we will examine

- Input devices

- Software to assist with input

- Output devices

- Software to assist with output

- Resources for further information

INTRODUCTION

It is said that microcomputers are just tools: What you get out of them depends on how you use them. Perhaps what is so amazing about microcomputers is the almost unlimited variety of input devices, output devices, and software programs. Many devices and programs have been developed specifically to enable people with disabilities to benefit from microcomputers.

INPUT DEVICES

Input devices allow the user to tell the computer what to do. By far the most common input devices are the keyboard and the mouse. These and other devices can be manufactured in a variety of forms to address specific disabilities.

Alternate Keyboards

A common alternate keyboard is a programmable device that can be customized for specific applications. The *Intellikeys* keyboard by IntelliTools is a popular example of a programmable keyboard. It is a large, flat panel that has 576 individual touch-sensitive cells. Overlays are placed on the panel, and individual or groups of cells are programmed to produce keyboard responses when they are touched. Overlays can resemble large versions of standard keyboards, or custom overlays can be designed, printed, and laminated to work with almost any commercial software on the market. (See fig. 10.1.)

A second approach is to design keyboards for individuals who have limited but accurate movement of their fingers. These keyboards are often small, and some have a reduced number of keys. When only a few keys are used, keys are often pressed in multiple combinations to produce text. Some of these keyboards can also be programmed to produce full words or even phrases with combinations of simultaneous key presses.

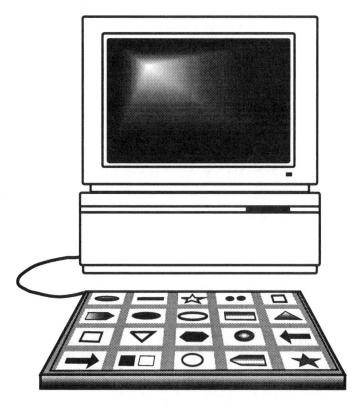

Figure 10.1. Alternate Keyboard.

Joysticks and Track Balls

Joysticks have long been used for video games, but they can also replace computer mice for people with limited use of their hands. In many cases, a joystick can directly replace a mouse; sometimes software drivers need to be modified or replaced. Once properly installed, however, a joystick can be used with most commercial software that would otherwise require a mouse.

Track balls are not as common in the microcomputer domain. A track ball is like a mouse that has been turned upside down. Instead of pushing the housing around on a flat surface, a large ball may be rotated directly by a person's fingers. Because the track ball does not move around the desktop, it is much easier to use than a mouse when a person has limited arm motion but good control of the fingers. A similar device is the finger mouse, which is commonly found on laptop and notebook computers. Finger mice can control the cursor with a single finger. Track balls and finger mice are designed to directly replace mice; there is usually no need to make any changes in the software.

Touch Screens

Computer monitors with touch-sensitive screens can also be used when a keyboard or mouse is not practical. The software drivers for touch screens are designed to replace the input created by a mouse, so a person can "click" on a portion of the screen simply by touching it. Touch screens may be purchased as special-purpose monitors, or they can be add-ons, such as the *TouchWindow* by Edmark that slips over a computer monitor.

Switches

Switches are simple input devices that are plugged into programmable keyboards or other interface devices. They are usually large, durable, and colorful. Switches can be used singly or in combinations for specialized purposes. For example, one or two switches might be placed so that the feet can activate keyboard functions such as function or shift keys.

Pointing Devices

Sometimes simple sticks can be strapped to the arm, held in the mouth, or worn on the head to serve as pointing devices to activate keyboards, touch screens, or switches. More advanced pointing systems include optical or ultrasonic devices that can be strapped to the head, such as the *HeadMaster* by the Prentke Romich Company and *HeadMouse* by Origin Instruments. This device is for people who have good control over their head position but little or no control over their hands or feet. A sensor on the computer monitor detects head movement and positions a cursor accordingly on the screen. Simple switches, sometimes controlled by air pressure from the mouth, then make appropriate selections.

SOFTWARE TO ASSIST WITH INPUT

A variety of software programs can function on their own or in combination with other input devices to assist individuals with disabilities with inputting information into a computer.

On-Screen Keyboards

One of the most common software techniques for inputting information is the on-screen keyboard. The software places a standard or modified illustration of a keyboard upon a computer monitor. (See fig. 10.2.)

Various selection techniques are then used to allow an individual to type information into the computer. In some cases, a cursor continually scans across all the keys one by one (*Click It!* by IntelliTools is an example of this technique). At the moment a desired key is highlighted by the cursor, an individual initiates a key switch and that key is selected. The scanning process continues until the

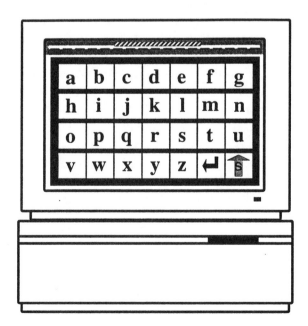

Figure 10.2. On-Screen Keyboard.

text or command is entered. Touch screens, track balls, joysticks, and head-pointing devices can all be used as selection tools for an on-screen keyboard.

Voice Recognition

As the power of computers has continued to improve, so has the efficiency of voice recognition software. It is now possible to use voice recognition software to issue computer commands, such as "Save file," or even to take dictation. As one might expect, voice recognition software still has some limits with words that sound alike, but these programs always have options that allow spelling individual words when needed. Voice recognition usually requires a period of training to adapt to an individual's voice. To some extent, the individual also adapts to the strengths and weaknesses of the voice recognition software itself. Over a period of time, however, the recognition process can become efficient.

Word Prediction

When individual key presses are difficult and time-consuming for an individual and voice recognition is not an acceptable alternative, then word prediction software such as *Co:Writer* by Don Johnston, Inc. can be helpful. This software uses the first one or two letters to predict the likely word that the user wants to type, based upon common usage and the individual's previous writing style. If the desired word is not shown in the list after two key presses, then the third letter is typed. In almost all cases, the desired word appears before the entire word must be typed. In the cases in which a new word is actually typed in, the software enters that word into its database and keeps track of the conditions when it was used. Word-prediction programs can greatly reduce the total key presses required, thus speeding the overall typing rate of a disabled individual.

OUTPUT DEVICES

Hardware devices and software exist to help provide computer information to people with disabilities. The extent of a disability determines the type of output device. For example, something as basic as a larger monitor can be sufficient to help a mildly vision-impaired person see the characters on the screen. For more severe cases, software can be used to expand small portions of the screen so that just a few characters cover the entire screen at any one time. For people who are blind, text-to-speech systems can almost replace the computer monitor.

Screen Enlargement

The most direct way to enlarge information on the computer screen is to use a larger screen. In many cases, simply changing from a 12-inch or 13-inch monitor to a 17-inch to 20-inch monitor is all that is needed to allow visually impaired people to use a computer. Often a transparent glare-and-radiation shield is added to the front of these monitors to protect people who must sit close to them. A less successful technique is to place a flat enlarging lens in front of a standard monitor, but they almost always require darkened rooms and perfect positioning to work properly.

Braille Displays

A Braille display consists of a matrix of movable plastic or metal pins that make up from 20 to 80 Braille cells. Electromagnetic solenoids or other devices position the pins in the cells to represent a line of text. When the text has been read, the user pushes a button to move on to the next line of text.

Braille printers—properly called embossers—prepare permanent records of computer output by stamping indentations into paper. Some Braille embossers can print line-oriented graphics as well as standard Braille characters.

Braille displays and Braille embossers normally require translation software that formats standard text for Braille output. In some cases, this software is supplied with the equipment, while in other cases it must be purchased separately.

Speech Synthesis

Speech synthesis has progressed rapidly over the last several years. The hardware that is now used to produce synthetic speech creates sounds that are still a bit robotic, but they are much more natural. The software that converts text to speech has also greatly improved, and often there are several "voices" available (see chapter 4 for more information on speech synthesis).

SOFTWARE TO ASSIST WITH OUTPUT

There is no clear line between hardware and software with output devices. Most output hardware requires some form of software support. In a similar manner, most software enhancements require some form of special hardware to support them. The following tools, however, are probably more software than hardware.

Screen Windowing Software

Windowing software allows an individual to select a specific part of the screen to expand or "blow up" to fill the entire screen. A person with a vision disability is then able to examine the details of a portion of the screen. Windowing software is designed to work in the "background" with normal commercial applications, but it is not perfect. Products should always be tested with desired applications before they are purchased.

Text-to-Speech Conversion

Some speech-synthesis systems use firmware—programs stored on the sound card—to do the conversion, while other systems such as *Write:OutLoud* by Don Johnston, Inc. use software programs. In either case, the quality of the program determines the effectiveness of the conversion. While all text-to-speech programs are designed to convert text files to speech, some also allow real-time screen conversion of text into speech. These programs are a critical component in allowing visually impaired individuals to participate in E-mail and online "chat" activities of the Internet.

Special Applications Programs

In addition to the creation of hardware and software that handles input and output of information, publishers have been designing programs that address specific learning needs. In particular, individuals with specific learning disabilities have a rapidly increasing assortment of software to help them. Software ranges from early vocabulary development, such as the series by Laureate Learning Systems, Inc., to scanning math calculators, such as *Big:Calc* by Don Johnston, Inc., that talks to its users.

CONCLUSION

Computers are now tools that can help people with a variety of physical and learning disabilities. Because this is such a rapidly expanding area of computer technology, one of the greatest challenges is to keep up with what is now possible. Fortunately, there are excellent support organizations at the national, state, and local levels. A first step is to get in touch with one of these agencies and identify what is available at your local level. Some of these technologies tend to be expensive, and often local organizations are established to share and sometimes help support these expenses. Also, do not overlook resources on the Internet. You will be surprised by the wealth of information there.

ASSISTIVE TECHNOLOGY GLOSSARY

access software. Computer programs or "drivers" that support input to a computer by alternative devices.

alternative input device. Optical head pointing, voice, scanning, eye tracking, data glove, Morse code, touch tablet, or other devices that permit computer input.

alternative keyboard. A device that replaces or modifies the standard keyboard.

artificial speech. *See* synthesized speech.

Braille cell. An arrangement of raised dots. Each cell depicts a letter, number, or special character.

Braille input. A Braille-style keyboard or specific keys on a standard keyboard that function in Braille patterns.

Braille output. A device that produces raised-dot Braille on paper. Also devices that produce paperless, refreshable Braille as output from the computer.

Environmental Control Units (ECU). Devices that are usually connected to computers to enable individuals with mobility impairments to control lights, thermostat, television, radio, and various other appliances.

firmware. Software that is stored in permanent memory rather than on disks.

head stick/head pointer. A simple stick or advanced electronic system that attaches to a person's head. It allows the person to activate keyboards or make selections from the computer screen.

input. The process of giving information or instructions to a computer.

keyboard. The part of a computer that looks and acts like a typewriter.

keyboard-enhancement programs. Input devices for people who have difficulty using standard keyboards.

large-print display. Enlarged letters that are displayed on a computer monitor for individuals with visual impairments.

mouth stick/mouth pointer. A simple stick or advanced electronic system that is controlled by a person's mouth. It allows the person to activate keyboards or make selections from the computer screen.

output device. Devices that produce the results of computer activity. Output devices include computer monitors, printers, Braille devices, and speech synthesizers.

refreshable Braille. A device that has space for up to 80 Braille cells and for which the dots in each cell are electronically raised and lowered in different combinations to form all the Braille characters.

scanning. Software that causes a cursor to automatically move at an adjustable speed among selected symbols, boxes, or other "hot spots" on a computer screen. A switch or other alternative input device is then used to make the desired selection.

speech recognition system. Software that allows an individual's voice to be recognized by the computer.

speech synthesizer. An output device that enables a computer to speak.

switch. Devices that allow individuals to operate electric or electronic objects. A switch can be operated by hand, foot, puff of air, or a variety of other methods, depending upon the needs of the user and the configuration of the switch.

synthesized speech. Artificial speech that is generated by computers. A computer can then produce spoken E-mail output, for example.

ASSISTIVE TECHNOLOGY RESOURCES

Technology Resources

Berkeley Access
2095 Rose Street
Berkeley, CA 94709
510-540-5535

Don Johnston, Inc.
P.O. Box 639
Wauconda, IL 60084-0639
800-999-4660

Duxbury Systems
435 King Street
P.O. Box 1504
Littleton, MA 01460
508-486-9766

Edmark Corporation
P.O. Box 97021
Redmond, WA 98073
206-556-8400

GW Micro
310 Racquet Drive
Fort Wayne, IN 46825
219-483-3625

Hartley Courseware, Inc.
3001 Coolidge Road, Suite 400
East Lansing, MI 11766
800-638-2352

Henter-Joyce, Inc.
2100 62nd Avenue North
St. Petersburg, FL 33702
800-336-5658

IBM Special Needs Systems
11400 Burnet Road
Austin, TX 78758
800-426-4832

IntelliTools, Inc.
55 Leveroni Court, Suite 9
Novato, CA 94949
800-899-6687

KidTECH
3204 Perry Place
Bakersfield, CA 93306
805-873-8744

Laureate Learning Systems, Inc.
110 E. Spring Street
Winooski, VT 05404-1898
800-562-6801

Madenta Communications
9411A 20th Avenue
Edmonton, AB T6N 1E5
Canada
800-661-8406

Marblesoft
12301 Central Avenue NE
Blaine, MN 55434
612-755-1402

Mayer-Johnson
P.O. Box 1579
Solana Beach, CA 92075
619-481-2489

Microsystems Software, Inc.
600 Worcester Road
Framingham, MA 01701
800-828-2600

Origin Instruments
854 Greenview Drive
Grand Prairie, TX 75050
214-606-8740

Prentke Romich Company
1022 Heyl Road
Wooster, OH 44691
800-262-1984

R. J. Cooper and Associates
24843 Del Prado, Suite 283
Dana Point, CA 92629
800-752-6673

Telesensory
455 N. Bernardo Avenue
Mountain View, CA 94043-5274
800-804-8004

UCLA Intervention Program for Young Handicapped Children
1000 Veteran Avenue
Los Angeles, CA 90024

World Wide Web Resources

American Council of the Blind
http://www.acb.org/

Americans with Disabilities Act
http://www.usdoj.gov/crt/ada/adahoml.htm

Assistive Technology for Disabled Computer Users
http://www.iat.unc.edu/guides/irg-20.html

Assistive Technology On-Line
http://www.asel.udel.edu/at-online/
assistive.html

Equal Access to Software and Information
http://www.rit.edu:80/~easi/

University of Illinois
Project PURSUIT
http://www.rehab.uiuc.edu/

University of Waterloo Electronic Library
Disability Issues
http://www.lib.uwaterloo.ca/discipline/
Disability_Issues/index.htm

Western New York Disabilities Forum
http://freenet.buffalo.edu/~wnydf/

Other Resources

American Speech-Language-Hearing Association (ASHA)
10801 Rockville Pike
Rockville, MD 20852
(Voice/TDD) 800-638-8255

Baruch College Computer Center for the Visually Impaired
The City University of New York
17 Lexington Avenue, P.O. Box 515
New York, NY 10010
212-802-2140

Carroll Center for the Blind Computer Access
770 Centre Street
Newton, MA 02158
617-969-6200

Closing the Gap
P.O. Box 68
Henderson, MN 56044
612-248-3294

National Braille Press
88 St. Stephen Street
Boston, MA 02115
617-266-6160

National Easter Seal Society
230 W. Monroe Street, Suite 1800
Chicago, IL 60606
800-221-6827; (TDD) 312-726-4258

National Organization on Disability (NOD)
910 Sixteenth Street NW
Washington, DC 20006
202-293-5960; (TDD) 202-293-5968

Technical Aids and Systems for the Handicapped, Inc. (TASH)
Unit 1, 91 Station Street Ajax
Ontario L1S 3H2
Canada
800-463-5685

Trace Research and Development Center on Communication Control and Computer Access
University of Wisconsin-Madison
S151 Waisman Center
1500 Highland Avenue
Madison, WI 53705
608-262-6966

RECOMMENDED READING

Alliance for Technology Access. (1994). *Computer resources for people with disabilities.* Alameda, CA: Hunter House.

Armstrong, K., J. Brand, R. Glass, and L. Regan. (1995). Special software for special kids. *Technology and Learning* 16(2): 56–61.

Castorina, C., ed. (1994). *Equal access: information technology for students with disabilities.* New York: McGraw-Hill.

Lazzaro, J. J. (1993). Computers for the disabled. *Byte* 18(7): 59–62.

Lee, G., C. Groom, and F. Groom. (1996). Teaching visually impaired students in a multimedia-enriched environment. *T.H.E. Journal* 23(7): 88–90.

McCain, G. (1995). Technology-based assessment in special education. *T.H.E. Journal* 23(1): 57–60.

Salvador, R. (1996). What's new for the disabled? *Electronic Learning* 15(5): 10.

ASSISTIVE TECHNOLOGIES

An Overview Of

Dr. Ann E. Barron
University of South Florida

Dr. Gary W. Orwig
University of Central Florida

This brochure is an excerpt from:

New Technologies for Education

A Beginner's Guide

Third Edition

To obtain the complete book, contact:

Libraries Unlimited
P.O. Box 6633
Englewood, CO 80155-6633
800-237-6124

Special Applications

In addition to the creation of hardware and software to handle the input and output of information, publishers have been hard at work designing programs that address specific learning needs of disabled people. In particular, individuals with specific learning disabilities have an increasing assortment of software to help them. Software ranges from early vocabulary development to scanning math calculators.

Resources

For more information about assistive technologies, see the following resources on the Web:

American Council of the Blind
http://www.acb.org/

Americans with Disabilities Act
http://www.usdoj.gov/crt/ada/adahom1.htm

Assistive Technology for Disabled Computer Users
http://www.iat.unc.edu/guides/irg-20.html

Assistive Technology On-Line
http://www.asel.udel.edu/at-online/assistive.html

Equal Access to Software and Information
http://www.rit.edu:80/~easi/

Western New York Disabilities Forum
http://freenet.buffalo.edu/~wnydf/

Assistive output devices are often creative adaptations of more traditional output tools.

Braille Displays

A Braille display consists of a matrix of moveable plastic or metal pins that make up from 20 to 80 Braille cells. Electromagnetic solenoids or other devices position the pins in the cells to represent a line of text. When the text has been read, the user pushes a button to move on to the next line of text.

Braille Printers

Braille printers (also called embossers) prepare permanent records of computer output by stamping indentations into paper. Some Braille embossers can print line-oriented graphics as well as standard Braille characters. Both Braille displays and Braille embossers require translation software that formats standard text for Braille output.

Speech Synthesis

Speech synthesis has progressed rapidly over the last several years. The hardware that is now used to produce synthetic speech creates sounds that are still a bit robotic, but they are much more natural than before. The software that converts text to speech has also greatly improved, and often there are several "voices" available.

The devices that provide this data are called input devices.

Programmable Keyboard

A programmable keyboard is a device that can be customized for specific applications. These keyboards are often large, flat panels that have many individual touch sensitive cells.

On-screen Keyboard

Programs are also available that place an image of a keyboard on the computer screen. Various selection techniques are then used to allow an individual to type information into the computer.

Computers have almost unlimited combinations of input devices, output devices, and software programs. Many of these devices and programs have been developed specifically to enable people with disabilities to enjoy and benefit from computers.

The term assistive technologies is often used to refer to a device that increases the independence of a disabled person. Just a few years ago computers were all but inaccessible to many people with disabilities. Now these same people use computers as tools to enhance their abilities to work, to create, and to play. The hardware and software that make this possible are called assistive technologies.

Impairments in vision and mobility often create the greatest challenges to a student's access to computers. Through the use of assistive technologies, individuals with limited vision can have their computer translate E-mail into synthesized speech, or they can use a Braille computer system to display the text for tactile reading.

Students with limited muscular control can choose from a variety of tools (such as alternate keyboards, ability switches, headpointers, and joysticks) that enable them to enter text or commands into their computers.

Closing Remarks

The closing remarks of the second edition pointed out the dynamic nature of educational technologies. In conducting research for this edition, we discovered that the dynamics are still there and, in fact, are accelerating.

The increasing power of microcomputers has enabled dedicated hardware and software developers to create fantastic tools for individuals with disabilities. While such tools have existed in the background for several years, decreasing costs and increasing capabilities now allow them to enter the mainstream. Computers and all they bring with them are now available to many people who previously had very limited access.

Another rapid change is somewhat of a contradiction. Several years ago different computers had very different user interfaces. Now the graphical user interface (GUI) reigns supreme. Many popular programs such as word processors are available for a variety of computers. The programs look and behave almost exactly the same, regardless of the computer platform. The point-and-click nature of graphical interfaces has even extended into the Internet. In the previous edition we covered Gophers and other text-oriented Internet tools. Now these have been replaced almost entirely by point-and-click Web browsers.

Once again, there have been winners and losers in the technology race. Analog videodisc technology appears to have reached a plateau and will probably gradually fade from the scene as it is replaced by digital video technology. Schools should not immediately scrap their videodisc players, though, because the content of the videodisc programs will probably remain useful for several more years.

CD-ROM technology has had remarkable staying power. Faster drives and direct-write media have established CD-ROM as an ideal way to distribute new software and to archive important files. However, even CD-ROM technologies might be in for some incredible changes soon with the Digital Versatile Disc (DVD) format peering over the horizon. If commercial concerns over pirating of software can soon be resolved, DVD may replace many CD-ROM and analog videodisc applications.

Our advice remains the same. Continue to move ahead but with caution. If someone tries to sell you a wonderful new product, be careful. Do your homework and find other companies that support the hardware or software format. If it turns out to be a one-of-a-kind wonder, it probably will not be a bargain after the dust clears. Match software to curricular needs first, then examine the hardware needs associated with the preferred software. It does little good to buy state-of-the-art hardware that has no curricular function.

The best approach is to stay informed by reading, attending professional conferences, requesting demonstrations in your school, and asking many questions. Many school systems provide workshops for teachers and administrators. Select appropriate workshops and attend them. As you collect information and experience, you will develop a sense of how technology fits into your individual environment.

Index